SALES HUNTING

HOW TO DEVELOP NEW TERRITORIES AND MAJOR ACCOUNTS IN HALF THE TIME USING TRUST AS YOUR WEAPON

David A. Monty

Apress·

Sales Hunting: How to Develop New Territories and Major Accounts in Half the Time Using Trust as Your Weapon

ISBN-13 (pbk): 978-1-4302-6770-6

ISBN-13 (electronic): 978-1-4302-6769-0

Trademarked names, logos, and images may appear in this book. Rather than use a trademark symbol with every occurrence of a trademarked name, logo, or image we use the names, logos, and images only in an editorial fashion and to the benefit of the trademark owner, with no intention of infringement of the trademark.

The use in this publication of trade names, trademarks, service marks, and similar terms, even if they are not identified as such, is not to be taken as an expression of opinion as to whether or not they are subject to proprietary rights.

While the advice and information in this book are believed to be true and accurate at the date of publication, neither the authors nor the editors nor the publisher can accept any legal responsibility for any errors or omissions that may be made. The publisher makes no warranty, express or implied, with respect to the material contained herein.

President and Publisher: Paul Manning
Acquisitions Editor: Jeff Olson
Editorial Board: Steve Anglin, Mark Beckner, Ewan Buckingham, Gary Cornell,
    Louise Corrigan, James DeWolf, Jonathan Gennick, Jonathan Hassell,
    Robert Hutchinson, Michelle Lowman, James Markham, Matthew Moodie,
    Jeff Olson, Jeffrey Pepper, Douglas Pundick, Ben Renow-Clarke, Dominic Shakeshaft,
    Gwenan Spearing, Matt Wade, Steve Weiss
Coordinating Editor: Rita Fernando
Copy Editor: Kezia Endsley
Compositor: SPi Global
Indexer: SPi Global
Cover Designer: Anna Ishchenko

Distributed to the book trade worldwide by Springer Science+Business Media New York, 233 Spring Street, 6th Floor, New York, NY 10013. Phone 1-800-SPRINGER, fax (201) 348-4505, e-mail orders-ny@springer-sbm.com, or visit www.springeronline.com. Apress Media, LLC is a California LLC and the sole member (owner) is Springer Science + Business Media Finance Inc (SSBM Finance Inc). SSBM Finance Inc is a Delaware corporation.

For information on translations, please e-mail rights@apress.com, or visit www.apress.com.

Apress and friends of ED books may be purchased in bulk for academic, corporate, or promotional use. eBook versions and licenses are also available for most titles. For more information, reference our Special Bulk Sales–eBook Licensing web page at www.apress.com/bulk-sales.

Any source code or other supplementary materials referenced by the author in this text is available to readers at www.apress.com. For detailed information about how to locate your book's source code, go to www.apress.com/source-code/.

Apress Business: The Unbiased Source of Business Information

Apress business books provide essential information and practical advice, each written for practitioners by recognized experts. Busy managers and professionals in all areas of the business world—and at all levels of technical sophistication—look to our books for the actionable ideas and tools they need to solve problems, update and enhance their professional skills, make their work lives easier, and capitalize on opportunity.

Whatever the topic on the business spectrum—entrepreneurship, finance, sales, marketing, management, regulation, information technology, among others—Apress has been praised for providing the objective information and unbiased advice you need to excel in your daily work life. Our authors have no axes to grind; they understand they have one job only—to deliver up-to-date, accurate information simply, concisely, and with deep insight that addresses the real needs of our readers.

It is increasingly hard to find information—whether in the news media, on the Internet, and now all too often in books—that is even-handed and has your best interests at heart. We therefore hope that you enjoy this book, which has been carefully crafted to meet our standards of quality and unbiased coverage.

We are always interested in your feedback or ideas for new titles. Perhaps you'd even like to write a book yourself. Whatever the case, reach out to us at editorial@apress.com and an editor will respond swiftly. Incidentally, at the back of this book, you will find a list of useful related titles. Please visit us at www.apress.com to sign up for newsletters and discounts on future purchases.

The Apress Business Team

I would like to dedicate this book my fiancée Mary, who supported me through the entire process. She is always there for me, giving me the space and support to follow whatever idea I have. And to the four teenagers in the house—Carter, Caitlin, Jen, and Will—who had to put up with the clicking of the keyboard for a year, and the massive mood swing I had after losing six months of work to a faulty hard drive. Note to self: back up often, and to more than one source!

Contents

About the Author

A veteran of the U.S. Navy, **Dave Monty** has sold software and hardware solutions for over 20 years. He has been an account manager, regional manager, or director of sales, for such companies as Cisco, EMC, and Dimension Data. Monty has a passion for training, and for helping individuals and companies reach their full potential in sales. He currently lives in the Research Triangle area in North Carolina

Acknowledgments

I would like to thank Paul Kizakevich, who is the best sales manager I have ever had. Paul's passion for the craft of sales gave me pride in being a salesperson, and he inspired me to hone my knowledge and skills in sales. My only regret with Paul is that I did not meet him earlier in my career.

I would like to thank Wes Miller and Doug McFarland for having the patience to read early drafts of my book and to offer great feedback to help improve the content and flow. I would like to thank Jennifer Asciutto for helping me realize the value of a comma. Her initial edits helped me learn more grammar than I did in four years of high school English. Thank you to Chris Daltorio, with Costigan Training, who helped edit for content, and shared many valuable ideas that turned my strategies into actionable tactics. Lastly, I would like to thank Jeff Olson with Apress. Jeff was a pleasure to work with, and his insights truly made this book a better product than I could even imagine.

Introduction

Tom is a new salesperson about three months into his job. Tom was promoted from within the company because he was the number one inside salesperson. His job was cold calling to set appointments for the outside sales team. He is diligent, hardworking, and already understands the company and its products.

One day, he is out to lunch with some colleagues, and one of the more senior reps asks, "How are things going, Tom?"

His reply, "Things are great, I have been on many appointments. My boss is happy with the number of customers I have been in front of. My pipeline is very strong. I have not booked my first order yet, but I am excited. My second quarter will be huge!"

"How many customers have you visited?" the senior rep continues.

"Close to 25," says Tom.

The senior rep is impressed; this is a large number of appointments for his industry, so it's clear he is working hard.

So far, it sounds like everything is great. High activity, opportunities in his pipeline, a happy manager; the only thing missing is some closed business.

Three months go by, and Tom walks into the senior rep's office. He asks Tom the same question, "How are you doing?"

"Well, quite a few of my deals *pushed* [moved to the next quarter] or fell through this quarter, but my pipeline is even bigger, and Q3 will be huge."

"Tom, how does your boss feel?"

He replies, "I can tell he is a bit more concerned with the numbers. He loves my pipeline, but he is pushing me to start closing some of this business."

"What is his advice?"

"Keep pursuing leads. He says keep my pipeline strong, and deals will come."

The senior rep asks, "How many customers have you visited?"

"Maybe another 25 this quarter. Marketing is great—they keep the leads coming."

The senior rep then asks, "What are your top opportunities?"

Tom lists some companies. The senior rep recognizes that from a geography standpoint, he is often driving three hours in one direction, then four hours in another direction. He asks Tom, "Why are you driving all over the place?"

"My boss wants me running down the opportunities on these leads."

"So you have been in front of 50 different customers? How many different opportunities are you working?" The answer is an impressive 40.

The senior rep is starting to spot a trend. Tom is working on more opportunities than the senior rep himself. And he knows that in this industry, you can make your living with 10 accounts. So, he leads Tom by asking, "Tom, which of the 50 customers have you qualified as your best?"

Tom is confused, "What do you mean?"

"I mean where are you spending your time? Which customers are getting your time?"

"I have been following up leads, and trying close these deals, so pretty much where I have opportunity."

Instead of pointing out an issue, he gives Tom some direct advice, "Go back through the list of accounts you have visited, and figure out which customers are a fit for our company and for you. Note where they have money, where there is change, where they have aging IT infrastructure, and where you felt you had a good personal fit. You need to start establishing relationships and building trust with these customers."

Tom nods; the advice seems to make sense. But he's sure some of the leads he gets each week will take care of the problem.

Another quarter goes by, and he walks into the senior rep's office one more time. The rep asks, "How are things going?"

"Not so good," says Tom. "I barely closed anything last quarter. I had three large deals that we thought we had won, but we lost them to price at the last minute. My pipeline has shrunk. We cannot figure out what is going on, so my boss is starting to think I must be lazy, or I am just not a closer."

"Did you take my advice and identify your 'go-to' customers?"

"Well, no. I have been too busy trying to close deals."

This story does not have a happy ending. Tom was let go a few weeks later. How do you go from a hard-working inside sales rock star to being fired as a salesperson? He worked hard and had a strong pipeline, so why was he not closing business?

What Happened?

The approach that Tom took is how most salespeople approach sales hunting. And it's not surprising; the company trains them on its top-selling products. They are given a list of accounts or a territory, some sales training based on skills or process, a laptop, and a phone.

The advice—from managers, books, seminars, and other sources of sales training—for hunting typically goes something like this: "Work hard, get in front of as many customers a possible, work your leads, find opportunities, and close business. Go hunt!" If the salesperson is "lucky," he is probably given a common strategy. "Your goal is $5,000,000 in revenue. This equates to $1,250,000 per quarter. We close 30% of our deals. So you should have $4,200,000 in potential revenue in your pipeline at any time." In other words, find as many opportunities as possible; keep your pipeline full.

The sarcasm in that last statement was not meant to insult the many managers who have used that advice. I have used that advice myself in the past. On the surface is seems like perfect common sense. However, as you start to dig into why customers buy, look at the most important asset a new salesperson has (time), and understand why managers push for pipeline much greater than quota, you learn that this logic hurts more than it helps.

As this book will show, the senior rep in the previous story has the right idea about how to succeed: identify the most likely accounts, develop relationships, and build trust. But Tom—and most of the Toms in the sales world—doesn't hear this kind of advice often enough.

The Difficulty of Penetrating New Accounts

Penetrating new accounts is a daunting challenge for any salesperson, whether you are new or have been with the company for years. If you have been with a company for many years, for example, you know that new account acquisition never stops. There are a few accounts that have been on your target list for years, but you just can't get your foot in the door. You have tried everything, but the door just will not open. You finally get that important first meeting, but you just don't seem to get any traction. And if you have a new territory, your first year is nothing but penetrating new accounts.

If you are a sales manager, you know that one of the most anxious times you experience is when you hire a new candidate. You know how expensive it is when the new hire does not work out. You could be wasting six months to a year, and if the person does not meet expectations, you will have to start over with a new person. And there is no guarantee this next person will be any better. Many times, you hang on to average salespeople to avoid this risk.

Sales managers often wonder how to quickly determine if a new hire is a good fit for the position. What proactive advice do you have for penetrating new accounts, or for managing a new territory? Is your advice more than, "work hard"?

If your job is to develop new territories, penetrate new accounts in your area, or manage those who do either, this book is for you. I will show you how to develop new territories successfully, in half the time.

Costs of Poor Performance

Let's look at what's at stake for you personally when you are unable to ramp an area in a reasonable time. Assume that your on-target earnings are $150,000, consisting of 50% base and 50% leveraged compensation. Your annual commission target is $75,000. Assume you only make 50% of your number in the first year of sales. That is $37,500 not in your wallet, or approximately $3,000 per month. If you struggle in your first year with the wrong strategies, you are set up poorly for your second year, and performance will not increase as much as you would like.

And there are intangible costs:

- Stress of meager pipeline
- Increased scrutiny from management
- Bad selling behaviors caused by desperation that may alienate customers
- Bad reputation, bad references

Managers will also misunderstand your lack of success and assume you don't know how to sell or are lazy. The real problem? You just don't have the right strategies.

There's a personal cost for the sales manager as well: There is the stress of firing someone, lost time recruiting, and the fact that your team is a direct reflection of your capabilities. Your reps are most productive after the first year, so it's better to be managing a team that is producing rather than constantly hiring and training new reps.

Cost to the Company

And, of course, the company suffers. Here is a hard truth across all industry B2B sales: the turnover for new hires in sales is approximately 40% in the first year. How much does this cost the company? Rather than get into a specific cost example, let me just point out where the costs are, and you can do your own math. The cost is staggering and includes:

- Lost revenue or margin

- Cost of new hire training, sales training, and technical training

- Cost of time spent training and coaching existing salespeople

- Lost guarantees, or commission draws, if the person leaves

- Cost of lost marketing leads

- Cost of hiring new salespeople

  - Cost of recruiters

  - Cost of advertising for new position

  - Loss of relationship with customers

  - Negative perception of sales staff turnover

  - Time spent searching for new candidates, number candidates interviewed, and the number of people interviewing each of these candidates

  - Time training new salesperson

  - Ramp time of new person; loss of revenue and margin

  - No guarantees new person will be an improvement

The estimated cost of losing and replacing one salesperson is, at a minimum, three to five times the position's annual salary.

As you'll see, one of my goals in this book is to ensure that neither you nor your company incurs any of these costs.

Why I Wrote This Book

I have been a salesperson and sales manager, among other sales-related jobs, my entire career. My experience has been mostly in the IT industry. You will find many real-life examples and stories from multiple industries in this book, but the majority comes from the industry in which I spent my career. As you'll see, the advice is universal. Many of the examples come from when I was with a VAR, or value-added reseller. If the tactics and strategies work with a VAR, they will work for any B2B sales person. Resellers find it difficult to differentiate themselves from competitors. By definition, they do not have their own products. There are multiple companies in the same territory selling the identical products from the same vendors. This leaves the salesperson as the main differentiator to the customer. Veteran salespeople therefore learn early on that developing good relationships is the key to success. While most salespeople are concentrating on their products, the customer is looking at the salesperson and thinking, "Can I trust this person?" And that is the same in any industry. As you will see, the sales skills and strategies needed to succeed in this industry translate to any B2B sales environment.

When I started this book, I was a regional manager at an information technology (IT) reseller, or VAR. It was this new role as a regional manager that actually prompted me to write this book. I was given a territory that at one point had been one of the most successful regions in our company. Throughout the years, five salespeople were all at, or above, their quotas. However, in the two–three years prior to my taking over the region, we had turned over most of the team more than once. Our partners had lost faith in our company, and our customers were concerned about the health of the company due to the turnover of the sales force. This territory could support five to six salespeople. I only had three salespeople left and they were a mixed bag of experience, work ethic, and skills. One was experienced and performing, one had very little sales skill and was unwilling to learn, and the third was for the most part not showing up. So, my first job, which is not always easy, was to let the latter two go. My uphill battle continued:

- I had one salesperson, but I carried a quota for five salespeople

- I had to hire four new salespeople, and finding the right people takes time

- We had damaged customer relationships

- In the IT industry, as a VAR, it is not unheard of for a salesperson to take six months to get their first order

- It typically takes up to 12 months, if not longer, for a new salesperson to match pace with their monthly quota

I wanted to make money in my first year. I did not want to take the long ramp period as the definitive truth. I turned to several sales books I had purchased over the years, but I could not find one book on how to ramp a new sales territory. I reached out to colleagues whom I trusted in sales management roles, but the advice was pretty much the same: train the best you can, cold call, follow up on leads, and drive the pipeline. The main advice—or the belief—for success was to drive high activity. I always held the belief that high activity was important, but the wrong activity is purely a waste of time. I needed to identify which activities would help my reps start producing in the short term.

Lastly, I turned to personal experience. Before becoming a regional manager, I had worked as an account manager for this company for four years. Before that, I was a territory salesperson for two large, fast-growing manufacturers and a large VAR. I personally have ramped seven sales territories with varying degrees of success. (Of course, like any salesperson, I have had my share of losses, which I will be sharing with you as well.) However, I never stopped to think about why some territories never took off, why some took years to ramp, and why some were successful from the start. What was the common thread? What worked and what didn't? Why did 80% of our salespeople close an average of only five deals their first year?

I quickly learned that it had nothing to do with work ethic, as with Tom. I witnessed some of the hardest-working salespeople fail miserably. And my experience prompted additional questions: Why did only 20% of new hires reach quota? Why, in my most successful territory, did it take me four months to get my first order and why, by the end of the year, was I pulling in more business per month than most of the other salespeople at the company? Why did some of my own territories fail?

This desire to understand the first year of sales also led me to thoroughly research the science of selling, including buyer psychology, seller psychology, sales process, sales techniques, and behavioral change.

During the process of writing this book, I gained even more confidence as a salesperson and sales manager. In good conscience, and to be able to provide all the advice this book contains, I used the process I developed and outline here. I took a direct sales role with a new company. The new territory was a challenge and the previous two salespeople had failed by any metric you measure. They made very few sales, and secured perhaps two or three new accounts in about two years.

In my first year, my sales engineer and I secured sales with approximately 40 new customers and finished at 230% of our annual quota. While this is a small data set, I proved to myself that I was on to something with the system you are about to learn.

Traditional Sales Training Does Not Work

Here is the dirty little secret of sales training:

Sales training and materials are developed to be sold, not developed to work.

This may sound a bit harsh, but let's analyze the most popular topics of sales training. Sales books and training come in all shapes and sizes, but 80% of it falls into two categories:

- Sales skills

- Sales processes

Here's what I have learned and what the book will show you: Your success does not depend on your ability to manage opportunities, your ability to close, or your ability to "wow" with presentations.

This is a bold statement, but it's true. Salespeople with average skills can be very successful with the proper strategy. Most sales training, in contrast, concentrates on improving a salesperson's selling skills. I believe this is a lazy approach by management. Managers feel they need to do something to improve sales. So, they train the sales team on skills and expect better results.

This simply does not work. Management sees that the training does not work and they turn back to the trainers for help. The recommendation to solve this problem is, if they don't "get it" the first time, use repetition. Role play. Repeat over and over again. It sounds like common sense. The sales training community pushes the idea because it can sell more training time and materials to their customers.

Sales management buys into this because it is easy to blame the salesperson for not "getting it." They never stop to ask whether the salespeople are being tasked and managed effectively. You have probably seen this in training classes you have taken. You have a great teacher who motivates you. You are excited about everything you are learning. It all makes perfect sense. You role play over and over again until you have memorized the process. Then what happens when you get back in front of the customer? The ego kicks in. You now have something at stake, and you revert to your core ego-driven personality.

Ask yourself: Has sales training ever improved your skills? If so, you are in the top 5% of self-aware people. Someone needs to be completely self-aware to make significant change in personality.

I am no different. As I have already stated, I have read hundreds of sales books over my career, and I have taken multiple trainings, including some of the most popular training courses in the industry. It took me 10 years to realize I was one of the "talkers" who did not listen to customers enough. It has taken me an additional 10 years to improve on this bad personality trait. While I continue to improve, I am sure a 20-year return is not the quick results anyone is looking for. You want to see improvement today, not years from now.

The next area that is popular with sales training is the sales process. Again, the end customer is the VP of sales. One of their main responsibilities is to forecast accurately at a company level. Forecast accuracy is vital to the running of any company. Companies need to execute on business planning, and Wall Street is looking for revenue expectations. A good process should

- Help the sales force forecast more accurately.
- Drive proper selling behavior.

Most processes on the market are so cumbersome that management stops using them. However, at the end of the day, most companies hold on to old processes to justify the massive investment in tools. Salespeople are stuck using just the reporting aspects of the process, but selling productivity seldom increases.

This example highlights the issue of training focused in the wrong area.

The Charles Barkley Effect

A perfect example of the difficulty of overcoming ego is The Haney Project. Hank Haney is considered the one of the best golf instructors in the world. He has a television series on the Golf Channel, and each season, he takes one amateur and works with them to improve their golf game.

The first season is a classic. His amateur is ex-NBA star Charles Barkley. Charles's "natural" swing is horrid. He has glitches, stops in the middle of the down swing, and literally looks like he is going fall over every time he swings a golf club. (If you want see this swing, take a look at http://www.youtube.com/watch?v=WSx069MJ-cA.) Hank teaches the skill—how to swing the club—like we try to teach sales skills. They go to the driving range and practice and practice until Charles has a decently smooth swing. This practice is like sales role play. Then they go back on the golf course (the sales call), where the swing needs to produce results, and where there are consequences. What happens? The same horrid swing reemerges, as do your day-to-day sales skills. Why? Because under pressure, the subconscious mind takes over. The same thing happens to selling skills when you get back in front of a customer.

Skills vs. Strategy

Selling skills are of course important. Improper selling skills will hinder your ability to execute some of the fundamental strategies in this book. But let me be clear: the quickest road to better sales results is by shifting your strategy.

And that's exactly what this book shows you how to do. It has some selling techniques, some skills training, and some process, but majority is based on a strategy *anyone* can implement. Let's go back to the golf example. If you are an amateur golfer, you can spend months on the driving range with a golf pro, and maybe see a one- or two-stroke improvement. Or, you can go buy Jack Nicklaus's book, *Golf My Way*, which teaches nothing but shot preparation and golf course management. You learn how to aim at the right location, how to set up for the golf swing, how to aim away from trouble, which holes to attack, and which holes to play cautiously. He teaches you how to get the most out of your game regardless of your skill level. With these new strategies, you will see a five-six stroke improvement your first time back out on the golf course. And, they do not require you to improve your golf swing at all. This is the difference between strategy and skill.

You can work the strategies in this book in conjunction with the more popular methods like *Solution Selling* or the *Challenger Sale*. As with golf, I want the quick strategies to help my game *today*. But, I also continually work on the skills and methods that will improve my game in the long run. I believe you should do this as well.

You Picked the Right Book

If you want to sell more, and if you want to open up new territories successfully, congratulations. You have picked up the right book. It will not require you to deal with uncomfortable role play. It will not require you to change how you talk to your customers. It will not require you to change how you sell. The strategies it contains do not require you to change your personality. Instead, they help change the focus of your efforts, and they produce results.

Specifically, this book is intended to teach you the correct methods for gaining access and getting the all-important first order with new customers. You learn how to start building trust before you meet with the customer, how to engage new customers, how to message, how to identify real opportunities you can close, and how to plan your territory for rapid success.

This book is also for sales managers, who can use it to refocus their training efforts and achieve better results. (For that reason, I highly recommend that salespeople ramping a new sales territory share this book with your managers.) The sales manager will learn ways to measure early success, and it is not always in the form of expanding the pipeline in the beginning of the process. This requires you to demonstrate patience and insight, and to perhaps rethink what is the best for the long-term success in your region.

Roadmap to the Book

Here is what you will learn from this book:

- The major obstacles that plague most salespeople trying to acquire new accounts
- How customers make purchasing decisions
- A sales process to align with the buyer
- How focusing strictly on opportunity will sabotage your success
- Tactics for gaining access to prospects
- Skills and strategies for qualifying customers and opportunities
- Which prospects are worth your time, and which ones to cut loose
- Which products and services in your portfolio will give the greatest odds of success
- How to identify prospects who are ready to buy today
- How become the trusted, and therefore the preferred, vendor for potential opportunities
- How to manage and forecast opportunities

In short, you will learn how to win more new customers than ever before and cut in half the time it takes you to ramp a new sales territory.

Let's get started.

Setting the Foundation

Because if you have a strong foundation ... you can build or rebuild anything on it. But if you've got a weak foundation you can't build anything.

—Jack Scalia

Hunting Misunderstood

Sales Hunting Is a Science

Farming as we do it is hunting, and in the sea we act like barbarians.

—Jacques Yves Cousteau

In the sales world, people often talk of "farmers" and "hunters." Here's what they mean:

- A sales *hunter* finds new customers. The hunter is aggressive. The hunter takes no prisoners. The hunter must be tenacious at getting in the front door, and be adept at closing business quickly.

- A sales *farmer* manages existing accounts. Sales farmers have strong relationships with the customers to the point where customers often seek them out as problem solvers. The customer often presents the opportunity to the salesperson. Since the farmer understands the procurement and decision processes of the customer, closing business is fairly easy.

Put another way, the hunter has a slant toward the transaction, whereas the farmer leans more toward the relationship.

But are these conceptions of sales professionals backward? Think of farmers. They have a long process they have to trust. They plant seeds, water, fertilize, and wait weeks for plants to germinate. They water more, fertilize, hope the weather cooperates, and wait months for the plants to grow before they can harvest the produce. When developing a new territory, the salesperson is primarily dealing with all new accounts. This is a long process as well; salespeople need to find a way to get into a customer, develop a relationship, find an opportunity, see the opportunity through to the end, compete against an incumbent, and hopefully close some business. The farming process therefore seems to correlate with developing a new territory.

Salespeople with existing accounts—traditional sales farmers—are typically looking for new opportunities on familiar grounds. They know the customer, and opportunities pop up around them that they will easily "take down." In my view, this seems more like the hunting.

Learning to Hunt from My Barber

I have to thank my barber of 10 years for showing me that *hunting* is exactly the right term for securing a new customer. It was in listening to him talk to his buddies about hunting over the course of many haircuts that I realized how much I misunderstood hunting. The term hunter perfectly fits the act of penetrating and taking first orders from new customers. The problem was my misconception of hunting as a sport, a misconception that I believe is shared by most of the sales community.

Hunting is simple; you buy a hunting license, grab a gun, dress in camouflage or orange, walk through the woods, shoot the first deer you see, drag it back to the pick-up, and eventually eat it. This correlates perfectly with the advice given to most hunter salespeople. Grab a product presentation and wander through your territory. Find any customer who will listen to your presentation, put the opportunity on your forecast, close it, and cash your commission check.

In either scenario, however, your chances for success are not good. If you walk through the woods looking for deer, they will hear you and run. The same is true with sales. Yet most new salespeople do just this—they stomp around in their territories scaring off customers—based on advice from their managers.

The problem is, if you present your product or service to as many people as you can, you are "selling" at the most superficial level. Your customers might listen, but they will never allow you to fully engage in a real opportunity. Being focused on the initial opportunity, or your presentation, leaves you blind to the real opportunity: developing a long-term customer.

My barber taught me that hunting is a science. It is a game of patience. It takes preparation, knowledge, experience, skill, and a lot of hard work to be successful. When he hunts, or plans to hunt, he takes into consideration temperature, phases of the moon, wind, scents, ammunition selection, and proper gear. And if the land where he is going to hunt is new to him, he scouts it out first. And while this may sound obvious, he also needs to know what hunting season it is. He can speak for hours on the details of his science.

Let's look at how closely sales hunting and game hunting parallel each other.[1]

- The land on which you hunt is your customer at the company level. Your sales territory is made up of many hunting grounds, or many customers.

- Your prey, rather than an animal, is the opportunity or the deal.

- Getting in the door is much like finding property on which the owner will allow you to hunt. What is the best way to get permission to hunt?

- Camouflage hides hunters in the woods. Camouflage in sales is about looking different than your competition. Do you sound like every other salesperson and scare the deer away?

- Scouting a territory is parallel to qualifying a customer; what traits do you look for that indicate that there are deer here? What traits do you look for in your potential customers that indicate they are a match?

- Setting up your deer stand is equivalent to establishing trust with your customer. Do you try to shoot before your deer stand is set up? Are you even in the right hunting season? Do you know if you are wasting time working opportunities that have no chance to close?

- Selecting the right weapon and ammo is always critical. When you are ready to hunt for sales, which product should you lead with?

- You have to know when to squeeze the trigger and when not to. Do you have the sales skills necessary to build rapport, drive new opportunities, and then at just the right moment, pull the trigger and advance the sales cycle?

---

[1] Serious hunters reading this book will forgive me, I hope, for oversimplifying or misconstruing some aspects of hunting. The ignorance is my own—not my barber's.

- You have to know who you are in the hunting party. Hunting parties can consist of landowners, guides, sharpshooters, and so on. If you are in partner sales, or work with technical experts on your team, you need to understand your role in the sale, and what your customer expects from each person on the team. A good, well-oiled team can bring home many more trophies than an ill-trained team working out of sync.

Selling Is a Science

Sales hunting is a science, just as deer hunting is. There is a method, and a consistent approach, to growing sales with new customers. Selling is not randomly looking for opportunities and then relying on luck for the final outcome.

Although I will develop the hunting theme throughout the rest of this book—and point out where sales hunting takes its lead from deer hunting—I will not force the analogy on every concept discussed.

As I stated in the introduction, the principles in this book are based on years of selling and marketing experience, along with an abundance of sales research. This book is more about establishing and growing trust with your customers, just as a hunter learns to navigate and understand his hunting grounds to be prepared for an opportunity.

I believe that most people have trouble learning something when they don't believe the underlying principles of the material. And in my experience, too many salespeople pursue the "chase it down" form of sales. So, I will spend the first part of the book understanding why true sales hunting is all about preparation and developing the more subtle aspects of the craft. Then, together we will develop strategies to create trusted business relationships that will ensure if any new sales are to be had, you will book them.

Your success depends on developing a valued business relationship with your customer, not jumping on the first opportunity you find.

It's All About Trust

Customers do business with vendors they trust. But what is trust, or what elements of trust are important in a business relationship? I will use the four core elements of trust to build the model for sales hunting—Intention, Capability, Dedication, and Results. Customers want relationships with salespeople who have the intention of helping them, who bring value through personal, team, and solution capabilities, who are dedicated enough to follow through, and who help produce results that move their business in a positive direction. I will spend chapters on that last sentence.

Building trust gives you a position of strength with your customers. For example, you will learn when you have become the "chosen" vendor, which gives you the ability to hold firm in negotiations. It also gives you the ability to speak your mind with the customer. That's especially important, because your customers crave help from vendors they trust. A successful salesperson becomes, in essence, an extension of the customer's staff. You are there to help the customer drive success in their business. That means you have to accept responsibility. If you do not bring value, you will not be there very long, no matter how much a customer might like you.

Successful game hunters build a trusted relationship with the land. They do not chase the prey. They know that the relationship with the land is as important as learning how to shoot accurately. Without the relationship, there is never a chance to shoot. This holds true for sales. Any successful salesperson will tell you that they value the relationships they have built with their customers more than any specific opportunity. However, nearly every sales book, sales process, and training class revolves around an opportunity. Although they also teach skills to create better relationships, they rarely tie the relationship specifically to managing an opportunity. Relationships, after all, cannot be plotted on a spreadsheet.

(Well, as you'll learn, they can in fact be plotted on a spreadsheet—eventually. And in bigger numbers than opportunistic hunters will ever tally.)

To that end, I will define the tangible attributes of a trusted business relationship and discuss how to indicate the relative strength of each against your competition. These, too, are items you can put on a spreadsheet. I will also present clearly a structured map to develop valued relationships with your customers.

Although this model can be used for an entire sales force, this book is aimed at new account managers with new territories and salespeople trying to penetrate new accounts. It requires a fundamental shift in how you look at your business, but that doesn't mean you have to completely ignore everything you have been taught. I will build on a lot of basic sales processes, strategies, and techniques.

Get Ready to Learn—and Win New Sales

To make this a comprehensive book on new account selling, I am going to cover a lot of basic concepts in process, strategy, and tactics along the way. I believe that people learn better when they fully understand, and believe, the underlying foundation of the lesson. Put another way, "You must understand algebra before you can learn calculus." Be patient, as the book builds slowly from a fundamental foundation in sales process, through the phases of planning, to more advanced concepts such as business trust and buyer psychology. Stick with it and I can assure you that your sales will grow.

Summary

Put away your misconceptions about sales hunting. Forget the macho connotations associated with hunting and realize that it is a patient science that requires work and planning. Understand that there is a method to penetrating new accounts. Know that there is a learnable method for bringing in your first orders, or for booking much more than you have until now. Just as a good game hunter puts the land before the prey, you need to put the customer before the opportunity. As a wise man once said, "Opportunities at best will bring you a commission check; relationships build wealth."

> *Opportunities at best will bring you a commission check; relationships build wealth.*

—Chris Daltorio

Identify the Silent Sales Killers

You Never Had a Chance

Status quo, you know, is Latin for "the mess we're in."

—Ronald Reagan

Why are improved sales results so hard to drive in the first year? What are the root causes? To improve results, salespeople and management both grab onto tangible ideas like product training, working leads, work ethic, sales process, and sales skills training. But the difficulty in *ramping* (succeeding in) a new sales territory is often not rooted in the salesperson's lack of experience or sales skills. There are many *seasoned* sales professionals who fail to succeed in new territories. The reasons fall into the category of *status quo*.

There are many variations of the status quo:

- Potential customers are already doing business with an incumbent vendor

- Customers do not have a big enough issue to make a change

- Customers' fear of change and the risks it brings is holding them back

- Customers have fallen into the rut of habitual purchasing— the automatic use of an incumbent vendor, without thought

- Customers have competing uses for capital—they have more important projects than than the one you are proposing

- Customers are not in the market—they buy what you sell only every few years, or longer

Let's look at how each of these items works against developing new business in more depth.

"We Have a Guy for That"

Customers have standing relationships in place for almost everything they purchase. Whether they buy that product or service every week or every four years, they have a vendor. You may be a better, more caring, and more competent salesperson than the incumbent. You may work for a better company than the incumbent. And, you might have far better products or services than the incumbent. However, the incumbent salesperson has the most important asset in sales: the trusted business relationship.

Example

Here's an example. A reseller, VarTech, recently entered into a new relationship with a manufacturer, Brand Computer. Brand Computer has one of the largest product portfolios in the world, and they have resellers established in VarTech's region. As seen in Figure 2-1, the customer base has the option to buy through a value added reseller, or directly from Brand Computer. Being a new reseller competing against incumbent resellers, VarTech needs a strategy for how to ramp with this new manufacturer.

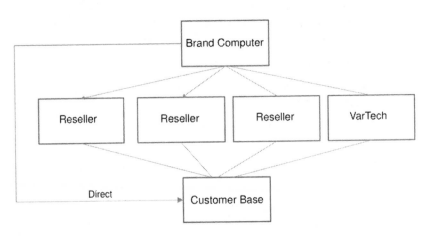

Figure 2-1. Path to market

Brand offers endless product training for VarTech's sales teams and engineers. Marketing programs are developed to introduce this new relationship to VarTech's customer base. Field sales teams from both companies conduct countless account mapping and territory planning sessions. Yet after six months, the reseller has very little sales traction. Looking for answers, sales management turns to the manufacturer for help. Brand Computer's answer is, predictably, more product training. Still, results do not improve.

A couple of months later, VarTech was able to hire two of Brand's senior, successful salespeople. These individuals interviewed very well. They passed the personality/sales profile tests. Their references checked out flawlessly. Their product knowledge of Brand Computer products is, naturally, well beyond any VarTech salesperson, since that's all they had been selling the previous five years.

Each of these new hires comes to the company with relationships with several customers. These relationships are at high levels, with the power buyers. That's reflected in their results—together they sold $30 million worth of products in the previous year. Clearly, these are senior salespeople—experienced, hard-working, and full of product knowledge.

This was the answer to VarTech's problems. The company's goal is to sell $3 million of the manufacturer's product in the first year. This goal is only 10% of what these individuals did the year before in their sales roles at Brand Computer.

But things didn't go as planned. In their first year at VarTech, they booked $100,000 in sales—99.7% less than they did the year before.

Here are two experienced, hardworking salespeople with track records of success. They had full support from the company. They had no trouble getting their feet in the door with their old customers. Sales managers went on high-level calls with them to most of their old customers. So, what was the problem? Why such horrific sales results which, incidentally, resulted in their terminations within 12 months?

To understand what went wrong, we must analyze their previous year of success. What made them successful during their tenure at Brand Computer? What was the sales model?

They did 100% of their business through resellers.

Let me repeat that. They did 100% of their business through a reseller like VarTech. These salespeople thus had more of a "how is everything going" type of relationship with the customer. The resellers, on the other hand, owned the valued business relationships with the customers. How do you think the calls went with their old customers now that they worked for VarTech, a competitor for many of them?

Let's analyze the initial conversation one had with an old customer. When asked by the customer, "Tell me about your new company," one of the new salespeople, Susan, and her sales manager spent 30 minutes with the customer reviewing the capabilities of their company. At the end of the appointment, the customer was at least honest with the new rep, "Susan, thank you for the overview of your new company. Sounds like there is a lot you can offer, and we value the relationship we have had with you. Thank you for the hard work you have done over the years. However, as you know, I also have a relationship with Jim at VPH (another reseller of Brand Computer). I can't just move my business to your new company. He has also been a great asset to our company, a trusted advisor. He probably has to screw up pretty big for us to change. They process our orders the way we like, our credit line is established, they are a preferred vendor in our system, and they have great engineering support."

In other words, "We have a guy for that."

The situation gets worse. The rep says, "We definitely understand that. I also liked working with Jim. So, what can we do to earn your business?" Two things here: She did not throw Jim under the bus. That's good. But she gave up all her power. That's bad.

The customer says, "Well as business comes up I can give you a chance to quote."

Susan replies with a smile, "Thank you. All we ask for is a chance."

Susan and the sales manager leave the call happy. The door is open! The customer is giving them a chance. The sad fact is that Susan and the manager think the only chance they have against Jim is to win on price, since he is giving them a chance to quote.

Does this turn out as they hope?

They get a chance, actually several, over the course of the year. However, Susan's replacement at Brand Computer is working with Jim, the incumbent. In the IT industry, the first company to register the deal with the manufacturer enjoys a significant cost advantage over competing resellers, making it nearly impossible for VarTech to use lower pricing as a strategy. So, Susan never has a chance to win on price, which in itself is a bad way to earn business.

Why? Let's say this "get a chance" strategy had worked. They get to quote on a project. The sales manager wants this customer, so they take the business at very low prices. With this strategy, they become the low-cost provider, a weak vendor, and not a partner. Winning on price just gives up your personal value to the customer.

But Susan never got even this far, and she was out of a job within a year. Later, I will outline the strategies Susan should have used to compete against the incumbent.

Habitual Purchasing

Habitual purchasing is a sales "relationship" in its lowest form: "We just buy all that stuff through Larry." Customers who have high transaction rates will often fall into this category. They have a preferred vendor, the order process is routine, and pricing seems fair. They might even have certain items show up month after month. They might not have seen the salesperson in months. But, nonetheless, "We buy our stuff from Larry."

Example

Let's say a newsales person, Sara, is trying to sell dental supplies to a busy dentist. She visits his office every week, in the hope she can actually catch the dentist to talk to him. This dentist had a relationship with a salesperson, Ben. Ben was a relationship guy. He won over the dentist when the dentist was just starting out. For 10 years, the dentist bought all his dental supplies from Ben's company. Ben retired two years ago, and Chris replaced him. Chris barely steps foot in the dentist's office. Chris is young, and he has nothing in common with this dentist. Nonetheless, the dentist keeps ordering from Chris's company.

Over the years, the dentist has had to deal with so many different salespeople, he got to the point he does not even take calls or appointments from anyone new. His automatic response, and his defense against new salespeople is, "I buy my stuff from Ben's, or that new kid's, company." He probably repeats this so many times that he almost believes he is not allowed to go anywhere else.

This is habitual purchasing. The dentist has a "relationship," but it is more out of habit. He does not have to think about it. At the end of the month they tally up their inventory and just send an order over. The dentist even says, "What I like about this new kid is that he does not try to sell me." He views new salespeople as just trying to sell him something. He views the kid who he doesn't know as his preferred supplier, "Because he understands I just want to order and not be sold." In reality, Chris does not understand anything about this dentist. he has tried to meet with him often, and the dentist rebuffs him, saying, "We are good. We use you; no need to come in." Chris eventually will just stop calling.

So, the new person, Sara, coming in has practically no chance. What can she do to talk to this dentist? I will share the strategies she uses to eventually win this dentist's business later in the book.

Don't give up on customers in "habitual purchase" mode. They meet the best quality of any customer—they are purchasing. Eventually they will understand that salespeople can help them do more business or save money.

Not in the Market

In most B2B sales, buying cycles are lengthy. I will define *buying cycles* in detail later, but here is a simple definition for this chapter—it's the period of time between customer purchases. Do they buy what you sell every week, every year, every four years, 10 years, or 20 years? Your only chance of beating an incumbent vendor is to beat them to the punch. You need perfect timing to engage the customer when they decide they need to buy and before they call the incumbent. This window of opportunity is very small. If they purchase—or consider a vendor change—every four years, this window of opportunity is maybe two months prior to the customer seriously considering the solution. That is a probability of 4.2% to engage the customer at just the right time. I will explore this at length in Chapter 7, Build Business Relationships.

Most sales processes have you believe that if you can create enough pain, or expand on an issue the customer has, they will suddenly be in the market. This is not the answer. What if the customer just purchased? What if there really is no issue? What is your strategy at that point? Customers live with pain all the time. While pain must be present for the customer to make a purchase, you cannot always manufacture pain for the customer. Plus, customers often live with pain for various reasons.

Example

The best way to demonstrate customers living with pain is through an example we can all relate to on a personal level. On a day-to-day basis, you live in a house. Typically, you buy what you can afford at the time. Over the course of the years, you start to make more money. You have your first kid. You start to accumulate more stuff, and the house starts to feel too small. Every day, you drive past a new neighborhood that is closer to work and where the homes are larger and nicer than the home you live in. You would love to move, and you now make enough money to afford a new home in this neighborhood. Even your ego is kicking in; your internal voice is saying, "Move up, you deserve it."

You drive up to your existing home and see all the work you have put into the yard, you walk into the living room where you have laid the hardwood floor yourself. You see where your child took their first steps.

The next morning it's Friday, but you are stuck in traffic and late for work, and you are sitting in front of that new neighborhood, "Wow, it would be nice to have saved 15 minutes on my commute. I would be past this traffic by now." Then you start to seriously consider a move. As traffic eases up, you think about the effort it would take to move. You have to list your house, which means finding an agent. You will have to keep your house immaculate for the next three months. On the other side, you might have to deal with builders in the new neighborhood, and timing the sale of your current house with having the new house be move-in ready. The hassle of the physical move itself is a huge consideration. The new home will be bigger, which means you will need new furniture. You just finished hanging blinds in every window of the old house after five years. You will have to landscape and hang blinds in this new house. The list continues in your mind.

On the way home you start to wonder what your weekend plans should be, but you have nothing planned. You start to think, "The weather is great. You know what, I think I am going to go look for a new boat this weekend." Thoughts of a new house have evaporated ... for now.

This example points out several reasons why customers live with pain.

1. They are emotionally tied to a solution they presently have. In a business setting, they made a significant purchasing decision at some point. They may have tweaked the solution over the years. They are comfortable with their solution. They know the ins and outs of their current solution.

2. The thought of change, or of the unknown, is too overwhelming. The act of change will not be easy. They fear the learning curve of a new solution.

3. They have other uses for their money. They have more urgent projects.

In this example, you hate the commute and really want a new house that is bigger and in a better location. You know you have a long commute. You know you keep tripping on toys in your small home. But, you are not willing to change for a variety of reasons. Even if a real estate agent came in and starting selling features and benefits of the new home and neighborhood, you are still not ready to make the emotional decision to move. *It is just easier to do nothing.*

Understand that in many cases it is easier to do nothing than to entertain the idea of buying what you are selling. Even if your solution is superior, the thought of changing is too daunting for many. But there are ways to get people to look to you first when they do decide to buy.

More on the Status Quo

What I just described with the sections "Not in the Market," "We Have a Guy for That," and "Habitual Purchasing" is *status quo*. Status quo is also known as making no decision. It's the act of keeping the same solution, or doing business as usual. So even if you can convince the customer there is a need, how do you beat the incumbent? How do these challenges present themselves? How do you know when the customer is not in the market or if you are in a competitive environment? The customer will not always be direct. And here is the interesting part—in status quo, regardless of which category the buyer falls in, she will present the same way, usually with silence.

The most frustrating part of being a new salesperson is that prospects don't bother to call you back, return your voice messages, or acknowledge your e-mails. After all, they not only have a guy for that, but they have 10 other salespeople waiting in line to provide that service or product.

It's frustrating. You make 50 cold calls a day. You attend networking events. You join lead-sharing groups. You do your education on the customer. You have the greatest new product on the market. But, your customer does not acknowledge any of this. You are just another person, and they hit delete before the voicemail system has a chance to play the message through to your name.

We have all been customers, and we know what customers face. Think about it, how many voicemails do you get a day, how many e-mails? Think about the inbox of your personal e-mail account. How many spam e-mails do you get? When you don't recognize the name, do you bother to read the e-mail? When a telemarketer calls you, don't you want to hang up as quickly as possible? Business customers are people with busy lives. They do not feel any different.

Throughout the book, I discuss tactics and methods to get past the silence and gain access to prospects.

Understand the Opportunity Trap

The "opportunity trap" is how you learn about the power of the status quo. Thanks to your efforts, you engage a customer with an opportunity. They seem to want your input and bid. But they have no intention of awarding you the deal. You can identify you are falling into this trap over and over again because you have a large pipeline but never seem to close anything. Most managers will come to believe that you have a problem with closing business.

In your first year, if you go straight after opportunity, your relationship is not nearly strong enough to unseat other vendors with more established relationships. You probably are losing most of your deals to "the guy we have for that." The difference is now you have skin in the game. You now see the opportunity, spend time on the opportunity, forecast the opportunity, and usually lose the deal. The problem is that customers need to look at more than one solution, or proposal, whenever there is a large purchase. They need to do this either because of policy, where they require three proposals, or because they are looking to negotiate against their chosen vendor. The other vendors they use for comparison are called "column fodder."

I have devoted an entire chapter to the opportunity trap and becoming "column fodder." For now, let's take an example that has nothing to do with sales, but will drive home the point: *American Idol*. If you have been living under a rock for the last 10 years, or this book is still in print 50 years from now, and you have not heard of it, *American Idol* is a singing contest television show. Each season, they start with literally thousands of contestants, and, through a series of eliminations, they crown one winner. Here is how the process works. Before the season starts, they go to eight or nine cities. They advertise for contestants and fill up a football stadium in each city with the hopefuls. Each meets with a producer of the show, to see if they can get a chance to perform for the celebrity judges, with a potential to get on TV in the early rounds. The celebrity judges then select maybe 200 contestants to advance in the competition. The 200 contestants over the course of a week get whittled down to 15 contestants who make the live shows. Then, viewers vote on their favorite singer, and the one with the least number of votes gets eliminated each week until there is a one winner.

In the very first elimination event, the producers screen thousands of hopefuls to put in front of the celebrity judges. The four types that make it to television are:

1. The great singers.

2. The singers that the producers need a second opinion about. They may have a unique quality or voice.

3. The "fun" people who do crazy things that will be fun to watch. They have no chance to win, and they know it. They are just happy to get on television.

4. The people who think they are good but are just awful. These people make for the best television because they can't believe they are not good, and they go insane when they are eliminated from consideration.

How does this relate to sales? In sales you have a champion, a primary point of contact at the customer who guides you through the sales cycle. The champion is analogous to the producer. As with the producers, the champions have a mission, one that is in the best interest of the show or the company. Who does the champion advance in the sales cycle?

1. The incumbent, "the guy," the great singer.

2. The hopeful, "the new guy they like." The second option singer.

3. The vendors they are going use to beat up on price to keep the first two companies honest. But, unlike the category 3 singers on *American Idol*, you still might have a chance at this stage. Later, you'll learn different strategies. Or, if they stick you in this category and you know it, you can minimize wasting your sales time by bowing out early.

4. This is the worst position as a salesperson. You think you have a great opportunity. And, you work it to the bitter end. You forecast it. You waste your time and company resources. However, you never had a chance in the first place. This is column fodder.

Where would you rather lose a deal—before the producers, or before the 20 million TV viewers? Would you rather qualify the deal out early or waste time—hours, weeks, or months—holding on to hope? On the show, the singers with little talent who are told by the producers they are good are devastated when they learn the truth from the celebrity judges. Salespeople in this category are frustrated and confused, because all along their "champion" was telling them they were winning the deal.

I will help you identify if you are number 1, 2, 3, or 4 in the process. This will help you understand why you lose so many deals in the first year, and it will help you avoid wasting that precious time. I will also help you identify if opportunities you uncover are worth working, or reporting in your forecast. But most importantly, I will discuss how to take advantage of opportunities that you do have a chance to win.

Avoiding the opportunity trap is not an easy problem to overcome. You will be pressured to build a pipeline. Since your numbers are not great when you are starting a new territory, you will have personal and managerial pressure to work these deals hard to the bitter end. Along the way, you may feel your only chance to start doing business with a customer is through aggressive pricing. This is a mistake. It will only hurt your long-term relationship. Still, there are some managers out there who will have you work bad deals and answer bad requests for proposals (RFPs). "A 15% chance of winning just means you have to answer eight RFPs to win one," the manager might say. This is a classic case of working hard, not smart. How do you get around this?

In the introduction, you read about Tom, a typical first-year salesperson. Tom is hardworking. He has no problem getting appointments with new customers, which is the first challenge. He uncovered, and worked, many new sales opportunities. However, he closed very few deals, and eventually it cost him his job. He exhibited the classic behavior of chasing opportunities. He has a strong pipeline but never seems to close a deal; he is great at getting appointments but has trouble winning any business. The reason for this is simple. When he finds an opportunity, he is not in a position to win the deal. It's like spotting a deer out of hunting season.

I will soon cover this trap in depth—how to avoid it, and, if you are in the trap, how to recognize and get out of it.

How Buyers View You

Beware of opportunities early in your relationship with potential customers. I have used the *American Idol* example to loosely define column fodder. An educated buyer will look at more than one vendor to compare and negotiate pricing. Professional buyers are taught to engage with three or four vendors with each deal. Let's label the vendors as A, B, C, and D.

A is the vendor that the customer wants, the customer who has the trusted relationship. Determining if you are this vendor should not be difficult. Vendor A can be the incumbent, or the vendor that helped the customer discover a need and establish the purchasing criteria. This is the vendor that probably spent the most time with the customer. Vendor A will get access to the true decision-makers.

The customer can live with Vendor B, if they do not get the pricing or terms they believe are fair from A. You can identify yourself as B if you are not the incumbent but helped identify a need for the customer. You have a unique solution that offers greater value than A. The customer has spent a considerable amount of time with you. Vendor B has controlled access to power.

Vendors C and D for the most part are there to help negotiate the pricing of Vendors B and A. The customer spends very little time with these vendors. These vendors are late to the game and are given the requirements of the project, but they have no influence over the criteria. A lot of times, Vendors C and D will receive a call asking for pricing. Or, on the first few visits to the customer, the customer may say, "Great timing. Yes, we have something we need. Here are the criteria. Can you get us pricing?" If you are answering an RFP that you had no input on, you must consider yourself Vendor C or D.

If you didn't help shape the RFP you are bidding on, understand that you are most likely a third- or fourth-tier vendor and have your work cut out for you. Or you have no chance of winning the sale no matter what you do.

Most sales processes teach that one of the criteria you must have to win a deal is a champion. This is an individual at the customer site who guides you through the process, sharing information like decision criteria, who the players are, who the competition is, and so on. Educated customers are taught to assign a champion to all the vendors in the running, even the ones they have no intention of purchasing from. Keep in the back of your mind the questions, "Did we earn this level of support from the customer?" If the answer is no, you most likely are Vendor C or D.

Here is the basic strategy of the multivendor approach, which is taught to most buyers. Each vendor is assigned a champion. The champion helps the vendor understand the requirements of the project. Champions for Vendors C and D will make them think they are winning, but they need better pricing. The customer will keep Vendors A and B insecure, never giving them the feeling they are winning.

Vendor D thinks all they need to do is provide better pricing, so they do. The customer takes that pricing and negotiates with Vendor C for better pricing. With a good price in hand, the customer now approaches Vendor B who, remember, has been kept insecure, and asks them for even deeper pricing than Vendor C. Now they have a strong price, a solution, and a vendor they can live with, Vendor B. They will say to Vendor A, "We have a vendor we like. You are now in the lead, but you need to match or come close to Vendor B's offer."

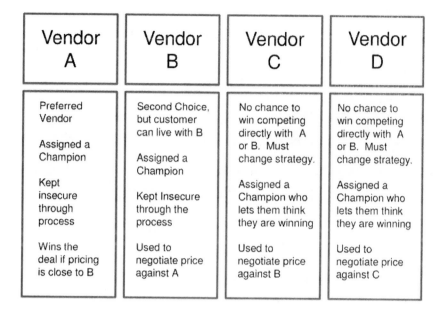

Figure 2-2. Column fodder

The trap is, if you are Vendor C or D, you have been engaged on this opportunity by the customer very early in the relationship. You have not built trust. You must question why they would trust you with such a large project. Have they investigated your capabilities? Probably not, which is a telling sign. That's why you do not want to spend a lot of time on these opportunities early in the relationship. In short:

1. You will be forced to use lower pricing. This will pigeon-hole you as the low-cost vendor.

2. You will get out of alignment with your customer if you think you are losing. You try too hard.

3. The deal becomes about your quota and not their project. Your perceived intentions with this customer can be forever damaged.

4. You can waste a ton of time on these deals and you can spend your time better establishing relationships with customers who might actually buy from you.

The opportunity trap becomes a vicious cycle that is hard to get out of. You end up wasting time on opportunities that you do not have a chance to close. So, your pipeline is weak, and you look for more opportunities that have little chance to close. This lack of strategy will kill the first year of sales, and put your job in jeopardy. It is the same strategy as the hunter grabbing a gun, walking into the woods, and chasing deer. The hunter is much better off understanding the land, setting up his deer stand, and allowing the prey to come to him.

These Leads Suck

Here's another problem plaguing new salespeople or those developing new areas. You have a great marketing department. You get three to four leads a week, or a day, depending on your industry. You seem to be working harder than anyone, not passing up any lead, and working them until they close or die. The issue is that these leads are opportunity-focused.

Say you get a lead from marketing. It has all the details.

- Contact name
- Contact number
- Contact e-mail
- Brief description of interest
- Date for an appointment
- Expected purchase timeframe

You go into your Customer Resource Management (CRM) system and accept the lead. Next, you call the customer to confirm the call. Approximately 50% of the time, the customers will say they need to reschedule, and to please call back in a couple of weeks. But this time, the customer confirms. You are excited that you have an appointment, a "real" lead. You drive to the customer and start, "So you are interested in X." The customer is confused and says, "That's not what I told the person on the phone. I told them maybe next year." So, you start to back-pedal a bit and begin to qualify the customer. The customer seems a bit guarded and does not share that much information. You go back to the office, sign into the CRM system, and update the status of the lead as dead. But, you put in a callback reminder six months out.

What went wrong? Why was the lead information wrong? What could you have done differently?

Your manager will track success with leads. Do you follow through with them? What close rate do you have? Marketing will want to cost-justify their lead programs and will also track the success of the leads passed to the field. Not being near your sales goals, leads become a crutch. You work every lead to the end. That's what your gut instinct says to do, and your manager keeps saying, "Success will come; keep working your leads."

Leads are a great tool, but only if you use them correctly. Leads are not the opportunity—leads are a foot in the door. Concentrating on the details of the lead will focus you specifically on opportunity, which means you'll fall into the same dilemma as before: they have a guy for that. They engage you on deals you have no chance to close, or you don't run into a dead end talking about a specific opportunity. If you start to qualify the customer, you leave the door open.

Example

A company's finance department is having a review with the president. The CFO brings to the president's attention that an incumbent software provider is delivering less-than-acceptable support. The discussion becomes whether or not the vendor can be replaced. The CFO says that they are pretty much locked into the incumbent solution. Even though they do not like this vendor, it would be too costly and cumbersome to change the technology. So, what do they do to get better service from this vendor? The president says, "We need to find a competing technology. Our current vendor needs to think this is a real threat. The new vendor needs to think they are winning, so we can get a great proposal we can leverage against our current vendor."

They engage a new vendor with all intentions of deceiving it. They are going to give some salesperson hope, but no chance. Would they do this to a vendor who has been working for their business? No, they actively seek out a "stranger."

This is not an isolated case. I know of a major customer who has a strong relationship with a vendor. They need to refresh the equipment every four years. Every four years they find a competitor who is willing to "compete" for the business. Every four years, they take the competing proposal and negotiate price with the incumbent, and the incumbent wins. This customer has done this over the last 20 years, so most people in the industry know that working this deal is a waste of time. But, every four years, they find a hopeful, with "happy ears," who is willing to take the bait—even when partners and other people in the industry are telling the salesperson they have no chance. This new salesperson wastes months of work on a losing effort.

Example

You do the same thing as a consumer. You are buying a car and go to your nearest dealership. You negotiate what you think is a good price, but you head home to think about it. You want the car, but you want to make sure you are getting a good deal. When you get home, you call a dealer that is two hours away and you say, "I am looking to buy a car. I would be willing to drive the two hours if you give a great price."

The salesperson on the other end of the phone says, "Let me see what I can do." He goes to his manager and says he has a customer willing to drive down if they can give him a good price. He is engaged in the sales cycle, getting management involved, and so on. He calls the customer back and says, "Yes, we can meet the price you are looking for."

The price is very similar to the local dealer's price. You got the information you needed, "Thank you, let me think about it."

The price from the original dealer is fair so now you know you got a good deal. Even if it was not fair, you most likely will take that price and try to negotiate with the local dealer. You never had any intention of driving two hours to buy from the other dealer, yet you engaged them with the carrot of a sale. You intentionally wasted a salesperson's time. It happens all the time!

Summary

This chapter outlined the major challenges you face when trying to win business with a new customer. The number one issue is that they are unwilling to change the current solution or current vendor. I will explore each of these challenges in more detail and discuss the strategies you need to first gain access, then win the trust of the customer, then focus on opportunity, and finally close the deal. You need to think outside the opportunity. However, that is where I will start, with the basics of an opportunity. The best place to start learning about opporunity is to understand the process your customers follow when making purchasing decisions. I will cover that process in the next chapter.

The Buyer Process

Laying the Foundation

Don't reinvent the wheel, just realign it.

—Anthony J. D'Angelo

You need to lay a foundation on which to build the strategies needed to win new customers. The first place to start is to understand the process the buyers follow with every purchase, small or big. This is a naturally occurring series of stages; the goal is to define each of the stages to give you common ground to build upon.

The Buying Cycle

Books regarding selling and buying cycles fill the shelves of stores. They go into much more detail. (More information on cycles can also be found in the reference section at the back of this book.) There are many different sales processes companies use, and most likely your company has a process in place.

My model is a simplified version that encompasses the main concepts of most processes (Figure 3-1). The core buying processes are the Needs Analysis, Evaluate, and Purchase phases. In total, this model defines the entire vendor-customer relationship cycle.

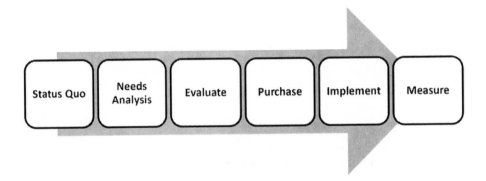

Figure 3-1. Buying process

This process applies to every purchase a customer makes, from consumer-based purchases to multi-million dollar business-to-business purchases.

Let's look at each of the steps in order.

Status Quo

Customers are conducting business as usual. They have their preferred vendors, and they may be evaluating purchases today. They are influenced by industry trends. They are constantly being asked to drive cost down. In some cases, depending on which department is the target of your sales efforts, they may be asked to increase revenues. Today, the customer is living with issues. They may not be aware of the issues they have. They may have inefficiencies that they may not be aware of. Customers always want to simplify their lives, so a lot of times they have vendor-reduction programs underway. They have 30 other people just like you calling them daily. At a certain point, a compelling event—called a *trigger*—will occur that will cause them to move to the next step.

Needs Analysis

An event has happened, or a business need arises that influences a particular department. The customer is now tasked with understanding the issue. Depending on the complexity of the issue, customers will look for external help to define their needs further and start exploring options to solve their issue. Once they feel they have a solution, or even multiple solutions, they proceed to the next phase.

Evaluation

Customers look at each option. They ensure the solution works to the specifications the vendor has promised. Once they settle on the most helpful solution, they move to the purchase phase.

Purchase

The purchase phase for the customer involves budget approval, if not already done; negotiations with the vendor(s), contracts, terms, and conditions; and purchase orders.

Most buyer and sales cycles stop after the close, since they are typically focused on the sale. I want to discuss two more steps that truly complete the buyer/seller relationship. These steps are important in the process of understanding your main competitor, the incumbent. I will discuss later how the stages impact trust and how they create an unfair playing field that you must be aware of.

Implement

Buyers will implement the solution or utilize the product they purchased. The buyer can implement the solution by themselves or with help from the seller. The buyer is evaluating the ease of implementation. Are there any surprises? Challenges? Did the seller stay past the close of the sale? Was implementation easy or hard?

Measure

Does the solution live up to the buyer's expectations? This step is often neglected by both buyer and seller. In most B2B sales, an ROI is presented. Does the solution in fact meet the ROI objectives? This is one of the most important steps in maintaining customers, and lead to easier referrals; both internal to the customer and external.

The final two steps in the sales cycle—implementing and measuring—are areas that most salespeople neglect. If you want to be a superior salesperson, pay attention to these final steps in all sales. The good news for the hunter is that the typical incumbent's lack of focus in these stages is a weakness you can exploit. Again, I will discuss this in further detail later in the book.

The Buyer's Four Concerns

Concentrating back on the main purchase phases—Need Analysis, Evaluate, Purchase—the buyer balances four psychological concerns. These concerns are need, cost, solution, and risk. As Figure 3-2 shows, the relative level of concern for each of these shifts throughout the buying process.

Buyer Concerns

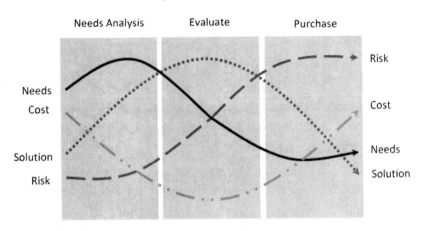

Figure 3-2. Shifting buyer concerns

When buyers first enter into the buying cycle, the primary concern is need, followed by cost, solution, and risk. When you enter into a decision to purchase, you know you need something, and you know about how much you can afford, or how much a solution might cost. Today this has never been more true with pricing information on the internet. In the first phase, buyers start off not as concerned with the solution. As buyers progress through this stage, they evaluate their needs in more detail and start to get a better sense of what they are looking for—the solution. Notice that cost concerns start going down. Risk starts to rise since the buyer is spending more time on this purchase—the risk of lost time.

In the evaluation stage, customers are focused on the solution; they may test-drive a car, look at a house, try ice cream flavors, demo your solution, or conduct a formal evaluation. During this phase, buyers stop focusing on the need, and start focusing on the features and functions. Cost concerns are very low. Risk continues to rise as they invest more time in the process.

In the purchase phase, the focus moves to risk. Buyers are concerned about whether they are making the right decision. Do they sign on the bottom line? What if they make a mistake? In a business setting, this can affect a person's career if the purchase is large. The concern with cost rises in this stage, but notice that cost is never top of mind in any stage. It is also important to note that need and solution are nearly out of mind in the final stage.

Example

This example illustrates the activities and concerns as they shift throughout the buying cycle. It revisits the house scenario discussed in Chapter 2.

In status quo, everyday living, you have been thinking about moving. But you decide you can live with the pain of the commute, and you are okay with the smaller house. The thought of the cost and chore of moving has you cringing. You get home Friday after work, and walk into the kitchen to talk to your wife about your idea of buying a boat. Before you open your mouth, your wife, smiling, says, "Guess what?"

"What?"

"We are going to have another baby!!"

Being smart, you tuck the bass boat idea away. "Wow that's awesome honey." After some hugs and kisses, you say, "You know, we need to buy a new house."

You just had a compelling event, a *trigger*. There is no way your current house will provide enough room for two kids.

Most likely, you do not have real estate agents cold calling you, but over the years you have made friends with one or two, and you call the one you feel will help you find the home you need, someone who knows the market.

Needs Analysis

As far as the seller is concerned, this is when the buyer enters the market and into needs analysis. Assume that you are sitting down with the agent for the first time to go through your needs. In the early part of the sales cycle, your needs are loosely defined: you know about where you need to look, how much you are willing to spend, and you probably have an idea of the number of bedrooms. When you meet with the agent, she will start to define your needs in more detail, probably by asking a series of questions. How old are your kids? Are you looking for a sidewalk neighborhood, or more in the country? How long of a commute are you willing to tolerate? Does the age of the home matter? Would you like new construction? Number of bathrooms? How much land are you looking for? Do you care which school district? And, so on.

Just as in the buyer concern graph, you come in with some needs, and then start to more clearly define them. During that process, the buyer is also starting to form a better idea of what they are looking for, or the solution. While defining the needs, cost is not discussed past the initial range you give the agent. At this point you are just developing a wish list.

Evaluation

Now that the agent has a good idea of what you are looking for, she will go online and do a quick search of homes for sale that meet your criteria. Now starts the evaluation period. You sort through all the listings and, based on gut, pictures, pricing, narrow down the list to 5–10 houses to evaluate. You and the agent spend the next week, or longer, touring houses. You look carefully at every house to see if it meets your criteria, while looking for good and bad features.

Look again at the buyer concerns. The buyer's original needs, or criteria, are becoming less of a concern since most of the houses should have the basics. But, you now are looking at the condition of the house, the wow of the kitchen, the smell of pets. You are more concerned with the bells and whistles of the solution. Cost goes out the window. "What an amazing view of the lake," you might say, even though the price of this option may be completely beyond your original price range. The evaluation stage closes with choosing a house, and having an inspector make sure that everything is up to code.

Purchase

The purchase stage starts with making an offer. Concerns and emotions can run high at this point. Risk is the highest concern; you just spent two weeks running all over looking at one house after another, and you and your wife "fell in love" with one. Concerns with solution and need are both at an all-time low. Now it's about the risk and the price. Price is not the main factor in closing. Rarely do homebuyers go for the lowest-price house they look at. Risk is two-fold in the last stage—the risk of not getting what you need and the risk of signing. Now it's time to sign the mortgage papers. You and your wife sit in the lawyer's office signing 40 different documents. You have seen the numbers for the last two weeks, but now is the time to sign, and that's when risk is a huge concern.

Exercise

It would be a great exercise for you to imagine any purchase you have made over the last week, and think through the entire buyer process. For example, you are driving around with the family on a hot day. The kids are getting antsy, so you decide to stop for some ice cream. You just went from status quo to needs analysis. You go through each step by evaluating (sampling), purchasing, implementing, and measuring results (tasting). Will you get this flavor again, or use this ice cream shop again? Every purchase goes through the process and different levels of buyer concern. The magnitude of the purchase determines the effort spent on each phase, and the range of buyer emotions you will experience. Think through going to a restaurant, buying a car, or purchasing a vacation.

Summary

Customers go through each stage of the buying process with every purchase. In some cases, parts of the process are condensed or simplified. You will learn that customers might make the process easier for some vendors and harder for others, depending on the level of trust they have with each. In the next chapter, you will see that sales cycles are nothing more than aligning with the buyer cycles.

The Sales Process

Align with the Buyer

Sales is like a dance; you and the customer take the same steps. The successful salesperson is not afraid to take the lead, or step on a few toes.

—Dave Monty

To start to define the sales process, let's start with the end in mind. Ultimately, you want the customers to use and gain value from what you sell them. However, you must win the sale the sale first. So what do you need to win a deal?

- *Pain.* Every sales process revolves around the concept of pain. Without pain, or need, there is no order. Throughout my career, I have learned that a compelling event is more important than mere pain. A compelling event is pain with a time element. This is the best type of pain because it makes predicting and closing business easier. "Compelling event" means the customer has a deadline. Without a deadline, opportunities will drag indefinitely, which can be a huge drain on the sales rep's time.

- *Solution.* The customer needs to envision that your offering will solve the pain, or fill the need. The customer needs to see value. There has to be a return on investment (ROI). What they spend must either increase revenue or reduce cost greater than the investment.

- *Authority.* You need a "yes" from someone within the organization who has authority to purchase (otherwise known as power).

- *Understanding.* You need to identify and understand the purchasing decision process.

- *Relationship.* You must have a trusted, valued business relationship with the customer.

So how do you bring the customer from need/pain to purchase? Better yet, what does the customer need to identify their need and decide to make a purchase? The buyer follows a psychological process called the buying process (defined in the last chapter). The sales process simply needs to align with that process.

The Sales Cycle

As with the buyer cycle, the sales cycle can have many more stages. Again, I will stick with a basic sales process in order to build deeper concepts. Figure 4-1 shows the process and how it correlates with the buying cycle. When working new territories or breaking into new accounts, your focus will be mainly on the first two stages of this process—Plan and Qualify.

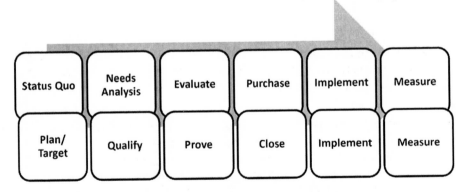

Figure 4-1. The sales process involves defining the buying stages from the sales persective

Let's look at each step in turn.

Plan

Sellers must plan how they will develop their customers and territories. You must align with your customers even before you meet or reach out to them. You need to learn everything there is to know about your industry, and begin the process to learn about your customer. This knowledge can be found online, from company annual reports, from partners in your industry, and through ongoing interactions with the customer. Based on vertical markets, you can also make assumptions on customer needs. Planning also involves strategizing where to spend your time wisely.

Qualify

Understand the customer's needs. With most models, the emphasis is on qualifying the opportunity. Does it meet all the criteria for an order to be placed? Is there pain, a decision process, a yes from power, and a good solution? You guide the conversation slowly toward your solution based on initial customer needs. You expand the needs to fit the solution. Paint a vision for the customer for how your solution can help them solve their problem or issue. Understand the evaluation process.

This model will shift the emphasis from qualifying the opportunity to qualifying the customer. In the traditional model, the main question you need to answer in this stage is, "Is the opportunity worth spending time on?" In this model, the question becomes, "Is the customer worth my time regardless of an immediate, qualified opportunity?" At this point, I am laying the foundation of the sales cycle. I will spend chapters on this shift in focus.

In either model, this stage is the most important, as this is where a solid foundation of trust is built.

Prove

This stage is all about understanding the decision criteria your customer is using to make a decision. It's also about providing a demo of your product, as well as your service capabilities. Give customers the product to evaluate in their setting.

Close

Closing is, in the context of this sales process, the act of taking an order. Closing sales is an art that is present at every stage of the sale. The act of closing, if you have qualified right, and have proved your solution meets their business requirements, should be the simple acts of negotiating, working out the terms of contracts, and completing purchase orders.

Implement

Implementation is simply the customer using your service or product. Depending on your offering, this can be a simple process or take years. The buyer or the seller may be responsible for the implementation. However, it is important for the seller to stay engaged at this stage to ensure it runs smoothly for the customer.

Measure

Measure the results after implementation. As mentioned earlier, this stage is often neglected. For a salesperson, this can be the most powerful stage. This stage takes work and diligence and may require input or work from the customer. It is important that the buyer is shown by the seller that the value that was presented in the earlier stages is true. Notice that these last two stages are actually named the same in the buyer and seller processes. Up through the Close/Purchase stage, the buyer and seller may work closely together, but the agenda of each is different. There are still issues of pricing, terms and conditions, competition, and so on. After the purchase, the customer and the seller are partnered in solving the problem.

Your focus in the early stages of developing a territory should be on the customer and not on the opportunity. Figure 4-1's steps are simple to help you stay focused on your goal, which is a sale. If you would like a deeper dive, look at my recommended reading list at the end of the book.

Example

Let's continue the real estate example from before, focusing here on the seller's experience during the sale of a home. The sales agent needs to align with the buyer right from the beginning.

Let's say a real estate agent meets a potential new homebuyer at a party. Eventually the homebuyer asks, "What do you do?"

She says, "I am a real estate agent."

"We have been thinking of moving, but we are not ready right now."

The agent asks, "Why are you thinking of moving?"

"Well, I am not very happy with my commute and our house is getting too small," says the buyer.

The agent makes a mental note. *I need to keep in touch with this client; he is close to moving.* He is not ready to move, but he is one compelling event away from moving. So she does the smart thing and stays in touch with this new buyer. In six months she gets a call. The buyers are expecting a new baby. The compelling event she had been waiting for occurs.

She gets the listing on the old home, and now she turns her attention to looking for a new home.

Here, the buyer relays the basics of what they are looking for—the number of bedrooms, cost range, town, and so on. For any salesperson, this is the *most* important stage of the sale. It's in this stage that you show your knowledge, and how much you care about the customer. When qualifying a customer or opportunity, the more you know, the better and easier the sale and evaluation stage. For the real estate agent, effective questions include, "Why are you moving? When are you looking to move? Is your current house already on the market? Have you secured financing? How old are your kids; does school district matter; are you looking for a neighborhood with amenities? Where do you work; how long of a commute is ideal?" The goal here is not to teach you to be a real estate agent, but to give you a sense how the right questions show that you know your business, and that you care about the customer.

On the opposite side of the coin, imagine the agent skips the step of further qualifying the needs, and says, "I have the perfect house for you." The agent can't ignore the most important concern, real need, and jumps straight to the solution. I know I would feel uneasy, and that jumping straight to looking at houses would seem like a waste of time. Unfortunately, this is exactly the mistake 80% of salespeople make—they jump to product discussions well before needs have been analyzed in detail.

During the evaluation stage, the agent needs to show the houses. During this phase, the buyer can become overwhelmed with the options. What happens to cost concerns of the buying in this stage? This concern goes way down. It's at this time that agents will stretch the buyer's budget. Since concern with cost at this point is so low, this tactic goes largely unnoticed. She knows the buyer might pay for a lake view, even though it was not one of the original needs. The agent is taking advantage of the buyer concern cycle. I use this example to illustrate the point that cost is of little concern. In business-to-business sales, your repeat business is more important than the first sale. So, your concern should be for the best interests of your prospect's business, not the size of your commission check.

Now comes the time for the buyer to make that big decision and purchase. The biggest concern is risk. The buyer is about to commit a great percentage of his paycheck for the next 30 years. A good agent in this case remembers the sales cycle, and keeps reminding the buyer of the needs and solution.

"You are going to look great cooking out on that gorgeous back deck. Wow, what a great location, only five minutes from work. Now you don't have to worry about finding a hotel in between homes."

Exercise

As you did at the end of the last chapter, think through a purchase you have made recently that involved a salesperson. How did the salesperson do? Did she align with you in the buyer process? How did you feel if the person was completely aligned, or how did you feel if she was not aligned?

The degree to which you evaluate needs and the solution usually correlates to the size of the purchase. You drop your mobile phone and break it. You walk into the mobile company's storefront. The salesperson asks what you what brought you in. Does this person instantly start showing you phones, or do they get to know what you use your phone for? Do they take the time to understand your needs? Do they help you narrow down your choices? Do they allow you to try the phone?

After you place the order, does the salesperson help you learn the new features of the phone? Most salespeople don't do this, but did you get a call a few weeks a later asking if your purchase is meeting your needs? Think through other scenarios you encounter on a daily basis. Take eating at a restaurant, where a good waiter is a good salesperson. Or, think through the last car you purchased. Did the seller align with you at each stage: Status Quo, Event, Needs Analysis, Evaluation, Purchase, Implement, and Measure? If not, how did you feel?

Summary

The sales process mimics the natural steps each buyer takes when buying anything. In later chapters, I address each stage of the sales process, as they are all important in establishing trust with the customer. Trust and the sales cycle are a symbiotic relationship. Put another way, trust is developed through a sales cycle, and the sales cycle can be defined by trust. The next chapter discusses in detail what I mean by trust in a business setting. Then, in the following chapter, I show how trust and the sales cycle affect one another, and why it is so important to understand the level of trust you have built relative to your competition.

Trust

The Grease for Sales Success

*Technique and technology are important, but adding trust is the issue of
the decade.*

—Tom Peters

The goal for any salesperson should be to become the customer's trusted
advisor. The phrase "trusted advisor" is, however, thrown around too easily.
At one company I worked for, we had an account-planning worksheet. The
form was used to rate the level of relationship with the customer. The options
were:

- No engagement
- Engaged without first order
- Doing some business
- Vendor
- Preferred vendor
- Trusted advisor

I sat through quarterly business reviews for approximately 40 salespeople. We
reviewed several accounts for each. Almost half the accounts were marked
as trusted advisors. Many of the accounts we reviewed had been through
one sales cycle and our company won the business. Management never once
challenged the salesperson on the trusted advisor designation. Finally, I could
not take it anymore and asked a couple of salespeople to define their definition of trusted advisor. "Well, when the customer wants to buy widget X, they
purchase from us." Or, "I have a customer security badge."

Neither suggests trusted advisor status. Trusted advisor is a simple concept; your customer includes you in their business-planning sessions. Acme Technologies is looking to expand manufacturing into South America. Are you at the table with the customer when they are strategizing the feasibility of this expansion? Are you treated like an extension of the company? Do you have the ability to add value above and beyond the customer's team? If the answer is yes, you are a trusted advisor. Do not confuse this with being told they are expanding, and then being asked to quote something to support that initiative.

A trusted advisor is not the "relationship" guy or the "people person." Relationship being an all-encompassing word, it is worth pointing out that I am talking about a business relationship, a valued business relationship. I am not talking about the guy the customer likes. This is not the vendor who buys lunch all the time. It's the vendor who is part of the customer's team, at a peer level, the person who brings value. If an employee is not offering value, he is not part of that company very long, no matter how much he is liked. Same goes with salespeople. You are an extension of the customer team. They are looking for someone they can trust and gain value from.

Being the trusted advisor is a lofty goal that you may never get to, but one you should strive for. So, what is the operative word in trusted advisor? Trusted. Your goal should be to establish trust. Trust starts before you set foot in the door and is hopefully strengthened by every step you take with your customers.

What do I mean by *trust*? In a sales relationship, the seller must demonstrate the core elements of trust. The customer from the beginning will judge you on these trust characteristics. They are:

- Intent
- Capability
- Dedication
- Results

Let's define each of these in detail.

Intent

Proper intent makes sales a noble profession. There are so many negative stereotypes regarding sales, all of which come from salespeople with wrong intentions. The major theme of this book, shifting from opportunity focus to customer focus, is a shift of *intention*.

I never thought I would be in sales. I am an educated electrical engineer. I was a nuclear-trained naval officer. I was waiting for a job to open up in a local nuclear power plant when I took an "interim" sales position 20 years ago. My father was a salesman in the 1970s and 1980s. He always wanted me to do better. So, when I started to sell, and the engineering position I was waiting for didn't open up, I felt stuck in sales. It took me years to realize that sales is a great profession. When I changed my intention from "sell them something" to becoming a salesperson who wanted to educate and help my customers, my outlook on my career changed, and my sales results skyrocketed. My day-to-day interactions did not change, and my skills did not change overnight, but that small shift in attitude allowed my customers to perceive better intent.

Your customers know your intentions. They see it in the first two minutes of conversation. Are you there to help them or to sell them something?

If you are there to help them, you will sell them something, and if you are there to sell them something, they will help you directly out the door.

Intention and sales skills are tied at the hip.

"We tend to judge ourselves by our intentions; we tend to judge others by their behavior."
—Stephen M. Covey

If you are talking non-stop about your product or service, the perception from your customer will be that you are there just to sell something. If you truly get to know the customer, by understanding their needs first, the customer's perception of your intent is to help them. If you lack the necessary skills to ask questions and listen, your first step in changing that behavior is to have good intention. Most people believe they are of good character, and that they have proper intent, but your customer can only see your behavior. If you care, you will listen. First and foremost, the customer must perceive you are there to help them. They want to see you are truly listening to their needs. Do you have a hidden agenda or do you have the best interest of all parties in mind? Your intent is to drive value for the customer. We have all heard the 80/20 rule of sales—80 percent of sales are done by 20 percent of the sales team. Nothing is more powerful in putting you in the top 20 percent than proper intention.

Capability

Do you have the necessary skills, knowledge, competence, and abilities to help your customer? In the ever-changing world of sales, capability is increasingly important. Your customers are inundated by requests for their time, both internal to their organization and externally by sales professionals. They want to learn from their vendors and will make time if they believe you have the capability.

You must demonstrate competence. You must show industry and product knowledge. All too often, the focus for sales management is about understanding the features and benefits of your products. It is much more than that. You must demonstrate that you understand how business is done—budgets, project timelines, decision processes, and so on. Are you capable of educating your customers on better ways they can do things? Do you show a propensity to drive results? Do you drive thought leadership? Can you get the customer to rethink their current way of doing things? In other words, do you bring value as an individual? Does your company bring value? Do the products or services bring value?

Your capability as a salesperson is directly tied to your ability to show proper intention. Are you skilled in sales; do you ask the right questions; are the questions good; do you show you care?

Capability is the one area you can control most while ramping a new territory, so take advantage of the wealth of knowledge around you. I discuss many ways you can improve your knowledge and talents in the chapters on planning. While you show capability in front of the customer, it is developed on your own time without pressure.

You do not have to be all-knowing. You can show your competence by being a good resource manager. If you lack in any knowledge area, you can utilize others to fill the gaps. That's why it is fine to bring engineers, managers, partners, and subject matter experts to sales calls.

Dedication

Customers want you to demonstrate as much effort toward their success as they do. They want salespeople who follow through on promises. They want salespeople who can help drive the sales process. They have needs that must be filled, and sometimes they are so busy they rely on their salespeople to keep them on track with their own projects. Are you diligent with helping the customer? Are you dependable? Do you take control of the situation? Do you push through with the decision process? Do you follow through with your commitments? Are you dedicated to your own solution?

I ask those questions, because trust, and especially dedication, is about character. If you show weak character in any area of the sales process, you lose the confidence of your customers. The classic place this happens is during negotiations. Most salespeople take the attitude that they must give in to every customer demand, and every pricing request. They believe that is the way to earn customer trust and loyalty. In fact, this weak behavior actually has the opposite effect. What you are showing them is that you don't believe in the value of your own services, and you lack commitment and dedication to your own company. The customer might be happy that they get better terms and conditions they are looking for, but they will slowly lose their trust of you. Of course, negotiations require compromise, but you must demonstrate strength throughout the process.

All your actions make up your character, which determines the trust your customers have for you. If you are playing golf with your customer and bend the rules, your customer notices. Every aspect of your character counts, so always think through the message you are sending to your customer. While it's important to remain dedicated to helping the customer, you cannot forget to protect the value of your time, product, or company. Giving in on price, for example, can actually hurt you as much as getting caught cheating at golf.

Intention is shown, capabilities are demonstrated, results are measured, but dedication is where you earn the trust of your customer.

Results

You must deliver the results you promised. You must deliver on time. In order to be fully trusted, you need to measure the return on investment you said would be achieved with your solution. Ultimately it doesn't matter what your intentions are, how dedicated you are, or how smart you are; in the end you must be able to deliver results. The reason you are there is to help strengthen some aspect of the customer's business.

You buy a used car. The salesperson and everyone at the dealership were incredibly helpful; they listened to your needs and were instantly able to find a car that fit your requirements perfectly. They knew every specification and feature of every car you discussed. The salesperson understood the purchase process, including leasing, financing, trade-ins, titling, and delivery. You feel that you worked out a very fair deal on the car. In other words, you saw impeccable intent, capability, and dedication. You drive five miles down the road and the car stalls. How do you feel about this salesperson and this dealership now? Without results, nothing else matters. You are not in direct control of the results your company can deliver. However, the act of measuring results—good, bad, or indifferent—will go a long way toward building trust.

The act of measuring results can be just as important as great results. Most salespeople, or companies, do no take the time to measure and share results. I believe most people are afraid to measure, because they are afraid the results might not be as desired. Your customers know whether they are getting value from your solution. By taking the step to measure results, you show you are dedicated to their success. If the results are great, you are in good shape. If the results are bad, you have identified something that needs to be addressed. You will gain more trust by fixing any issues.

A discussion about results can seem a bit out of place in a book about penetrating new accounts. It is true that measurement of results will help you with repeat business with a customer. However, if you know results are an important part of trust, you must figure out a way to show results before a sale. I will discuss many ways this can be done.

It All Matters

When developing trust, you are building a sense of power with the customer. Ask yourself, whom do you trust in a crisis situation? Do you trust the person who makes sure that everyone is comfortable, or do you trust the person who takes control? Authority is powerful. Authority is powerful in sales. While you cannot change your personality, as already mentioned, authority is built as you build on the trust elements. Knowledge will also give you confidence, which leads to trust and authority. Confidence is important in many aspects of a sale:

- Confidence in pointing out issues your customer might face.

- Confidence in your solution.

- Confidence to have a peer-level relationship with your customer. You don't cater to their every whim.

- Confidence to stick to the value of what you are selling and not always giving in on price.

- Confidence in driving your customers to make progress toward their goals.

Each trust element is crucial. If you are missing any one of them, you are not completely trusted. Analyze each of these elements as if you are missing one. It does not matter if you have the best intent, and are capable and dedicated, if you can't deliver results. Customers are looking for results.

If you can produce results, but your intent is only to sell the customers something, they will sense that you do not have their best interest at heart. Trust will not be established. To establish full trust, each element needs to be addressed. You can go through the exercise on your own. Think through situations where three of the trust elements are satisfied, but one is left out. Think to yourself, "Do I fully trust this person to deliver for me?"

These are the qualities your customers are looking for in a trusted advisor. Figure 5-1 shows your goal with customers.

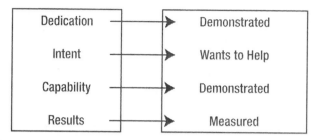

Figure 5-1. What customers need from the sales team

The trust meter (Figure 5-2) for the trusted vendor is full. That means you have demonstrated or measured each element. It is okay to show how you have delivered results for another customer, but it is critical that you demonstrate you can produce measureable results for them. They need to be shown, not just told. I will use this pie chart as a trust meter. Figure 5-2 shows a completely shaded, or full, trust meter.

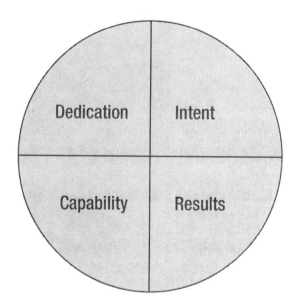

Figure 5-2. Full trust meter

During the buyer's status quo stage, they have vendors they are already doing business with. Each of these vendors has developed a certain level of trust. Although they may not be at trusted advisor status, or have all four core trust elements in proper alignment, you must assume they are farther along than you.

Your alignment stage to the buyer's status quo is plan and target. The incumbent vendor has demonstrated integrity, has shown their intent is to care, has solved problems, and has measured results.

Figure 5-3 shows what your customer thinks of you when they hear a voicemail from you, or you are on your first sales call.

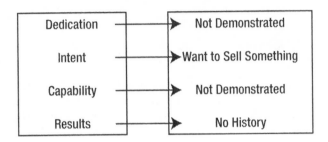

Figure 5-3. Customer perception of a new salesperson

As a new vendor, the customer has no trust in you. Your trust meter is empty (Figure 5-4).

Figure 5-4. Empty trust meter

I will discuss strategies you can use at each stage of the sales cycle to improve your trust meter.

"People buy from people." You have heard that a thousand times. Let me take this a step further, "People buy from people they trust."

The Value of a Personal Relationship

Do not underestimate the value of a personal relationship. I could easily add a "P" section to the trust pie. Some salespeople have that natural ability to forge quick personal relationships with customers.. However, the P section is one small aspect of the relationship, so people skills get you only so far. At the end of the day, the customer has a job and goals to meet. Here is a direct quote from a customer I know, "He is a great guy, but I can only have so many lunches before I feel like I am wasting time. I have a job to do."

As mentioned earlier in this chapter, your customer evaluates trust with everything you do. If you are establishing a personal relationship with a customer, do not compromise the business trust you built with low-character activities, like cheating in golf, drinking too much over dinner, or acting unprofessional, to mention a few. There is no distinction between personal and business character—it is just character.

Example

I was working for the industry leader in data storage and trying to break into an account that was held by my competitor. I did most of the right things. I even called high and met with the CIO. I found an issue that my competitor was not in a position to solve.

It was a hotly contested sales cycle, and I was competing against a trusted incumbent. The customer needed more performance in their computing systems, and they determined that the type of technology installed from my competitor was not the proper technology. The incumbent did nothing wrong; over time, new computing needs out grew this particular technology. The customer needed to improve performance. In order to do this, they were convinced they needed a certain type of technology, a technology in which my company was the industry leader. We had thousands of customers running this technology in their environments who experienced great improvements to system performance.

My competitor, the incumbent, was just entering the market with this technology, and it was widely known in the industry that they had a ton of bugs. They had one reference customer—themselves. The referral they used was their own internal IT department. We had better technology and references, competitive pricing, and a powerful position within the organization. Slam dunk!

On a Monday night, I was eating pizza outdoors at a restaurant, and I get a call from the customer. "Congratulations Dave, we are going with your technology." Well, dinner became more of a celebration.

The next morning, with my head a bit cloudy, I get a call from my new customer, "Dave, can you answer one more question?" I was thinking, "Where is this going? Something is not right." They had already said I had won, why another question?

I answered the technical question to the customer's satisfaction. That afternoon, I got another call. "Dave, we decided to go with the incumbent." I had better pricing, technology, references, and so on. Why did I lose? They trusted their incumbent more than me, the new salesperson.

Remember that the sales cycle breaks the Qualify/Develop stage into distinct sections. Establish trust then qualify. In my eagerness to win a "slam dunk" sale, I skipped straight to qualifying the technical aspects without first establishing trust. I sold the product first, then the company, and then myself. But any buyer buys in this order:

1. You. Do they trust you to help them with moving their business forward?

2. Company. Is the company stable; will it stand behind what they sell me?

3. Product. The product needs to meet their needs, but they will not consider product until trust is established.

In this example, I definitely had company and product advantages, so I have to assume I did not have their trust. I will wrap this chapter up with the conclusion of this story. I lost that opportunity, but using the strategies in this book, I gained that company as a long-term customer.

Summary

When you know the customer is looking for trust, and you can break down trust into tangible components, you can shift your strategy at each stage of the sales cycle to address each component. Always keep in mind that you must show that your intent is to help. You must continually improve your knowledge and skill to show proper competence. You must follow through on your commitments, large and small, to your customer. And, most important, your customer is looking for results. You must demonstrate you can deliver what you promise before and after the sale. In the next chapter, I explain how trust evolves through a typical sales cycle. Then I explain how trust actually changes the sales model.

Trust Sales Cycle

The Trust Meter Shows the Way

Trust…affects the quality of every relationship, every communication, every project, every business venture, every effort in which we are engaged.

—Stephen M.R. Covey

Focusing on the foundation of the relationship, this chapter analyzes how trust is developed from the beginning of a buyer-seller relationship. The natural progression of trust through an opportunity cycle looks like Figure 6-1.

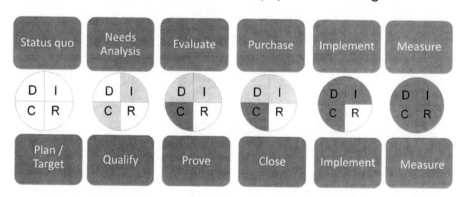

Figure 6-1. Trust progression

It takes a while for your trust meter to fill up. You are an unknown entity to your customer as you enter into the sales cycle. You have not established intent, capability, results, or dedication. Your trust meter is empty (Figure 6-2).

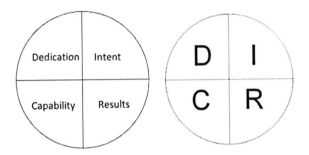

Figure 6-2. Empty trust meter

Let's look at a possible scenario of how trust might progress through one sales cycle. If you are able to gain access to your customers, and you properly engage them, you can quickly start to show that your intent is to help or educate. As customers get more comfortable with you, they will share more as they define their needs. During this process, if you act as a consultant and focus on the customer, you can start to show capability. However, there is still some skepticism by the customer, so elements of intent and capability are shaded in a light grey on your trust meter (Figure 6-3). Capability has been demonstrated via sales skill and knowledge, but you have not yet demonstrated your product's capability.

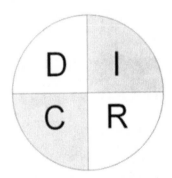

Figure 6-3. Trust meter early in the new customer acquisition phase

You start to show your dedication through the evaluation and closing stages. Their evaluation of your product or service is in line with the features and capabilities you sold. You are dedicated through the contract and negotiation process. You remain dependable, but you also show that you value your own solution. You continue to follow through on your commitments. You have not proved you will stick around after the sale yet, so you get only half the marks for dedication at this point. Your capability strengthens as you show more depth of knowledge for your own product and start to understand their business more deeply (Figure 6-4).

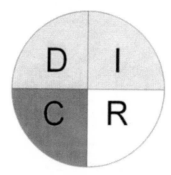

Figure 6-4. Trust meter as a customer begins to gain confidence in you

Next, your company implements the solution the customer has purchased. As a salesperson, you stick around through the implementation, ensuring there is a smooth transition from pre-sales to post-sales. So, your dedication quotient goes up. Your intent is now completely in line with the customer. The success of the implementation is as important to your company as it is to theirs (Figure 6-5).

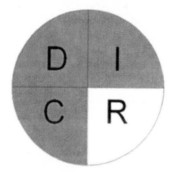

Figure 6-5. Trust meter when you make your first sale

The top salespeople are not afraid to come back after the implementation and determine if the solution they sold to the customer actually produces the business results they promised during the earlier parts of the sales cycle. By demonstrating that you and your company can produce results, you fulfill the entire trust process (Figure 6-6).

Figure 6-6. Full trust meter

You can be considered the incumbent at this point. However, becoming a trusted advisor comes only by repeating this process several times. As trust grows, you get the chance to work on projects that are more important, and that have more impact on the business objectives of the customer.

Almost every sales process falls short when salespeople do not take into account relationships, competition, or timing. Remember, the structure for most models is focused 100% on the opportunity. With a full trust meter, subsequent sales cycles become a non-linear process, as shown in Figure 6-7.

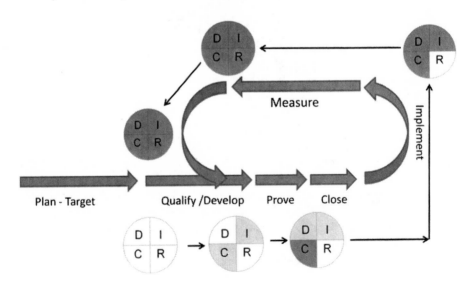

Figure 6-7. The sales cycle with the trust overlay

Once you have earned the customer's trust, the next time you enter into another opportunity, you do not have to start at the planning and target phases of the sales cycle. You now enter during the needs analysis stage (buyer process) or the qualify stage (sales process). Not only do you enter at a later stage, you don't have to earn full trust from the beginning. You understand the customer's business already, so you don't have to spend as much time qualifying the customer. You can start to analyze the customer's needs. Having already shown proper intent in a previous sales cycle, the customer will trust you and open up to you with more information.

To steal a phrase from the movie *Meet the Fockers*, you are now in "the circle of trust." (See Figure 6-8.)

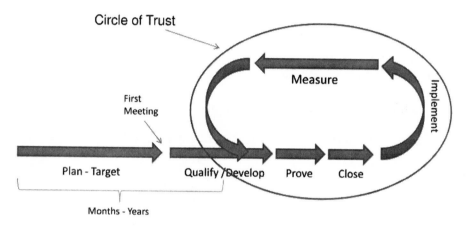

Figure 6-8. The Circle of Trust

Broken Model

While this all sounds great, the model is missing one huge element—"the guy," or the incumbent. With the introduction of the incumbent, a model that is focused on opportunity breaks. At the beginning, your trust meter is empty and you must assume the incumbent's is full (Figure 6-9).

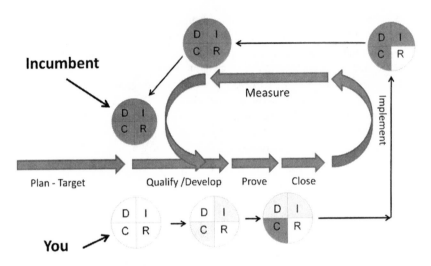

Figure 6-9. Incumbent vs. new salesperson in the sales cycle

Once a vendor has established trust, they enter back into the next sales cycle at their earned status. The incumbent's existing trust meter is the major challenge you face in your first year of sales, or anytime you're trying to engage a new customer (Figure 6-10).

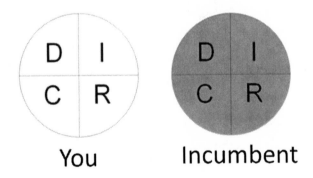

Figure 6-10. Incumbent trust vs. new salesperson trust

Even if you try to focus on customer needs during your first sales cycle with a new customer, you may not be invited into the circle of trust. Without enough trust, customers will not always open up to you about their problems. Or, they share much more information with the incumbent. They may engage you with a proof of concept (the testing of your solution against customer needs) in the prove stage, and they may even bring you to negotiations, but the incumbent is trusted and you are not. Look at the close stage in the previous model. While the incumbent's trust meter is full, your trust meter at best looks something like Figure 6-11.

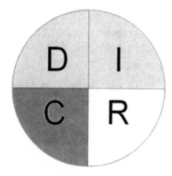

Figure 6-11. Trust meter that shows what you are up against even when you have proven your concept to the customer

This simply is not enough trust to compete.

Looking at the fully trusted sales cycle of the incumbent, you can see the process is completely condensed. They don't have to plan and target, nor try to gain access to the customer. They enter into the qualify/develop stage ahead of a new vendor. If the incumbent is smart, they will spend the time qualifying and defining the needs of the customer. Since there is more trust, the prove stage is condensed. There is less scrutiny versus a new vendor. The close stage for the existing vendor is shortened because they have experience with the process. They are set up in the purchasing system, credit lines are established, and relationships may have been built with the people in the purchasing department. It is easier and less work for the customer to continue using their existing vendor (Figure 6-12).

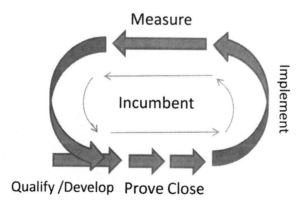

Figure 6-12. The condensed sales cycle of a trusted incumbent

This is a position of power for the incumbent vendor. Early in your relationship, it is like you are playing baseball on two entirely different fields. When the incumbent steps to the plate, they only have to run to third base and then back home for a run.

Knowing it is not a fair game, your strategy must shift away from getting the opportunity and toward building the relationship. The new sales cycle is shown in Figure 6-13.

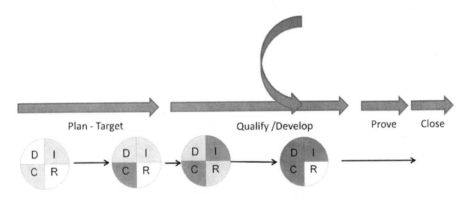

Figure 6-13. Trust before opportunity

With a new customer, 90% of all sales happen during planning and qualifying. In order to compete with an incumbent, you must build trust in the first two phases of the sales cycle. Ideally, you want to win the first opportunity you engage with a customer, and the only way to do that is to focus on building trust as much as you focus on the opportunity. This is the major focus of the book, so strategies to accomplish this kind of trust are presented at length.

Summary

When competing against the incumbent, or the status quo, any sales model that focuses on the opportunity is broken. The simple realization that you're not playing on a level playing field gives you huge insight—you go into the situation with open eyes, which can help you build trust and ultimately win business. The next chapter discusses in detail the advantages of focusing on establishing trust with new accounts versus focusing only on finding and closing opportunities.

Build Business Relationships

Job #1

If every instinct you have is wrong, then the opposite would have to be right.

—Jerry Seinfeld

On the television show *Seinfeld*, George is complaining about his life. He feels that every decision, every instinct he has, has been wrong. So, Jerry's advice is to do the opposite. As salespeople, every instinct we have is to focus on the opportunity. Managers, after all, measure our progress by opportunity. However, if your focus with a new customer, or a new territory, is only to find opportunities, you will fail.

Although it's not exactly the opposite of targeting opportunity, you need to build business relationships first. Once you gain access to a customer, the focus needs to remain on the customer. Focus on the customer's needs and adding value to the customer's experience before you look to fill your pipeline.

Every sales skill is about focusing on customer issues, or finding a solution that will help them. This is the foundation to the establishment of trust. However, every sales process implemented today only tracks what is in it for the salesperson, focusing on going after tangible opportunities. This forces salespeople to lose their way with new customers. I illustrated several times in the previous chapters that opportunity can't be trusted. You need to start by forging a relationship. The sales managers out there are probably thinking, "You can't forecast on or close a relationship." I understand that relationship is only part of the equation. It's just that without it, there is no sale. Let me also reassure you that, by forgetting about opportunity during your initial engagements, you will find many more opportunities within the first year. Opportunities you actually have the chance to win.

The Outcome of Good Relationships

Focusing on relationships has three major effects. One, it opens the window of opportunity. The more time you spend with the customer, the better chance you have to hit a purchase cycle and or a compelling event. Two, once you are engaged in an opportunity, you are more trusted; you are in a position to win. Three, by qualifying the customers you will make better use of your time. You will understand which customers fit with your product. You can start to be selective with your customers.

Going back to the example of Tom in the Introduction, where Tom chases opportunities in his first year and struggles, what advice should Tom's manager have given him after Q1? Had I been his manager, I would have said, "Tom, let's go down your list and see which customers best match our ideal customer profile. Of these customers, which ones do you feel a personal connection to? How much time are you spending with these customers?"

I would go on to say that I wanted him to spend half his time on establishing more trust with these customers. He can, for example, meet other people who are part of their decisions. He can organize "lunch and learns" for the customers. He can provide educational industry training or provide road maps detailing future products or services. He should provide this in the spirit of education, not with a goal of trying to sell something. He can also introduce his contacts to different people from his own organization. I will explore these in more detail, and show how such efforts help you establish trust with your customers.

Trust the System

This is where you need to trust in the process. It is not easy to do. There is nothing in the forecast to warrant the time and resources Tom is devoting to this customer. Then why do it?

You hear this all the time: "Sales is a numbers game." Just as we are changing the concept of hunters and hunting, we need to change the concept of the numbers game. Looking at sales as a numbers game traditionally focuses on volume: volume of cold calls, volume of sales calls, volume of opportunities, and volume of pipeline. It means hard work, and a ton of wasted effort.

It also means that you expect failure. I have worked with many organizations that require salespeople to carry a pipeline-to-quota ratio of 3:1, even up to 5:1. Assume your annual goal is $5,000,000 in sales, meaning that in a given quarter your quota is approximately $1,250,000, or 1/4th the annual quota. Your pipeline at the 3:1 ratio should be at a minimum of $4,200,000. The company sets this threshold because, historically, their sales team has a 30% close rate. Look at it in the negative: that is a 70% failure rate. That is 70% of your time on wasted deals, wasted conversations, and wasted administrative work.

Continuing this train of thought, if you need to have $4,200,000 of pipeline and your average deal is $120,000, you need 35 deals in your forecast. If your sales calls-to-pipeline identification is 2:1, you need to go on 70 calls. If it takes eight calls to set one appointment, you need to make 560 calls.

Sales is a numbers game. However, the numbers that you need to focus on are probabilities, not volume. Volume has a compounding effect of wasting time. Increasing your odds of winning frees up your time to work on even more qualified opportunities. In Las Vegas, for example, your best odds are at the black jack table, where the odds of winning are at best 48%. (This is a gross simplification; the odds of winning are based on many house rules, and your ability as a player to make the right decisions.) With a 48% chance of winning, in the long run, you lose. Some people think it's crazy to play roulette where the odds on the simplest bet drop to 47%. No matter how many times you spin that wheel, in the long run, you will lose. In fact, the more times you spin the wheel, the more you lose. It is no different in sales. Turning up the volume of activity with lousy odds will just cause you to fail even more. It is better to work on the odds.

Adding more volume to low-odds activities will compound your failure. Working to increase your odds of success at each stage of the sale with compound your success.

The tragedy in all of this is that the data has been staring us right in the face, but we ignore it. If you look across a large data set of all salespeople within a company, the close rate might be 70%. So, at first glance, it makes sense to use the 70% close rate as a metric to set pipeline targets. However, this includes the 80% of the not-so-good salespeople. Sales management ignores the pipeline rules for their top performers. Since Johnny has a great close rate, we will not pressure him for the higher ratio in pipeline. Since Johnny does not fit the model sales management expects, or manages to, he is labeled a sandbagger— someone who underforecasts their deals to look like a hero at the end of the quarter. Management looks at Johnny as the anomaly. *Instead, why not use him as the role model?* He is a top performer, so let's look at his numbers, pipeline, close ratios, behavior, and selling strategy. Does it make any sense to manage to the non-performers? Instead of labeling Johnny as a sandbagger because of his low pipeline ratio, look at Johnny's close rate. Now figure out why Johnny has a better close rate and teach the others some of his techniques.

I guarantee you one thing: He is not being pressured to waste his time managing bad deals.

Don't play the volume game unless the odds are stacked in your favor. If you insist on seeing the numbers, look at the numbers from the proper angle.

Here are the questions you (and sales management) should be asking: How do we increase prospecting success rates? How do we improve the number of calls we have to make to get an appointment? How do we increase the rate of sales calls to opportunities? How do we better qualify customers, so we are spending our time only on high-odds deals? How do we know when the odds of winning are bad? How do we stop managing to a 70% failure rate?

Why Trusting the System Makes Sense

Purchase cycles are long in most B2B sales; sometimes there are up to 7–10 years between decisions. Again in IT, telephony equipment, networking, or data storage, purchases are made every four years or more. Assume for example that the customer uses a four-year purchasing cycle. Out of the 48 months between purchases, the customer might start looking for new product or vendor, if they do not automatically go to their preferred incumbent vendor, about four months in advance. Now assume that they interview two or three vendors in the first two months of this buy cycle. Your window is down to those two months at best. That's two months in four years, a one out of 24 chance of hitting the customer at the right time.

You can see this in Figure 7-1. The larger circle is 24 times bigger than the smaller circle. The small circle represents the two-month window you have to hit an opportunity. The medium-sized circle represents a one-year window of opportunity, or customers you are establishing relationships with.

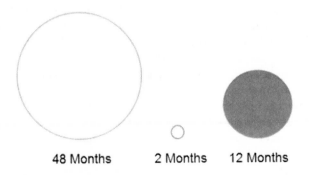

| 48 Months | 2 Months | 12 Months |

Figure 7-1. Window of opportunity

To play the volume game, you aim at 50 different customers, or you are look-ing for opportunity in 50 customers. So you give yourself 50 times the chance to find an opportunity. However, you know nothing about the customers. What are their decision criteria, who are the power players, what are their budgets, is there a strong incumbent? The list goes on. This is like hitting a moving target (Figure 7-2).

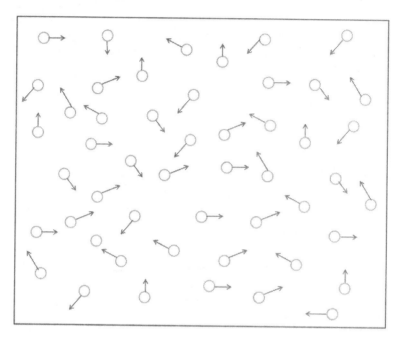

Figure 7-2. Moving target opportunities

With a change of focus, you move from targeting opportunity to establishing a relationship with a customer. That will give you a much bigger target to aim at over time (Figure 7-3).

Figure 7-3. Stationary customer targets

Establishing trust takes time, so assume now you can aim at only half the customers, or 25. With this new approach, qualifying customers first becomes important. There is no sense in aiming at customers who are not going to buy. Customers in this case are no longer moving targets. They are stationary. Customers are there for the entire first year; they are not fleeting opportunities.

Which of the targets looks easier to hit? The 50 small moving targets, or the 25 stationary targets?

Not only is it easier to hit the stationary targets, but when you do hit an opportunity, you have a much better chance of closing business. When aiming only at opportunity, you become column fodder—the vendor uses you to keep their preferred vendors honest—meaning your chances of winning are greatly diminished. Nonetheless, most sales managers tell you to shoot more arrows, make more sales calls, and work harder. I have seen some reps succeed on sheer will, and some on luck. Most of us are not that lucky, and most of us are unwilling to work *that* hard.

The secret, once again, is to focus on the customer, the relationship, instead of the opportunity. Don't aim at the small circles; aim at the larger ones. Work on building the relationship when there is no opportunity. No matter if you are cold calling, networking, or getting to the customer through referrals, your main goal should be to understand the customer, and start building trust.

If you find opportunity, you must be honest with yourself and truly qualify the deal. Do you have a chance to win? Or are you the column fodder I have discussed?

If you don't find opportunity, and the customer states they are not in the market—"I am not looking for X at this time"—your answer should be, "That's okay, I would prefer not to start our business relationship in the middle of your buying cycle. We can spend time now understanding your needs, which gives us time to show our value and earn your trust."

Your intent quickly goes from "they want to sell me something," to "they are here to help our business." Taking this approach builds trust instantly.

When you are willing to spend time with customers not currently in the market, they begin to trust you more. They will more readily believe you want to help their business grow and relieve problems.

Do the Math: Opportunity versus Relationship

In the previous example, I showed how the right focus improves your chances of finding real opportunities. But, how does the math work? What happens to your pipeline? In the previous example, you were aiming at 50 customers, and you had a 48-month buying cycle, so your window of opportunity is maybe two months long. To be more generous, I will give you a window of three months.

Your chance of finding any opportunity with a customer, real or not, is only 6.25% (3/48). Now multiply that by 50 customers, and you are working a total of three deals. I am going to be generous with this example again, and say that you sell multiple items and now you find twice as many deals, or six.

Remember you are mainly column fodder if you don't have a relationship, but I will be incredibly generous again and award you a close rate of 33%. (It is probably closer to 15%.) Congratulations—you will win two opportunities in a year. In the IT industry, where vendors have direct relationships with the customer, with no help from a partner, this is typically what you see from 80% of new hires. (I will discuss partner dynamics in a later chapter.) The numbers will be slightly better if the company has existing relationships with the customer.

Here is the math if you aim for the big circles, possible only when you aim at establishing the relationship with the customer before you chase opportunities.

First, work 20% smarter and aim at only 40 customers. Now, do not look for opportunity, but look to qualify customers, and spend time with them. You are engaged with the customer whether or not there exists an opportunity. Again, how you stay engaged without opportunity is covered later in the book. The window of opportunity of each customer raises on average from three months to nine. With the same 48-month sales cycle, you now have a window of opportunity of 19% (9/48). Over 40 customers, you will see 7.5 targeted opportunities.

However, here is the real strength of this strategy. In actuality, you will see many more opportunities. In your educational approach, you will pique the interest of your customer about opportunities they may not have been thinking of. And while spending time with the customers, once you have established trust, you will find they will start to bring you more opportunities. Conservatively, this will double the number of opportunities you're exposed to. For our purposes here, that's four opportunities per engaged customer.

Increased trust also brings higher close rates. In this example, I will be ultra conservative and use a slightly higher close rate than when you did not have a relationship, or 50%.

This math now works out to this way:

40 customers X 19% window X 4 opportunities per customer X 50% deal close rate = 15.2 deals

There are many circumstances that influence all of these numbers. But in general, you are looking at five times the number of won deals. Typically, with this approach you will not only have more deals, but the deals will be bigger. The "numbers game" shows that establishing relationships will drive more opportunity. Focusing on opportunity does not correlate into driving relationships.

When you chase opportunities, you have a limited number of relationships built by the year's end. In year two, you will still be chasing opportunities and working any deal or customer you can find. In the other scenario, you have purchasing relationships with at least seven customers. And, you have started building trust with up to 20 more customers. You can stop chasing opportunities, because with the trust you have built, customers will start presenting opportunities to you. This will also lead to more referrals. This is the difference between chasing deer, and knowing the land like the back of your hand.

Summary

The goal of this chapter is to drive home the point that focusing solely on opportunity is not the most productive use of your time. I have stated this a few times, but it's worth repeating. Your success does not depend on the first opportunity you find, it depends on a long-lasting relationship with the customer.

Now that I have explained the strategy, you need a way to track progress. In the next chapter, I will combine the aspects of opportunity and trust to give you the equation you need to win business. This equation will help you develop a process to follow, and help you determine your ability to compete with more established vendors.

Understand the Sales Equation

Why Chasing Opportunities Does Not Work

Every sale has five basic obstacles: no need, no money, no hurry, no desire, no trust.

—Zig Ziglar

I have discussed that chasing opportunities is setting the sales person up for failure. However, it is obvious that you need opportunities to close business. The goal of this chapter is to introduce relationship, or trust, into the discussion about an opportunity. I will develop a simple formula that equals sales success with new customers.

In Chapter 4, I listed these elements as the core to winning deals.

- *Pain.* Without pain, or need, there is no order. A compelling event is pain with a time element. This is the best type of pain because it makes predicting and closing business easier. A compelling event means the customer has a deadline. Without a deadline, opportunities will drag on indefinitely.

- *Solution.* The customer needs to envision that your offering will solve the pain or fill the need. The customer needs to see value in your solution. The increased revenue or cost savings of the solution you provide must be greater than the cost of your solution.

- *Authority.* You need a "yes" from someone within the organization who has the authority to purchase. Otherwise known as power.

- *Understanding.* You need to identify the purchasing decision process.

These are the items that customers need to make a decision to purchase, but are they the items they need to purchase from you? The answer is no. Each bullet can be claimed by you—*and* by a competitor. If the customer has a compelling event, it's a compelling event for you and for your competition. The competition will have a valuable solution. You hope you have more value. Both you and the competitor could have access to power. An incumbent most likely will have greater access. Both you and the competitor understand the decision process. Again, the incumbent will most likely know this better than you.

One last bullet needs to be added to the discussion.

- *Relationship.* You must have a trusted, valued business relationship with the customer.

I have been discussing this last bullet at length. I believe I have demonstrated how important it is to value the relationship as part of the sales equation. Without a good relationship, there is no sale. When you lose a deal to price, most likely you are losing because you did not have a good relationship. Price is the excuse the customer gives you because it is definitive and impersonal.

You must have all these elements for a sale, from which I can derive a simple formula for sales success:

$$CE \times V \times P \times DP \times (TR)^2 = Sale$$

Here's what each of the elements stands for:

- CE – Compelling event
- V – Value
- P – Yes from power
- DP – Decision process
- TR – Trusted relationship, which is squared due to its importance

The equation is multiplicative, meaning that if any one of the elements is zero, the sale does not exist. Therefore, with no relationship, there is no sale. The equation also squares the trust element. Trust has an exponential effect on your chances to win. When you are new, you have almost no trust, and with zero trust, you have zero chance to win. You must assume that the existing vendor is fully trusted (Figure 8-1).

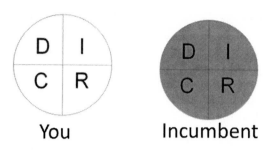

Figure 8-1. Trust difference

What is the formula for trust? I have one, but first let me say that I understand relationships can't be measured with a number or represented by a formula. The intent of this formula is to give you a mechanism to measure your relative strength against a competitor's, using metrics rather than just gut feeling. It also helps you determine how to systematically drive toward a trusted relationship.

So here is a simple "formula" for trust.

$$Trust = I + C + D + R$$

Again, here's what each item stands for:

- I = Intent
- C = Capability
- D = Dedication
- R = Results

Here, then, is the expanded sales equation:

$$CE \times V \times P \times DP \times (D+I+C+R)^2 = Sale$$

While this might look a bit complicated, it really is simple. In order to win a sale with a new customer, you need to be concerned with every element of this equation, such as the opportunity-focused sales criteria of a compelling event, value, power, and the decision process. Especially with new customers, the trust elements must be taken into account: Intent, Capability, Dependability, and Results. This formula offers a deeper level of inspection of each opportunity.

Concentrating on the trust elements, each is rated 0 to 2. A score of 0 means you have not addressed this trust issue, so you must assume the buyer rates you a 0. Give yourself 1 point for trust that can be assumed based on referrals, or when you have implied a certain amount of trust through actions in the sales cycle. 2 points indicates that you have made an effort or otherwise measured within the element. For example, you have provided education to show good intent, done a product evaluation to show results, conducted seminars to show capability, and so on. This points system is obviously subjective. It is better to overate your competition and underrate yourself. You do not want a false sense of security. It's better to identify weaknesses and take positive actions to strengthen them.

Figure 8-2 shows 0 points for results, 1 point each for dedication and intent, and 2 points for capability, which is a 4 out of a possible 8. You do not have a fair shot at the business, unless you have a unique value, a niche product, or are within 1-2 points of your competition.

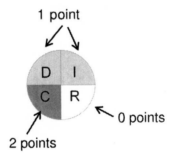

Figure 8-2. Trust points

If you can get to the point where you have 6 out of 8, as shown in Figure 8-3, you have a much better chance of winning than with 4 out of 8.

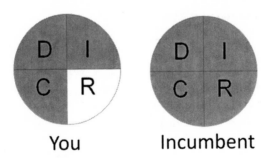

Figure 8-3. More Equal Trust Levels

There are any number of trust combinations that will work. There may be cases where the incumbent has lost some element of trust with a customer, and that gives you a chance to compete or even have an advantage. Maybe there is a situation where you have demonstrated dedication, some intent, results, and capability. Maybe the incumbent has demonstrated results and capability, but dedication and intent have suffered due to lack of ongoing attention. Suddenly you just leveled the score to 5 vs. 5. Now you can compete evenly (Figure 8-4).

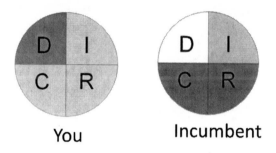

You   Incumbent

Figure 8-4. Equal Trust Levels

Allow me to repeat myself. I understand relationships can't be measured. I understand that there is a mix of personal and business relationships with each customer. This method is a way to analyze your relative strength against your competitor's. Your goal is not to walk into a customer like a robot with a relationship checklist. The intent of these strategies is to ensure you have taken conscious, proactive steps in developing a trusted business relationship.

The Great News

While the task of competing against an incumbent may seem daunting, it is by no means insurmountable; otherwise, new salespeople would never make it, nor would new companies ever get off the ground. In fact, it can be easy to unseat the incumbent. While you are focusing on systematically building trust, the incumbent is taking their customer for granted, looking for new customers, and waiting for their existing customers to call them with new orders. Figure 8-5 shows the buyer's concern about relationship versus the typical salesperson.

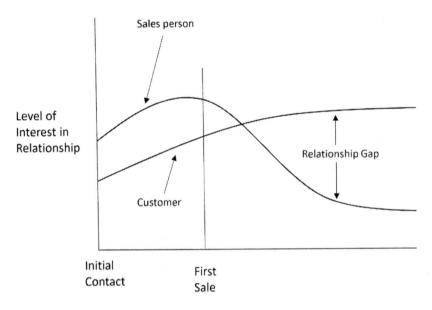

Figure 8-5. Vendor-buyer relationship gap

As you can see, once a salesperson makes a sale, they typically don't come back around and measure results or stay focused on the customer. Before the sale, the relationship is more important to the salesperson than to the customer. However, after the sale, the customer wants a stronger relationship. A lot of times the salesperson is off looking for other opportunities, or assumes the customer will just present them with the next opportunity. As a result, the trust meter of the incumbent is not as full as it could or should be. The customer's expectations of the vendor are typically not met after the sale.

However, you must assume that incumbent trust is full and systematically address each element of trust so you can compete with confidence. It is possible that, by the time you've developed an opportunity with a new customer, you could be more trusted than the current vendor(s).

Always assume the incumbent vendor has a trust meter that is full or close to it. That will encourage you to develop your relationship fully and do your best to provide value that makes a difference to the customer's business.

Summary

I have harped on relationships. But I think it is important to drive home the point from multiple angles. Your entire sales training—how you have been managed, how you have been measured and, intuitively, how you have tackled your territories—focused on opportunity. I hope by now I have shown, demonstrated, beat you over the head, and just repeated this concept to the point that you understand how important relationship-building is.

Now that you have the *why* behind you, you're ready turn to the *how* in the succeeding chapters. It is easy to tell salespeople to work on building a relationship, but you need systematic, creative approaches to build this trust. You must build trust before you have a chance to work on opportunity, so you will spend most of your time in the following chapters learning how to build trust in the planning stages, how to gain access to the customer, and how to qualify customers.

Understanding First Stage Selling

Success is neither magical nor mysterious. Success is the natural consequence of consistently applying the basic fundamentals.

—John Rohn

Preplanning: Prepare Yourself

Get Ready to Start

Confidence is preparation. Everything else is beyond your control.

—Richard Kline

As I've stated several times, most of your sales activity in the first year, when trying to penetrate new accounts, will be in the first stages: planning and qualifying needs. As part of the planning stage, I want to ensure that you have the tools you need once you're engaged with a customer. In this chapter, I address the "homework" activities you must do. This chapter helps you:

- Address your capabilities and learn to develop sales skills and product knowledge.

- Develop some simple messages that will engage your prospects in conversation rather than just deliver a monologue on what you do or sell.

- Construct an online presence that will instill trust in your prospects before you even talk to them.

Capability

Customers will evaluate you the moment you walk in the door. Trust is earned over time, but one element they can and will make an instant judgment about is your capability. Capability can be broken into three elements.

- Sales skills

- Industry knowledge

- Product knowledge

The demands on the salesperson are greater today than ever. An average salesperson working 10–15 years ago could get away with being a walking datasheet. The only way customers learned about new products was from salespeople visiting with them face to face. Customers had to listen to a salesperson go on about their products. Now, with the Internet, customers have instant access to your professional profiles, as well as your company and product information. Your customers have a good understanding of your products before you step foot in the door. They do not need a salesperson to tell them what they already know.

Today, customers expect their salespeople to bring value. That's why you need product knowledge beyond the datasheet. They want to see that you are experienced and understand how your products fit into the larger picture at their company. They want salespeople who understand their company and issues. They want salespeople with industry knowledge. They want subject matter experts.

Let's look more in-depth at the three elements that make up capability.

Sales Skills

Ongoing sales training must be part of the planning process. This is your career, so treat it as so. It is ironic that the most important function in any company is sales, because salespeople are the least trained people in their craft. Sales brings revenue, and without revenue, there is no business. Lawyers, HR, IT, and finance all require four years or more of education. Each one of these also requires ongoing education, training, and certifications. Yet most salespeople have one sales course, which they half pay attention to, every two to three years.

There is a wealth of information on sales skills, strategy, and process. Aim to learn something daily.

Early in my career, I worked hard, but I just showed up. (By the way, showing up will put you in the top 50%, and working hard will put you in the top 30%.) I understood my products and services, and I followed up with customers. However, I was by no means a student of my career; I just winged it from a skills standpoint.

A few years back, I was eating lunch with a coworker at a sports bar. ESPN was on the big projection screen running a story on an all-pro linebacker who came into NFL training camp out of shape, and his job was in jeopardy. I remember saying to my friend, "What an idiot! If I was making $4 million a year, hell $500k a year, I would make sure I was in shape." Coincidently, earlier that month one of our top salespeople made a huge sale, with a commission that propelled that salesperson to a commission in that range.

It then dawned on me. "I can make $500k selling. Why am I out of shape?"

Learn your craft, know your industry, and understand your offerings. Once you learn about them, learn to do them better. An all-pro athlete never stops training, a doctor does not stop reading medical journals, and your customers do not stop learning about new ideas on how to solve their problems. You should never stop learning.

There is one chapter in this book devoted to selling skills (Chapter 16, "Sales Strategies"). I have already stated my opinion on sales skills. They are very difficult to change. As with golf, the quickest way to get better results is through better strategy. Continued improvement of your swing is still a must if you want even lower scores. Same with sales. Start by learning proper strategy, and then learn the sales process to keep you organized. But continue to become a better-skilled salesperson.

Here is the simplest advice on sales skills ever: Be aware of you how much you are talking. After each sales call, ask yourself if you learned more about the customer than she learned about you.

Industry Knowledge

Research your industry and your customer's industry until you know it inside and out. This will give you a much better idea of your customer's potential problems. It will also help you position your offerings much better, help you with messaging, and add value with your customers.

Also research the job titles of the people you are calling on. There are web sites specific to almost any title.

- www.ceo.com
- www.cfo.com
- www.it-director.com
- www.hr.com
- www.thelawyer.com

No matter your target prospect, there is plenty of information regarding the issues and trends that affect their roles. This knowledge helps you gain access to prospects and shows the customers that you can help. For example, if you are meeting with a CIO, and you know the top five concerns of CIOs at this time, your conversation with her will be much more than just about product. Your potential customers want to know how you can help them with their concerns before they want to hear anything about your product.

If you do not have immediate access to a prospect, share industry trends and news on a proactive basis via e-mail or regular mailings, which will get more attention. These items can be online articles, information your marketing department provides, or ideally content you have personally generated. You might not be in the position to do this if you are new to an industry, but if you can provide these kinds of materials, you will start to show expertise (capability) even before you speak to a prospect. This is more effective than sending product literature. Sending product literature before you qualify your customer needs will only put you out of buyer alignment. So don't send product information unless it's requested.

The other effect of doing this research is that it will give you confidence when you do engage your prospect, and you will better understand their pain and issues. This enables you to better position your solution. Plus, your conversations will have much more meaning for the customer.

Product Knowledge

This may sound illogical, but there can be some dangers to having too much product knowledge. I have been saying all along your focus needs to be on the customer. When they have an abundance of product knowledge, most salespeople have the tendency to talk too much about the product. It is okay to be an expert in your field, but you must concentrate on customer needs first.

Look again at the buyer concerns graph (Figure 9-1).

Buyer Concerns

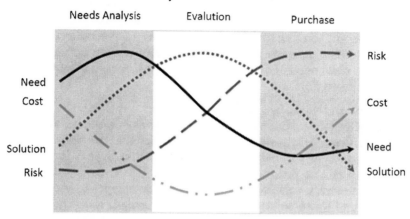

Figure 9-1. Shifting buyer concerns

The most important element of trust is intent. All too often, salespeople feel that capability of their products is the most important thing. Staying in alignment with your customer will allow you to show your capability in due time, without sacrificing intent. There is a time to focus on the solution, and it's toward the end of the needs analysis stage. To help fight the urge to talk product too quickly, you need to define product knowledge beyond the features and benefits. Figure 9-2 shows general levels (categories) of knowledge you can have with your offering. The categories of product knowledge are slightly different for each industry, so I have attempted to make these as broad as possible.

Focus	Stage	Buyer Concern	Category	Sales Priority	Team Member
Business	Evaluation	S	Impact to Stock or Bottom Line	Nice to Have	Manager
		S	ROI Analysis		
		NS	Business Value Proposition Business Problem	Sales Sweet Spot	Sales Team
		NS	Business Problem Solved		
		N	Business Needs Questions		
	Needs Analysis	N	Business Pain		
Technical		N	Technical Pain		
		N	Technical Need		
		NS	Questions to Uncover Pain		
		NS	Operational Benefits		
	Evaluation	S	How Product Works	Nice to Have	Technical Team
		S	Features and Benefits		
		S	Product Specifications		
		S	How to Use the Product		
		S	How to Set Up Product		Product Experts
		S	How Product is Designed		

Figure 9-2. Knowledge matrix; N stands for Need, and S for Solution

Again, there is a slight slant toward technical sales in Figure 9-2, but this matrix can be adapted for any industry. First, align the knowledge categories with the buyer concern graph. Start with analyzing the need from the business and technical aspects. You must understand the pains your products help alleviate. Then you need to know which questions will help you better qualify the customer and their needs. For clarity, in the Buyer Concern column, N means Need, and S means Solution.

The line between the Business and Technical focus is meant to be the highest level of knowledge. As you move up the categories in business, and down in technical, the depth of knowledge increases. Notice that the high-level knowledge corresponds to the Needs development of the Buyer Concern graph (Figure 9-1). Again, as you move away from the high-level knowledge, buyer concern shifts toward solution information. As you migrate toward the evaluation stages and more solution information is needed, you may need assistance from management on the business side, and from the technical support team on the technical side.

The amount of knowledge you have on any subject can be endless. Which categories of knowledge will benefit you most? Figure 9-3 shows the sweet spot of sales knowledge—it's all about customer needs. The major problem most companies have with training is they believe product training needs to be done by product experts. Experts are asked to "dumb it down" for the sales teams.

The product experts stay focused on the product, taking the simplest information about the product, and using it to educate the sales team. Look at the lower-right corner of Figure 9-3; you can see that they completely miss where sales should be focusing their conversations.

Focus	Stage	Buyer Concern	Category	Sales Priority	Team Member
Business	Eval-uation	S	Impact to Stock or Bottom Line	Nice to	Manager
		S	ROI Analysis	Have	
		NS	Business Value Proposition Business Problem		
		NS	Business Problem Solved		
		N	Business Needs Questions		
	Needs Analysis	N	Business Pain	Sales Sweet Spot	Sales Team
		N	Technical Pain		
Technical		N	Technical Need		
		NS	Questions to uncover pain		
		NS	Operational Benefits		
		S	How Product Works		
		S	Features and Benefits		Technical Team
	Eval-uation	S	Product Specifications	Nice to	
		S	How to Use the Product	Have	
		S	How to Set Up Product		Product Experts
		S	How Product is Designed		

Figure 9-3. Knowledge matrix showing what product experts think are the most important items compared to what good salespeople know are the most important things

This problem is compounded with new salespeople. Here's why. As mentioned, 90% of the time spent with new customers is in the planning and needs analysis stages. Your product experts are aiming the sales team past that stage, and directly at the evaluation stage. I will explore the importance of this in establishing intent with the customer in Chapter 16. At this point, just make a note that you cannot sacrifice intent for capability.

When you are studying your product, make sure you can talk in the sweet spot. Starting from the Business/Technical focus, first understand the business pain, along with the technical pain your solution can help eliminate. Then learn which questions can help you uncover that pain. Have a story about how you can help solve the customer's business pain, and have a story about how your offering helps address the business pain.

Do not be satisfied with the product training provided by most companies. You might only have basic product training. If management will not provide you with this level of knowledge, analyze the customer's pains and determine the questions you need to ask on your own.

Example

Let's go back to the example of purchasing a home. Although Figure 9-3 is set up for a business-to-business sale in the IT industry, in this case I will define the categories of knowledge for a real estate agent who works in a new development/neighborhood.

The technical aspects become the housing and neighborhood data. I will start what is most important to the customer.

1. Why customers move in general.

2. Why this customer is moving, and what they are looking for in a home and community.

3. High-level knowledge about the community.

4. High-level knowledge on the quality of home construction.

5. Detailed specs of each home.

6. How the home was designed and built.

7. How the framing was done, electrical specs of the home, and so on.

As you can see, the depth of knowledge can increase exponentially. However, the selling sweet spot includes levels 1-3 and possibly 4. If the customer has more detailed questions about home specs, the real estate agent can rely on the contractor.

Now look at this from the business/money side.

1. Understanding the budget—minimum, maximum, and stretch budget

2. Understanding home owner dues or fees

3. Understanding the financial information required to qualify for a loan

4. Understanding the types of mortgages available

5. Understanding how each type of mortgage works

6. Understanding how the underwriting process works

Again the details can get overwhelming, and the real estate agent can get help from a mortgage broker. The selling sweet spot is 1 and 2, and possibly 3. When you stay in the sweet spot, you are showing intention.

You don't ask an electrical subcontractor to teach the real estate agent how to sell the community. But this is exactly what happens in most business-to-business sales—the product experts teach product knowledge. You therefore need to educate yourself on buyer concerns to get an idea of what matters to your customers.

What Do You Do?

You need to learn to answer the question, "What do you do?". This seems like a very simple exercise, but when you ask most salespeople this question, it takes them way too long to answer. Whether it is on the phone, on a web site, in an elevator, or during your first meeting, you need to be prepared for this trap. I call this a trap because it pushes you in the direction of presenting a monologue, when your goal should be a conversation.

Be careful, because even management is directing you into this trap by making every salesperson memorize an "elevator pitch." This is typically a 20–30 second monologue about how the company is great and how they can help the customer. Elevator pitches come across as memorized; they all sound the same, and are filled with buzzwords and marketing hype. Worse, the customer stops listening 10 seconds in (and I am being generous). It should be called the elevator shaft. Your goal is a conversation with the customer.

So, what should you do when asked about your company? Instead of an elevator pitch, you need to develop an elevator "hook." An elevator hook helps you start a conversation with the customer. I will take some time here to set up the concept of the elevator hook, but it will take no longer than eight seconds to deliver it. The hook returns the focus to the customer and initiates a conversation.

Selling is simple; ask questions to stay focused on the customer.

The elevator hook engages the customer in a conversation and includes a reference story that implies a referral. With customer referrals, you gain more trust. With conversations, you show more intent, and therefore more trust. This process will keep you in alignment with buyer concerns. This keeps you in the qualifying stage, focused on needs, rather than jumping straight to the solution, which is well into the buying process.

The first objective is to turn the question "what do you do?" into a conversation. The best way to start any conversation is with a question. So, when you are asked, "what does your company do?," you respond with a question. That's the hook. You ask a question that engages the customer. A question solicits a response and curiosity from the customer. Come up with questions centered on issues that you know affect most of your customer base. These questions should solicit a quick yes or no. There is a time for opened-ended questions when you are exploring the customer needs. However, in this case you want to box the customer into a yes response. If you understand your customer, the industry, its challenges, and how you can help, this is simple.

These questions are simple to develop. You can simply Google "top concerns for hospitals, CFOs, CIOs, universities, manufacturing, IT organizations," or what have you. You can have different questions for different job titles and vertical markets. Again, your goal is to hit an obvious issue confronting your customers today. Examples include:

- "Do you think you spend too much on paper copies?"
- "Do you have issues with explosive data growth?"
- "Does the introduction of mobile devices by your employees onto your network cause you problems?"
- "Do you know how complex it is to set facility security properly?"
- "Are your receivables at the level you would like?"
- "Do you know how hard it is to accurately forecast 90 days out?"

You now have the customer set up with the elevator hook. If you hit on an issue customers have, their response should be, "yes." This will grab their attention, and you already got them to admit they have an issue. And, the yes is an invitation to say what you do, but without the details. Your response at this time is simple: "We help with that."

You have checked for interest. They said they have the issue, so they will want to know how you can help. Now you can proceed with a reference story, one that starts to build trust. I will break this down further, but frame your reference story like this:

A good illustration of how we help is by what we did for a customer in your industry. This company had issue X. We helped them fix that issue, or we delivered a solution that added Z value. With our solution, the customer experienced Y results.

The goal of this method is to build your trust meter (Figure 9-4) with a simple paragraph. The elements of trust need to be woven into the story. Let's break down the story based on the trust elements:

- Intent: You helped the customer.
- Capability: You understood their problem. You brought a solution that fixed their issue.
- Dedication: You stuck around to implement and measure results.
- Results: The customer was able to achieve what you promised.

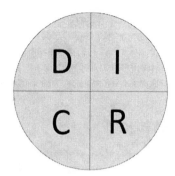

Figure 9-4. Trust meter after your reference story

Here is quick example of a good reference story.

We helped Acme (intent) by evaluating their supply chain inefficiencies and made recommendations on how to improve their systems (capability). The implemented improvements increased their inventory turnover rates by 100%, resulting in $2,000,000 of savings. (We remained after the sale, which shows we are dedicated. And we measured results.)

Use the 15 seconds the customer gives you to build trust, not to bore the customer with the canned elevator pitch. You need to practice these reference stories just as you practice the company pitch. But with questions, hooks, and stories, use conversational English, not marketing hype. Unlike with elevator pitches, you do not need to include the latest buzzwords or marketing fluff. Don't try to include everything you can do for the customer. Focus on an unique value you bring to customers. If you offer something unique, there is a better chance the door will open.

Here's a personal story. As a reseller, we sold products from many manufacturers. We had regular training. Almost every training session included the vendor's current elevator pitch. It was comical how they all sounded identical. They used the same marketing and buzzwords. Every year in the IT industry, there is a new focus or direction the industry is taking. One year, the new direction was embodied in the word "consolidation." For six months, every elevator pitch included the term consolidation. The next six months after that, every pitch included the word "green." The next year, the word "cloud" was in every pitch. The funny part was that these buzzwords were tacked on half the time, and were never integral to the core offerings of the company. "We help customers optimize their IT spend by consolidating excess computing power, blah, blah, blah . . . green and sustainability blah blah . . . Oh, yeah and we do cloud."

As you can see, the elevator pitch is not the most effective tool. Using an elevator hook, in contrast, helps you start a conversation, pique interest, and frame a customer reference story. This is much more powerful. Once you have the reference story down and deliver it to the customer, you should focus right back on the customer by asking more about their business.

Your Online Presence

What is the opposite of cold calling? Customers call *you* when they want to purchase something. If you want to purchase something, whom do you call? You want to call the best. So does your customer. If your customer does not already have a relationship with someone who can provide something they need, where do they go? Google.

If you cold call a customer and pique their interest, what is the first thing they are going to do? They will Google you, your company, or both.

Google yourself! What comes up—pictures of your last New Year's Eve bash, or a professional LinkedIn profile? Knowing what you look like online is the first step.

Today's leading networking site for professionals is LinkedIn. What does your LinkedIn profile look like? Is it like most others? Does it stand out? Does it offer anything to the customer? Is it simply a resume, or does it express the value you can offer?

You need to use your profile to show proper intent and strong capability— the value you can bring to customers. Most profiles are nothing more than a resume import. LinkedIn actually guides you into this mistake by importing your resume to build your profile. Although it is okay to show your career history, it should not be the first thing people see. So do not be lazy here! The intent you need to demonstrate is how you can help your potential customers. Customers do not care about your resume. They want to see the value you can bring to them.

The first things your customers see on your profile are your name and headline. Use the headline to indicate your specialty, or your area of subject matter expertise. The next section in LinkedIn is the skills section. List your industry expertise in more detail. When describing your skills, concentrate on customer trigger points:

- "I help customers develop their disaster-recovery strategies."
- "I help doctors increase in-office revenue streams."
- "I help customers drive business efficiencies."
- "I strive to understand my customer's business first."

If you truly want to be aligned with the buyer cycle, ask questions in your skills section. You are using the elevator hook to keep them interested, so they will read on:

- "Is your data storage a bottleneck of performance?"

- "Does your broker become a stranger after he collects his portfolio management fee?"

- "Are government regulations bogging down your finance department?"

- "Are you concerned with patient security?"

You can make the skills section as long as you like. I recommend that you make it long enough so that the customer has to actively scroll to see your work history section. Positioning your skills section in this manner can show proper intent and capability. That way, you can get a jump on building your trust meter (Figure 9-5).

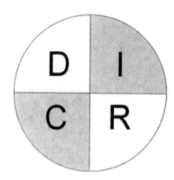

Figure 9-5. Trust meter when you do a good job with your online profile

You can demonstrate dependability via recommendations. Do not hesitate to ask colleagues for recommendations that talk about your character. Expect to be asked to reciprocate by writing a recommendation for them.

As part of your profile, list industry articles you have written, as well as blogs you write. This is the "give to get" mentality discussed earlier.

As part of your profile, do not forget to include your contact information; if someone is looking for help, help them find you!

Once your profile is up to snuff, it is time to ramp up your activity and contribute to the industry.

Proactive Online Presence

Your professional profile is a passive entity that gets no attention unless you are proactive. How do you become proactive online to get yourself noticed? First, understand which groups your customers are members of. When you connect with customers and colleagues, take the time to look at their groups. Join those groups.

Look for discussion threads that you can participate in.

Become a subject matter expert, a thought leader. Much like in the earlier planning stages, you do this by subscribing to industry magazines, regularly checking in on industry web sites, and then formulating your own thoughts, posting comments, or starting a discussions. If you are not an expert, look for whitepapers, industry articles, or professional development material you can share. Just make sure you give proper reference to others' work. Your goal is to develop an active online presence. With increased activity you become more visible to peers and potential customers. You want others to view you as an expert, thus increasing the chance they will call you.

Personal Profile

When preparing to sell, sales reps and management need to be honest with themselves about their capabilities and what level of salesperson they are. People do business with people. People do business with people they trust. People trust people they like. People like people they can relate to.

Can you realistically expect a green, behind-the-ears salesperson to relate to a 55-year-old CFO of a company? Will the CFO trust the new salesperson's capability? Will she believe the salesperson understands her industry, and that he can drive results? Will this salesperson be able to hold their ground, show dedication, and be respected? In most cases, the answer is no.

I am not saying that if you are new, you can't relate or bring value. There are younger rock star salespeople who show no fear, and who are respected by customers well above their organizational level. However, the initial impression new salespeople make on C-level executives is often poor; they have nothing in common with this person. After all, a 20-something is just starting out, worrying about paying back student loans, whereas a CFO is worried about paying for her daughter's wedding. The point is that it is easier to conduct business with people you can relate to.

While you are in the planning stages, prepare a list of traits that describe in your view a great customer. Also develop a list of traits that make someone an ideal contact for you, personally. At what level will you spend most your time? Do they have similar interests? At what level will you best relate? What outside hobbies do you have that you can share with your customer base? What is your religious affiliation? What organizations do you belong to? Are your kids the same age? Do you golf, fish, or play softball? Do you appreciate art? The list goes on. In the next chapter, we will use these traits to develop a ranking system to help you concentrate on the prospects and customers you should spend time with.

From personal experience, I can tell you that my most trusted business relationships over the years have been with customers with whom I have shared common interests. I am not saying if you are young you cannot call high. I am saying that you need to understand how that person views you. Develop strategies to put yourself in front of people like yourself. Build a team around you that can relate at any level. Understand yourself; understand where you need to augment your sales team. This not to say that you cannot sell to people who are not similar, it's just easier with a connection. Differences can be put aside for the common goal of solving problems. For example, in the IT industry, it's common to sell to engineers, and engineers and salespeople typically have dissimilar personal interests.

Develop a list of traits/activities you would like to see in a contact, and when you are qualifying customers, start qualifying contacts with the prospective organization. You can start to keep a ranked contact list exactly like the ranked customer list. Chapter 11 explores this idea in detail.

Summary

When you are establishing your territory, or trying to penetrate a new account, you will spend 90% of your time in the planning and qualifying stages. As you progress, planning becomes easier. The information you need to gather will already be at your fingertips. Planning becomes more of an updating exercise. When you are new, all this up-front planning will pay off. With everything you are doing to plan, make sure you have the end game in mind—building trust. The next chapter discusses what service or product is best to use when securing new customers.

Niche Selling

Lead with Something Unique

Attack him [the enemy] where he is unprepared, appear where you are not expected.

—Sun Tzu

The first major tactic in approaching new customers is putting relationship before opportunity. The second major tactic for approaching new customers or a new sales territory is to determine which product or service to lead with. Using the concepts of trust, I will develop a model that you can use to make this determination.

With all the talk about relationship and qualifying the customer, you eventually have to sell something. In the sales situation with Tom (the person who chased opportunities, had a large pipeline, but never closed a sale), the manager suggested that he learn about, and lead with, the company's top selling product, the products that generate the most revenue, and solutions that are the most competitive in the IT industry. I will first point out why this is an incorrect strategy, then discuss the correct product selection.

The primary reason for this chapter is to determine which products or services to lead with. If you have only one item or service to sell, not all the concepts of this chapter will apply to you. However, there are some great sales concepts in this chapter. The secondary value of this chapter is understanding your customer's purchasing personality, and how you can use it to properly present the solution you are selling. If your company is bringing a new product to market, memorize this chapter.

To Whom Will You Sell?

Geoffrey Moore's book *Crossing the Chasm* describes how to bring a new technology to market. He adapted this concept from research done at Iowa State University, which describes the acceptance of new products based on customers' demographic and psychological characteristics. The original purpose was to track the purchase patterns of hybrid corn seed by farmers.

This model has been widely used. These concepts adapt to most sales situations. What you should get from this chapter is an understanding of personal buyer personalities, how they fit within an organization, and how you position yourself to get that first deal. In this chapter I adapt the methods for marketing new technologies to work when selling any technology.

The chapter's conversation is built around this model (Figure 10-1).

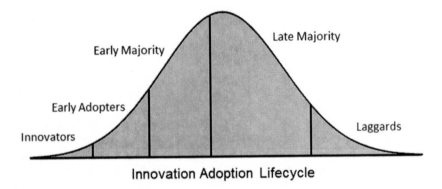

Figure 10-1. Innovation adoption lifecycle curve

As you can see, there are five buyer personalities. The premise is that you must follow a logical specific progression for each type of customer in order to successfully introduce a new technology. This is called the *innovation adoption curve* or *lifecycle*. The area of the curve indicates the relative size of the market. Here is a brief summary of each personality type, including how they buy, and what they require.

Innovators

The first category is the *innovator* or techie. The techie can be identified as the type of individual who likes to be at the early stages of a new product or service. This is the type of customer who just likes to be first. They have the first mobile phone, the first laptop, or the house in a new neighborhood. This is the type of person who reports software bugs. This report is made not out of frustration, but out of pride. They like to be recognized as helping define the final product.

In sales, the mantra is that customers buy in this order—you, the company, then the product. But in the innovator category, customers put product first. These people tend to be lower in an organization, but not always, as I will discuss later. Sometimes, meeting with an innovator might be your only way to get a foot in the door. But you must remember, this is a small number of people within a company, and typically their budgets are extremely small.

Visionaries

The second personality is the early adopter, or *visionary*. The visionary is the person who looks at a new product, and looks for ways to make magnitudes-of-order improvement in a process, or to their business. This personality type is viewed as a risk taker. Their ideas are grand. They like the big picture but get lost in the details. This buyer wants a working product; they want to implement the product, not trouble shoot it. They are more concerned with other things, like what this product can do for their company or career. In an organization they tend to be first-line managers, are younger, and are trying to move up the corporate ladder. Often, they are ambitious.

Pragmatics

Next is the early majority, or *pragmatics*. This is the first of the larger markets. By definition, pragmatics tend to be very practical. They are not risk takers, but are looking for products or services that are proven, and will help the company make small incremental improvements to costs or revenues. They want a product that has been proven in the market. They want a product they can purchase, and the companies they do business with must have references. These people are very well respected. They tend to be tenured within the organization, and carry director-level titles.

Conservatives

Conservatives, or the late majority, are about the status quo. Conservatives purchase a product once it has become mainstream. The product is "complete," tested, proven, and usually from the leading vendor in a particular market. From conservatives, you often hear statements like, "No one ever got fired for buying [insert big name here])." This type of buyer tends to be further up within an organization. They are tenured, but tend to have a "mitigate the risk" mentality of doing business. They are more interested in career preservation than career advancement. This is the largest group within a company, region, or market.

Laggards

Laggards, I will not go into detail with laggards, since they are a small market, and it's not necessary for the setup of our strategies. Laggards have an "old school" mentality; if it ain't broke, don't fix it. For example, some still don't see the need for a computer. "We always use manual ledgers; why would I need a computer?" This is an extreme example, but you get the point.

Customers in this category are usually related to the culture of the company. For example, buyers for a manufacturer of furniture will tend to be toward the back of the curve. But you do sometimes find a visionary working for a laggard company.

Laggard markets can be lucrative. In the IT industry, some customers hold onto equipment that is way past the support life of the manufacturer. So replacement parts become scarce and therefore expensive.

If you are in this type of market, just know that having a visionary message will usually be wasted on this type of buyer.

To fully understand the concepts around these personalities, consider these real-life examples.

Example: Techie in a Conservative World

My brother is in medical device sales. His company was introducing a new product that would reduce the need for some nasal surgeries. This device could be used in the doctor's office. The cost-benefit to the doctor was huge. He could do this procedure, as stated, in the office. It would take 15–20 minutes versus taking hours at a surgical center. The profit to the doctor was the same when you compared the surgical procedure versus the in-office procedure. However, for the doctor, the true savings lay in opportunity costs. He saved hours of time that he could use to see (and bill) other patients.

Given this great advantage to help doctors save time and make more money, my brother set out with his product. His sales in the first six months were almost nonexistent, and so were the results of the company. The main objection was that the product was not proven. Doctors tend to be conservative. They wanted to see that this procedure had been done safely for years. They want to be sure there are no long-term negative effects.

The message about large improvements to the bottom line was aimed at a visionary buyer. But in the medical field, the curve is shifted more to the right. Even visionaries in the medical field tend to be more conservative since they are dealing with human lives. So, the visionary market is very small in medicine. As a matter of luck, my brother called on a doctor who happened to be an inventor himself. This doctor was a straight-up techie. This is the perfect first customer for new technology. This doctor, without references, went straight to his patients and started performing procedures. As mentioned, innovators tend to be lower in the organization. However, in this case the doctor owned the practice. During the course of the procedures he pointed out issues he saw, made recommendations for improvements, and had ideas for add-ons to this product. The message of increased billings for this doctor was of little value. He wanted to play with the latest technology.

Leveraging the success of this doctor, my brother was able to grow his business. Outside events helped as well. For one thing, the company was smart enough to listen to the early clients and make improvements to the product. A couple of doctors saw the business vision and the competitive advantage to offering this procedure, and they built huge practices specializing in this procedure. This led to a wider use of the product that could ease the concerns of the conservatives.

The intent of the example is to show the progression that a new product takes coming to market. In terms of sales strategy, there are few takeaways. First, understand where your product resides on the curve, so you can keep an eye out for customers who properly fit. Second, know your customer adoption personality. Third, tailor your message to match the person. When dealing with a techie, your message should be about the product, and what it can do. If you are dealing with visionaries, the messaging is more about massive improvements. When dealing with pragmatics, you want to talk about experience, the stability of the company, and the proven track record of helping customers. Lastly, when dealing with conservatives you must either have the leading product, or a good message about how you can enhance the solutions they already own.

Example 2: Selling "Conservative" to a Visionary Doesn't Work

Here is an example of messaging from the other side of the equation. Early in my sales career I worked for Cisco Systems. If you are not in IT and do not know Cisco, they own 80% market share in computer networking. "No one ever got fired for buying Cisco." Their message was something like this:

> We have proven products. We have a huge R&D staff to keep ahead of the technology demands. We have 10,000 certified engineers. We have done proof of concepts with every technology on the market. Due to the volume of product we produce, we can offer competitive pricing.

How can you lose a deal with all this behind you? I did, and it was a large one. I had better pricing, a good relationship, and I listened to the business requirements. I actually helped the customer during the business planning. Plus, my product was more flexible than the competitors'. There was actually an investment protection program in place in case the technology changed. My competitor was shrinking, losing massive market share, and their R&D ranks were decimated. (Here is a quote from my customer about my competitor, "The one engineer who is working on this product has promised me he is staying with the company.") What's more, they were slightly more expensive.

How then did I lose the deal? Let me give you a bit of background on the prospective company and this person, and you tell me.

- This prospect was going to offer insurance through kiosks at a major retailer. They were the first company to deliver insurance in this manner.

- The owner of the company was young, and the company was growing almost too fast.

- The CIO, my main contact, was promoted from within. Just a few years before this, he was made head of computing because he knew how to operate both Apple- and Windows-based computers. Within four years, he was in charge of building out a 4,000-node network worth millions of dollars.

- The CIO liked to jump out of planes and scuba dive on weekends.

Why did I lose?

My approach was aimed at a conservative, but my buyer was a risk taker. The entire company was visionary. My competition played to the risk taker, the new technology, and the up-and-coming company (even though it was dying), and they assured him he could have access to the single design engineer. They risked their success on one person.

Getting back to theory, Moore's contribution to this model is the introduction of a break in the adoption model. There is a challenge between the visionary and the pragmatic, or the chasm. The pragmatics and decision makers of the company require references and referrals. These referrals can either be internal or external to the company. The problem is that early adopters of the technologies, the techies and visionaries, are not considered good references. The pragmatics view them as flakey, and their opinions are not valid.

The answer to this dilemma is niche marketing. For the purposes of this book, I call it niche selling. Niche selling is addressing a customer's need that is not addressed by a current vendor. Alternatively, you may have a product that addresses a specific need that does not involve much risk or investment. Niche selling is a powerful strategy for a new salesperson. You need to find a unique offering in your product or service line that your competition does not address.

Looking back at Tom's example, what did management do up front? They trained him on their big ticket, best-selling items, and their most competitive product set. Tom's challenge was manifold:

- Technology that is hard to replace at the customer.

- Dozens of other competitors in that market.

- Incumbents who have the customer's trust.

Tom would have been better suited if he were trained on products or services that were new to the market, or unique to the vendor. Your goal should be to sell to a customer base where there is not an incumbent.

Why Niche Selling Is Effective

Selling where there is an incumbent vendor shrinks your window of opportunity. Using the 48-month purchase cycle mentioned before, you might hit the window perfectly within the four-month sales cycle, but probably not given the 8% chance of hitting it. In reality, if they have a vendor for this type or purchase, your window is much smaller. If you happen to catch your competition sleeping, and can define the solution for the customer, your true window is maybe one month, or a 2% chance. If you hit the window perfectly despite the odds, you have an 80% chance of becoming the vendor they use just to keep the other vendor honest.

Now look at niche selling. You understand the customer issues around which you will position your product. You understand that being new, you need to establish trust, so your first deals might be smaller. When you position a new need to the customer, you create an entirely new purchasing cycle because this is a new concept. There is no incumbent. Your chance of engaging in a conversation that is open minded, not clouded by competition, is 100%. This method eliminates the window-of-opportunity concept. There is no cyclical purchase established for this particular product. You eliminate the need for perfect timing and lower the influence of competition. If your competition does offer the same solution, you put your competition in a defensive position with the customer. "Why didn't you tell me about this new product/service/technology?"

Trust in Niche Selling

When you're competing against a trusted competitor, you are looking to build your trust and find a weakness in the competitor's trust equation. If you lead with a niche product or service, you have a capability that is unique. You may not have demonstrated the capabilities or results yet. But since you are dealing in an area in which the incumbent cannot offer a solution, their trust meter for that specific solution is diminished. For that solution, the incumbent still has proved they are dedicated to the customer, and have good intention, but they do not have the capability or results for that solution. Always start by assuming the incumbent is fully trusted. So in this case, the incumbent trust meter moves to this level, as shown in Figure 10-2.

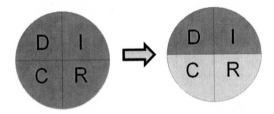

Figure 10-2. Lower incumbent trust due to lack of product offering in a needed area

When you are actually competing with an incumbent who did not bring unique values to the forefront, trust in the incumbent is degraded some. This comes in the form of showing a customer a new way to use their existing products, or solutions, that they did not think of. The incumbent can be hurt in the dedication and possibly intent elements. The incumbent is assuming that business will flow their way, and their approach to helping the customer comes into question (Figure 10-3).

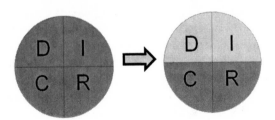

Figure 10-3. Lowering incumbent trust due to less than stellar customer service

You lowered the competition's trust profile without once being negative toward your competition. All you did was present an area where they are not capable.

During half time of a football game, the teams go to their locker rooms and you reevaluate the game plan. The first place you look is where you are having success, or where you can exploit a known weakness in the opposing team. If you are drawing up a play on the whiteboard, you would first attack the weakest link in the defensive line. Look at attacking the incumbent the same; where are they weakest? The defensive line for the incumbent looks like Figure 10-4.

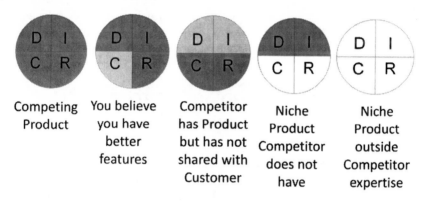

| Competing Product | You believe you have better features | Competitor has Product but has not shared with Customer | Niche Product Competitor does not have | Niche Product outside Competitor expertise |

Figure 10-4. Relative trust strength of incumbent vs. non-niche and niche products

If you have limited trust at the beginning of the sales cycle, your best play is moving toward the right of the line. Going head-to-head against a competitor with similar products is your toughest route. Even if you believe you have a solution with some better capability, you can see your situation does not improve much. The next trust meter shows a situation where you introduce a solution to a customer; a solution a competitor has, but has not discussed with the customer. The first niche trust meter shows a niche product that may replace, complement, augment, or possibly change a competitor's solution. The last situation is by far the best. You find a new product that is important to the customer, and they have no incumbent in that area. You are competing on a completely level playing field, or, ideally, you are the only team on the field.

Where Susan Went Wrong

Recall the example in Chapter 2 involving Susan, the salesperson who switched employment from the manufacturer to the reseller, where she had some good customer relationships. How her sales team approached her old customer base was with the products she had sold them in the past, but through another reseller. In each case, she chose to keep selling head to head, large product versus incumbent large product.

Since she had some personal trust developed with these customers, and the fact she had access, a better strategy would have been to find a unique offering they knew the incumbent did not have. For example, she could have found a niche offering within a small department. The deal sizes might have been smaller, but they would have been larger than zero. There are other benefits as well. She gets to work with a new person. Their company gets set up as a vendor in their system, which is huge. She gets the customer into a habit of buying from the new company. In addition, she has one more referral within the customer. She can start earning trust all over again. Ideally with new access, her company can bring new ideas to the customer. Compare that to what she did—wait for a deal to quote, which is passive.

Example: Putting Niche Selling to the Test

Let's take a look at this strategy in a company's effort to bring a new technology into its portfolio.

A reseller entered into a new contract to sell a large manufacturer's products and services. This manufacturer had a very broad portfolio in the IT industry, including servers, storage, networking, management software, and back-office software. Each of these product areas was supported by separate divisions of the manufacturer. They pretty much had everything you needed to run an IT shop. Yet the reseller was struggling in its first six months of engagement with this manufacturer. When we consulted with the reseller, we started by asking how they had engaged, what they had been trained on, who they had relationships with at the manufacturer, and so forth. Then we analyzed their pipeline.

Eight months into this new relationship, the sales teams across the reseller's five regions have done account mapping, training, and some joint sales calls with the manufacturer's server and storage teams. Servers and storage in this industry are highly competitive—in fact, the most competitive. Products are almost commoditized in these markets. Moreover, the products tend to be in sensitive parts of their customers' businesses, making them technically hard to replace. They are also on long purchase cycles, meaning that only a small percentage of their customer base is in the market at any one time. The reseller also faces competition from other resellers who also sell this manufacturer's products. They cannot simply position better features of the product. With these larger purchases, the sale teams were most likely competing against a seasoned sales professional who "owned" the customer relationship. Even when the customers are "in the market," they typically stay with incumbent technology.

Across five regions, they had 25 salespeople, and after eight months, they had a total of 10 deals in the forecast. The total revenue in the forecast was $1.7 million. We did not even bother to qualify the forecast based on their relative trust strength against the incumbent.

Our next step in the consulting process was to bring together the sales leaders from each organization. We asked the manufacturer to briefly review their product portfolio. We were able to identify a niche product that could be sold to a few different titles within an organization. We then looked back at the forecast and saw that two of the ten opportunities were with this product; this was without any focus on this niche product. We chose two regions at the reseller to roll out this strategy.

1. First, the reseller trained the sales teams on this niche product. Training was focused, and not scattered across the entire product portfolio. There was a simple story that both junior and senior salespeople could grasp.

2. They developed a marketing program that would bring customers to lunch-and-learn events. The promotion of the lunch-and-learn was focused on the issues customers face that this product solved. They did not focus on the product. With this focus, the sales and marketing teams were able to drive great attendance to the events. Over 50% of the attendees were net new clients to the reseller or the manufacturer. This is the power of focusing on issues that customers face.

3. After the lunch-and-learns, follow-up sales calls were conducted with the attendees.

The results were impressive. Remember, they conducted the events in only two of the five regions. In 37% of the time, 3 months versus 8 months, the company grew the number of opportunities 240%, from 10 to 24. The revenue in the forecast grew from $1.7M to $4.4M. 75% of these deals were in a "confident" stage. The interesting part of the scenario is that the niche product opportunities went from 2 to 7. That means the other opportunities, in the larger volume categories, increased from 8 to 17. The goal of the niche was to gain access to the customer and then have broader conversations, and that is exactly what happened. With these results, the manufacturer stepped up and paid for marketing events in the other regions. The other divisions of the manufacturer saw these results and were willing to put in money for marketing events, even though the niche product was outside their division.

Niche selling works because it gives every advantage to penetrating a new account. First, it increases the rep's chance to gain access to a customer. Next, it reduces the chances the rep will be going head to head against an experienced, incumbent competitor. Last, if you have a large product portfolio, it allows your company to focus training for new salespeople, and it gives a specific focal point for marketing to assist the sales team.

Summary

In this chapter, I assumed that you have a choice in products or services. If you do, pick something unique. If you do not have a choice, hopefully your offering is unique. If your offering is not unique, try to find a unique application of the product or service that has not yet been discussed with the customer. If it is not unique, at a minimum make sure your messaging is in line with your buyer's adoption personality, or job title.

The power of this strategy is that it does not require one ounce of sales training, or sales skills improvement. It can be done in a conference room with management. And, you can get the entire organization focused on supporting penetration of new accounts. It's a matter of simple physics. If you can apply the same amount of force in a smaller area, you generate much more pressure. If you push on a piece of paper with your hand using 20 pounds of force, nothing really happens. Now take that same 20 pounds of force, and focus it on the tiny area of a pencil tip. You will punch right through it. If you use marketing, events, cold calling, and training all focused on one niche product, you get the maximum pressure in penetrating new accounts.

Now that you are prepared to engage with the customer with a proper online presence, sales training, product training, an effective elevator hook, and you have picked a solution to lead with, it is time to figure out where to best spend your prospecting time, and which customers are worth your ongoing effort.

Rich Hunting Grounds

Which Land Has the Deer?

You don't hunt moose in Florida.

—Unknown

When hunting, you don't want to hunt on land that does not have prey. Likewise in sales, you must understand which companies are a good fit for your product or services. You are not just looking for any customer. You are looking for customers who will purchase your products. Qualifying customers for the potential to purchase from your company is one of the most important activities you need to accomplish using the systems you've learned in this book. Up until now, you had only one tool to determine where you spent your sales time—your forecast. While your forecast and opportunities are important, you need to spend time with customers who have great potential, and start establishing trust. The tools in this chapter help you determine and justify which customers you will target. The first thing is to figure out which traits and metrics to use to identify, measure, and track your customers.

You need help with this task. As a new salesperson, you should seek counsel from management, marketing, partners, and other successful salespeople in your organization to help create the ideal customer profile. This profile describes an ideal customer. The description should be based on elements that can be measured. You should rank every one of your target customers using the traits that make up the ideal customer profile. I discuss general traits shared by any organization that you can use to rank customers, and take a look at possible elements that might be specific to the customer vertical, or the products you sell.

You might know more about your customers than you think. The first sections of this chapter cover traits at the company level, traits at the individual level, and traits related to opportunities. You will use these traits to build a ranking worksheet. Chapter 12 then covers where to find lists of customers with information that will help you rank them.

Approach the planning stage as though the customer is completely new to you and your company. Being new, you have a completely empty trust meter. The goal is to start building trust before you engage with the customer. During the planning stages, there are strategies you can use that will help increase the customer's perception of you with capability and intent. The number one complaint customers have about sellers is, "They do not understand my business." By understanding their business and industry, you increase your capability and intent quotients in the eyes of the customer.

I use all the concepts in this chapter to help you build the ideal customer profile. You will use this profile to rank your prospects, and to start building a system to determine which customers deserve your time.

Customer Traits: Company Level

Before you start researching any one customer, there are traits common to all customers that you must understand. Customers need to be addressed from the level of the corporate entity and the individuals you will directly interface. At the corporate level, purchase decisions are based on how your product or service helps

- Drive revenue

- Cut costs

- Mitigate risk

- Maintain a positive image in the community

As you learn more about your customer base, industry, or the vertical market, you can extend the assumptions list. Here are some examples:

- Public schools can't drive revenue but are concerned with cost.

- Private universities are concerned less with revenue and more with image.

- Hospitals are very concerned with government regulations such as HIPPA.

- Public companies have large regulatory obligations.

- New companies will take more risks and are more concerned with revenue growth than cost.

- Manufacturing is a mature sector, so cost is a concern.

These are all simplifications, but they give you a starting point in approaching your customer base, or at least in understanding customer concerns.

One way to quickly show value to customers is by completely understanding their industry. This is easier for salespeople who sell only into vertical markets.

If your solution fits a broad customer base, you may want to specialize in one market and set yourself apart from the competition.

Regardless of the industry, all business customers have needs, issues, problems, and goals, both personal and business. All customers are working on some project today. All are planning their futures. Every day they are asking, how can they maximize profit? How can they drive cost down or increase revenue? They need to protect their assets or reduce the risk of something happening to the company. This is why they have lawyers, buy insurance, have disaster recovery plans, implement security policies, and so on.

Keep in mind that corporate image can be affected by many factors—banks losing customer financial data, web sites going down so customers cannot order online, product liability—the list is endless. Ten years ago, an issue would have to be huge to get media attention. However, today with social media avenues, small issues can be blown out of proportion. Consumers now can have the power to sway public opinion about a corporation with the speed of the Internet.

You must understand all these issues for your customers, so you can talk about the issues that concern them.

If you're selling to consumers, the concerns are the same. Consumers have the same objectives of driving revenue, lowering cost, mitigating risk, and protecting or enhancing image. With consumers:

- Instead of driving revenue, they want to make more money.

- Instead of cutting costs, they want to save money.

- Instead of mitigating risks, they want to buy insurance.

- Instead of maintaining a public image, they are aware of the images of the things they buy, from the cars they drive to the smart phone they use.

Each of these assumptions gives you some indication of the value you need to bring to the sales equation. When you understand these basic customer requirements up front, and address them when you initially engage a customer, you will increase your trust meter in the areas of capability and intent (Figure 11-1).

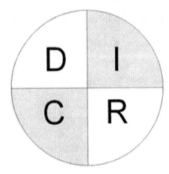

Figure 11-1. Trust meter with intent and capability

In gathering this general information, you must determine if there are traits that are worth putting into an ideal customer profile. Does the vertical market make a difference for what you sell? Does the cycle of purchases impact your ability to sell to this customer? Do you gravitate toward customers who are driving revenue or mitigating risk?

Customer Traits: Individual Level

The final assumptions you need to make about the customer are at the individual level. What level in the organization are you targeting? What are the personal goals of the customer? What assumptions can you make about the title of your customer? Every single person you call on has the same basic concerns you do. How safe is their job? Can they get a raise or make more money? How do they look to their peers? How do they meet management business objectives to maximize their pay? Is the person looking for advancement in the company? Most of these questions can be asked once you establish a certain level of trust. Here are some assumptions about individuals by title.

C-Level Traits

Goals at the C level are more closely tied to corporate goals relating to revenue, cost, risk, and image. Mitigating risk to their title is of most importance. There is not much farther up the ladder they can go, and they make more money than most people in the organization. Usually, their personal goals are about preservation rather than advancement. These tend to be the conservative buyers on the adoption lifecycle curve. This level will always have the power to purchase.

Director Traits

Director-level people (mid-level managers) are probably the busiest people in an organization. This level has to balance the need of the company goals with the ability to execute the goals by their direct reports. The IT department, for example, is the most targeted level by outside vendors. They are high enough in the organization to have good visibility into large projects. Director-level people are concerned with advancement, and they are willing to take some risks to advance their individual departments. On the adoption lifecycle curve, they are the pragmatics. This level might have the power to purchase. At a minimum, they can get you access to that power.

Non-Management Traits

Non-management employees often are the individuals who end up using the products and solutions you have to offer. They can influence decisions, but usually do not have the power to make corporate purchases. These individuals are most removed from corporate goals. They are concerned with having a paycheck, and having their lives the least complicated as possible. These types are important in a sales cycle but often only in the evaluation stage. These individuals will be all over the adoption lifecycle curve. They may also provide you access to higher-level decision makers.

Know Your Buyer

It is important to understand the distinction in these roles. Once it is time to position your solution, you want to make sure you are not talking about workforce reduction cost savings with non-management individuals. Conversely, you don't want to be talking about features of product with C-level employees.

Understanding the goals and concerns of the individuals you deal with will show your capability, intent, and dependability (Figure 11-2).

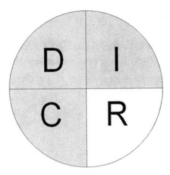

Figure 11-2. Implied trust when you understand the customer's individual role and concerns

---

On your ideal customer profile, is there a title that makes sense for you to target as a company? On the ideal customer profile or ranking worksheet, do you need access to C-level employees? Do your products have a direct impact on the bottom line? These answers will help you plan your approach and produce bigger sales sooner.

The Cycle of Purchases

I covered the purchasing cycle when discussing how to increase your window of opportunity. It is very important to track. How often does your customer purchase what you sell? Once? Every 3, 4, 5 years? Every 15 years? As you approach your customers, what are the chances that they are actually "in the market" for your product or service?

Let's say that a typical customer makes a significant purchase of your product every four years, and has a four-month buying cycle. If you are approaching a customer cold in this scenario, there is only an 8% chance they are in the market.

You can also define "in the market" at the consumer level. For example, I know Bosch makes one of the quietest dishwashers on the market. It is efficient, using less water and less energy. However, my standard GE washer works just fine. I am not in the market for a new dishwasher. I might be in the market every 8 years, when I look to remodel my kitchen. It does not matter that there is a better product out there.

Compelling events, or triggers, are also important. What events or conditions would cause your customer to look at your products or servers? If my dishwasher suddenly starts spilling water all over the floor, or the motor burns out, I am suddenly in the market. Understand these triggers for your product and customer base.

In the IT industry, customers make large purchasing decisions every four to five years on major purchases like storage, servers, and networking gear. However, issues like growth, consolidations, expansions, and building moves can also trigger larger purchase requirements.

In the medical device market, doctors are always in the market for breakthrough procedures and treatments. They rarely seek out new technologies on their own, however. They expect the market to educate them. A doctor might call you if she goes to a conference, or reads a medical journal, that highlights a breakthrough in treatment. But in most cases, you'll need to inform doctors of breakthroughs during sales calls.

Let's consider commercial plumbing supplies. Unless a new building is erected, or a plumbing problem materializes, companies are not in the market for plumbing. If the hot water heater in the building corrodes, the company is now in the market.

In the telecom market, companies replace their phone systems every seven to ten years, or when they are expanding, moving, or consolidating buildings.

These are all broad generalizations. It's important that you understand the purchase cycle and compelling events of your specific product or service.

What are the characteristics and compelling events you look for? Are they powerful enough to include on your ideal customer profile?

Example

A large manufacturer is the leader in its field. It has 80% market share. The target in this case is a large insurance company. This company is very conservative with its decisions. The insurance company happens to be in the backyard of one of the remaining competitors to the leading manufacturer. Year after year, the manufacturer puts a different salesperson on this account. Every year, this salesperson "fails." They have assigned this account to senior seasoned reps and junior hungry reps, but each year they fail to make their quota with this account.

Then finally they get a rep into the account who gets it! Management for the large manufacturer defines success as selling some very large equipment that is in the center of the company IT infrastructure. That means they have focused their previous sales efforts on selling their big ticket item head to head with the incumbent. This new rep has the benefit of understanding the account history from his predecessors. The customer purchased these central pieces of equipment two years ago, and the normal replace cycle is about four years. The rep, knowing the purchase cycle, told management that he would take the account only if he had two years to work the customer. He knew this core equipment was not due to be replaced for two years. In reality, he wanted to get room from management to be more relaxed and patient with the customer.

His goal was to build trust. He needs to show the customer he is sticking around and wants to help them. He needs to take the pressure of his quota for this customer. He needs to build trust. With what the salesperson knows at this point, he is setting up to show better intent, and to show dependability (Figure 11-3). I revisit this story in Chapter 21. However, understanding the customer purchasing cycle was instrumental in setting his strategy.

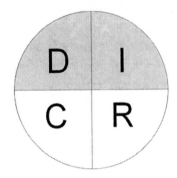

Figure 11-3. Building trust before opportunity

Traits to Consider

When developing your list of traits for the ideal customer profile, a good place to start is with traits common to all industries. This is by no means a complete list; just items you might want to choose to build your profile.

- Revenue
- Number of employees
- Vertical market
- Regional, national, or global company
- Number locations/branches
- Public or private company
- Growing or shrinking company
- Level of access you have at power or lower

- Level of trust built

- Buying style

Next, compile traits that are specific to a vertical you are targeting, your industry, and/or your product. Examples:

- If you call on hospitals, you might want to know the number of beds, and the number of doctors or nurses employed.

- If you sell automotive parts, you might want to know the number of units (cars) shipped annually.

- If you sell networking equipment, the number of locations or branches might be of use. However, if you sell data storage, you might track the amount of data they back up or the number of servers they have.

- If you sell mobile devices, discover the number of mobile users, drivers, salespeople, doctors, or what have you.

- If you sell turf, you might track the number of acres potential customers have.

I could go on with many more examples, but this is an exercise you have to complete with management, since it is specific to your industry.

Work with the End in Mind

The ideal customer profile is not intended to re-create your forecast. However, you need to determine which traits you might want to track that are related to the sales equation (for a refresher, see Chapter 8):

$$CE \times V \times P \times DP \times (D+I+C+R)^2 = Sale$$

Compelling event. While a compelling event normally identifies a trigger for an individual opportunity, you can also look for customer characteristics that identify compelling events. If your solution is sold in new locations, then you might look for companies that are expanding locations. If your sales are tied to the number of employees the customer has, then look for customers who are in growth mode.

This can work in reverse as well. Sometimes companies are shrinking and looking to save money. As you develop your ranking sheet, have one characteristic aimed at a compelling event. Also, keep in mind that different vertical markets will determine what they spend on your product. While everyone needs IT infrastructure, Internet companies need a lot more.

Value or budget. Do they have money, or will they buy if there is an ROI (return on investment?) Does the department you work with have money? If the customer does not seem to have money, the next question is, "Will they buy on value?" If they're shown a way to save money or make more money with your solution, do they buy? How do you determine if they have money? This can be done before you step foot in the customer's door. Run credit checks, or check financials if the company is public. Are there economic trends that affect a specific vertical? For example, when the economy is down, tax dollars are down, and state-run universities have very small budgets for improvements. The best way to determine if an organization has money is to check their reputation within the sales community. Talk with partners and with other salespeople who call on that customer.

Does the customer consider the value of the solution, or do they buy strictly on price? This can be good or bad, depending on your position in the market. Will this customer spend money to save money? Will they buy on ROI?

Power is defined as the people who can make purchasing decisions. This is simple in the ranking worksheet. Do you have access or not? You could rank the level of people you are dealing with. So this can be a range, rather than a yes or no.

As for *decision process,* there are a few items you can learn early on. Do they evaluate products, and then let purchasing beat up vendors on pricing? Are you on their preferred vendor list? Do they have a preferred vendors list? How closed is this list?

Not all characteristics fall under one category. For example, in state and local government, spending in the current fiscal year often must be budgeted in the preceding fiscal year. So decision timelines and budget availability can be lumped in with this characteristic. In addition, some characteristics like growth can have a direct impact on budget.

The last element in the sales equation is *trust.* I suggest you have a trust column and score it 0-8 based on the point system I developed earlier (see Chapter 8).

Here is a good list of options for your ranking sheet.

- Access to power
- Growing/shrinking company
- Vendor list
- Buys on value
- Adding locations
- Vertical market
- Has money

Ranking Customers

Traditionally, salespeople allocated their time based on where there were opportunities. If you are new to a territory, you will have no pipeline, and once you do have pipeline, you can't trust the quality of the opportunities. You need new metrics and a system to determine where you should spend your time. The ability to rank customers intelligently gives you the guidance you need. As you start to use this system, you will find it helps you no matter how mature your territory is. I found personally that using it helps me stay in touch with my most important existing customers as well as allocating time to hunt for new customers.

First, develop an ideal customer profile. As mentioned, an ideal customer profile requires you to choose attributes that are measurable, and that you can track for each customer. You can use the previous list for the attributes, or you can create your own. This exercise is very specific, based on your vertical market and your product or service. I am familiar with my industry (IT) and will use that as an example. This process is highly subjective. This becomes an art more than a science.

In information technology, even target customers will have different traits based on the product you are selling. For example, if I am selling networking equipment, the number of employees, the number of locations, or the number of branches customers have is a great indicator of their potential needs. However, if I am selling data storage devices, indicators of potential spending capability include the number of core servers they have or the amount of data they produce. Certain vertical markets generate more data, like hospitals, financial institutions, and software developers.

For this example, I assume I am selling data storage. Here are the metrics that make sense to consider. (It is not necessary you understand all these terms. Just get a feel of what is being done so you can apply the ideas to your own circumstances.)

- Revenue
- Number of servers
- Amount of data, if known
- Vertical market
- Our company trust meter
- Is the customer's organization growing or shrinking?
- Competition trust meter
- Do they buy on relationship, price, or something else?

An ideal customer profile would assign a range to each of these values. For example, your company might do well with customers who have revenues between $500 million and $5 billion. You use such characteristics to develop a ranking system for prospective customers, and to use once you start to gain access to customers.

The ranking system is meant to be a living document to help you determine where you need to spend your time. Traditionally, the only metric you had to allocate your time was your forecast, which is 100% opportunity focused. I have shown, several times, that opportunity with new customers can't be trusted. In short, this ranking system is the tool you need to determine which customers are worth your time.

I have developed an easy-to-use worksheet (Figure 11-4) that you can download from by web site, www.huntingwithtrust.com. In the first tab of the worksheet, you enter the attributes you want to rank or track. You then enter the unit of measure, the maximum value, and the relative importance of each attribute.

Attribute	Unit	Maximum Value	Importance (1-10)
Revenue	$ Millions	10,000	7
Servers	#	2,000	8
Amount of Storage	TB	2,000	8
Vertical Market	Rank (1-10)	10	5
Trust Built	8 Points	8	10
Company Growing?	Yes/No	10	7
Negative			
Incumbent Trust	8 Points	8	10
Buys on Price	Yes/No	10	5

Figure 11-4. Attribute worksheet in ranking system

There is a lot of judgment in this process. These numbers are a relative ranking. The weighting you assign to each value is also relative. You should experiment with the weights of each metric based on your experience. The negative attributes that work against you—the prospect has a strong incumbent or buys only on price—are automatically calculated with a negative number. This is a living document that changes as you add customers to the list, spend time with other customers, and generally learn more about your territory.

Notice that trust is one of the attributes. You can use any value you want, but for my example I am going to use the three-point system—0 points for no trust, 1 point for inferred trust, and 2 points for demonstrated trust. I then multiply that value by the four trust elements, for a total of 8 points.

The second tab in the file is where you enter customer data and then sort by rank. The limits on each cell are limited by the maximums you entered on the previous tab. Figure 11-5 is a view that shows the first columns.

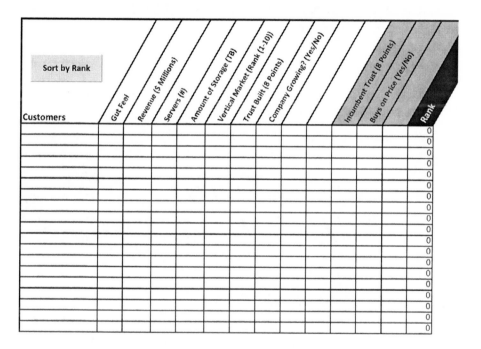

Figure 11-5. Blank worksheet that shows the attributes automatically placed as column headers

As you start entering data, an automatic ranking number will be given to each customer. Since values for each attribute can vary widely, like revenue in the billions, and trust points that have a maximum of 8, the spreadsheet will automatically normalize the numbers. If you enter the right information on the attributes tab, the spreadsheet will do the work for you.

It is not necessary to understand the algorithm, so skip this note unless you like math. Each attribute is normalized to a scale from 0-100 before it is added to the ranking score. For example, the trust meter only goes to a maximum of 8 points. But, in the background of the spreadsheet, an 8 becomes 100 points, and a 6 becomes 75 points. For the other attributes you define, the maximum value the attribute. The spread sheet will normalize the ranking score, once again, to a maximum of 100. For example, you enter a maximum value of $100 billion. Then, for a specific customer, you enter their revenue at $45 billion, the spread sheet will add 45 points to the ranking. This way, trust is on a level playing field with revenue. Once again, you don't need to know all the math; the downloadable spreadsheet does the work for you.

Let's walk through some examples on how to use this system. First, the spreadsheet gets populated with the raw data (Figure 11-6).

Sort by Rank	Gut Feel	Revenue ($ Millions)	Servers (#)	Amount of Storage (TB)	Vertical Market (Rank (1-10))	Trust Built (8 Points)	Company Growing? (Yes/No)			Incumbent Trust (8 Points)	Buys on Price (Yes/No)	Rank
Customer 1		1,000	150	150	5	2					10	168
Customer 2		50	100	20	10	4				6		115
Customer 3		1,000	175	200	2	2	10			8		185
Customer 4		2,000	200		7					6		93
Customer 5		100	35		5							71
Customer 6		150	750	1,000	5	5				5	10	211
Customer 7		5,000	700	1,200	2							236
Customer 8		25	120	20	2							66
Customer 9		75			10						10	18
Customer 10		120	20	45	10	8	10			4		258
Customer 11		250	30	50	6		10					178
Customer 12		400	50	100	6	2				6		123
Customer 13		650	50	120	7	2				6	10	91
Customer 14		2,000	500	500	9	7				7		238
Customer 15		2,500	350	1,000	8	2	10			7		290
Customer 16		50	200		2							83
Customer 17		90	25		3					8		1
Customer 18		45	10		4							27
Customer 19		1,500	225	1,000	7					2		219

Figure 11-6. Ranking worksheet with raw data before it is sorted

When you click on the Sort by Rank button in the top left. you will see the customer order change (Figure 11-7).

Sort by Rank

	Gut Feel	Revenue ($ Millions)	Servers (#)	Amount of Storage (TB)	Vertical Market (Rank (1-10))	Trust Built (8 Points)	Company Growing? (Yes/No)	Incumbent Trust (8 Points)	Buys on Price (Yes/No)	Rank
Customer 15		2,500	350	1,000	8	2	10	7		290
Customer 10		120	20	45	10	8	10	4		258
Customer 14		2,000	500	500	9	7		7		238
Customer 7		5,000	700	1,200	2					236
Customer 19		1,500	225	1,000	7			2		219
Customer 6		150	750	1,000	5	5		5	10	211
Customer 3		1,000	175	200	2	2	10	8		185
Customer 11		250	30	50	6		10			178
Customer 1		1,000	150	150	5	2			10	168
Customer 12		400	50	100	6	2		6		123
Customer 2		50	100	20	10	4		6		115
Customer 4		2,000	200		7			6		93
Customer 13		650	50	120	7	2		6	10	91
Customer 16		50	200		2					83
Customer 5		100	35		5					71
Customer 8		25	120	20	2					66
Customer 18		45	10		4					27
Customer 9		75			10				10	18
Customer 17		90	25		3			8		1

Figure 11-7. Ranking sheet sorted by clicking the Sort by Rank button

If you look closely, you'll see that the first column is called Gut Feel. This is the only fixed column in the worksheet. This field allows you to force-rank customers. Sometimes, the numbers just do not work out, and you know the customer is a great candidate—maybe from past experience, or your manager tasks you with penetrating a specific account, or you get a lead from a partner or referral from a customer. I've had customers who scored low, but through territory experience, I gave them a very high gut feeling, so they float to the top of my prospecting list. As an example, let's add to the gut feel on Customer 12. I also used a negative number to move down Customer 19, whom I don't think is a great prospect.

If you re-sort, you'll notice how Customer 12 rises to the top, and Customer 19 moves down a few spots (Figure 11-8).

Sort by Rank	Gut Feel	Revenue ($ Millions)	Servers (#)	Amount of Storage (TB)	Vertical Market (Rank (1-10))	Trust Built (8 Points)	Company Growing? (Yes/No)			Incumbent Trust (8 Points)	Buys on Price (Yes/No)	Rank
Customer 12	200	400	50	100	6	2				6		323
Customer 15		2,500	350	1,000	8	2	10			7		290
Customer 10		120	20	45	10	8	10			4		258
Customer 14		2,000	500	500	9	7				7		238
Customer 7		5,000	700	1,200	2							236
Customer 6		150	750	1,000	5	5				5	10	211
Customer 3		1,000	175	200	2	2	10			8		185
Customer 11		250	30	50	6		10					178
Customer 1		1,000	150	150	5	2					10	168
Customer 19	-100	1,500	225	1,000	7					2		119
Customer 2		50	100	20	10	4				6		115
Customer 4		2,000	200		7					6		93
Customer 13		650	50	120	7	2				6	10	91
Customer 16		50	200		2							83
Customer 5		100	35		5							71
Customer 8		25	120	20	2							66
Customer 18		45	10		4							27
Customer 9		75			10						10	18
Customer 17		90	25		3					8		1

Figure 11-8. Ranking worksheet with gut feel populated and then resorted

Once you have sorted the list, you can segment your customers into three segments: A, B, and C customers. Where you draw the line between each segment is up to you (Figure 11-9). In this example, I use only 20 accounts, total. The spreadsheet can handle up to 200 accounts.

Sort by Rank	Gut Feel	Revenue ($ Millions)	Servers (#)	Amount of Storage (TB)	Vertical Market (Rank (1-10))	Trust Built (8 Points)	Company Growing? (Yes/No)			Incumbent Trust (8 Points)	Buys on Price (Yes/No)	Rank
Customer 12	200	400	50	100	6	2				6		323
Customer 15		2,500	350	1,000	8	2	10			7		290
Customer 10					10	8	10			4		258
Customer 14	A customers				9	7				7		238
Customer 7		5,000	700	1,200	2							236
Customer 6		150	750	1,000	5	5				5	10	211
Customer 3		1,000	175	200	2	2	10			8		185
Customer 11		250	30	50	6		10					178
Customer 1		1,000	150	150	5	2					10	169
Customer 19	100	B customers			7					2		119
Customer 2		50	100	20	10	4				6		115
Customer 4		2,000	200		7					6		93
Customer 13		650	50	120	7	2				6	10	91
Customer 16		50	200		2							83
Customer 5		100	35		5							71
Customer 8		C customers			2							66
Customer 18					4							27
Customer 9		75			10						10	18
Customer 17		90	25		3					8		1

Figure 11-9. Ranking worksheet with customers prioritized by A, B, and C customers

Depending on your strategy to break into these accounts, you can now take action with the data to justify your decisions. For example, if you have an inside sales team, you might want to give your B and C accounts to them for prospecting. And, you might want to keep the A customers to target on your own. Or, you might have a partner strategy in dividing up targets. Again, once your territory starts to mature, this system will help you determine where you best chances of success are, therefore showing where you should spend your time.

Summary

This bears repeating: Coming up with the traits of good customers, and then assigning values to each trait, is a subjective activity. The values for each trait can be weighted based on importance. The individual numbers you assign might be a judgment based on the trait. Just as important, you can force some customers to the top based on experience. Remember, this is a living document. You will initially use it to rank prospects, but as you start to do business with these prospects, this sheet helps you allocate between qualified customers and prospects. Even though it is subjective, examining your accounts is powerful and can transform your sales career.

Once you have ranked each company, you will have a clear understanding as to which customers are worthy of more attention, and which customers you may not even want to target. Your top prospects get more attention during the planning process, as well as more direct focus during prospecting. The next chapter discusses where you get lists of customers, and where to start the process of filling in the values of each attribute.

Where to Find Customers

Develop a Target List

There is nothing like looking, if you want to find something.

—J.R.R. Tolkien, *The Hobbit*

Now that you have developed an online presence, chosen a product to lead with, learned about your product, and developed a ranking system to guide you to your targets, you need a list of targets.

When developing your list, there are two things to keep in mind—how you approach customers and how you determine if they are a good fit. The ranking you did in the last chapter addresses the issue of good fit.

The number of initial prospects you have is influenced by a few factors. First, are you in a transactional industry? Do you have a large quota, but what you sell has a smaller selling price? Are you new to a territory? All of these would indicate you need a large list of prospects. On the other hand, your list can be smaller if you have a new job, but are not new to the territory. Or if you have a set list of target accounts or just one major account. Further, if one deal can make your quota, you will have a much smaller list of prospects. Lastly, the more trust you have built with potential customers, the more likely you are to gain access, and the less need for a huge list of prospects.

First let's categorize customers by the levels of trust they have before you actually meet with them. I explain how that is possible in this section.

How to Approach Customers

There are three ways to approach customers:

- Hot: More than one element of trust is established.
- Warm: One element of trust is established.
- Cold: No trust established.

I'll paint a clearer picture by defining each one as it relates to the concept of trust. This will help you gain a clearer picture of how you engage with your customer throughout the sales cycle. Start by defining each element of trust as the customer sees you, based on your approach.

Cold Targets

A cold target is one who does not know you. You have no link or introduction to a cold target. They see you this way:

- Intent: You want to sell them something
- Capability: Unknown
- Dedication: Unknown
- Results: Unknown

In other words, your trust meter is empty (Figure 12-1).

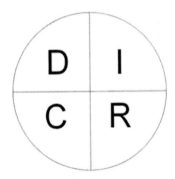

Figure 12-1. Empty trust meter when clients don't know you

The one element of trust your potential customer knows is your intent. Your goal is to sell them something. From their point of view, that's not necessarily a good thing.

Warm Targets

Warm targets include referrals from an existing customer, referrals from a partner, or internal referrals from a different division within the same company. The trust they have in you is based on their trust of the person offering the referral.

- Intent: You want to sell them something.

- Capability: They assume you have average competence until you prove differently.

- Dedication: They assume you have average dedication until you prove differently.

- Results: They assume you have produced some results for the referring party.

With a warm target, you have some trust in three areas (Figure 12-2).

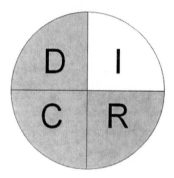

Figure 12-2. Implied trust from a referral

Hot Targets

A hot new target results when you are introduced by an existing customer or by an internal reference because they know you can help solve this person's problem. Here is how the potential new customer views you:

- Intent: You want to sell them something.

- Capability: You can do something for them.

- Dedication: They assume average dedication.

- Results: The assume you must have driven results for the person referring you.

The trust meter is looking better (Figure 12-3).

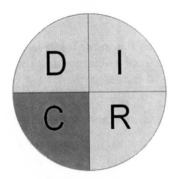

Figure 12-3. Trust meter from an internal reference

White Hot Prospects

The last target is no target at all, because he or she calls you. Customers will call you if they view you as an expert.

- Intent: You will educate them first.

- Capability: You are the expert.

- Dedication: They assume you are dedicated until you prove differently.

- Results: Experts produce results.

Figure 12-4 shows the trust meter in this situation.

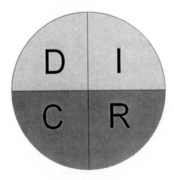

Figure 12-4. Trust meter of an industry expert

I will talk about techniques to accomplish this level of trust in the next chapter, "Cold Calling."

<table><tr><td>**THE VALUE OF TRUST**</td></tr></table>

The prospect-to-converted-customer ratio greatly improves when you use methods that establish trust up front. A few statistics tell the story:

- On average, you will do business with 2% of people you cold call.
- On average, you will do business with 36% of referrals.
- When customers call you, you'll do business with as much as 75% of them.

The number of prospects you need depends on many factors, such as how transactional your particular sales job is. If you are 100% cold with prospects, your list will need to be much larger. The average selling price of your product or service against your quota also influences the number of targeted customers.

Where to Get Prospects

Back to the original question: where do you get lists of customers? If you are a new salesperson, you must rely on management to provide you with customer lists and demographics. Over time, you will become familiar with the region and keep a master list of customers. The next sections discuss other places where you can get market intelligence.

Referrals

Your existing customers can be a great source of leads. This is one of the most powerful sources for new business. Yet, it is rarely used. As stated earlier, you have an 18 times greater chance of doing business with a referral than with a cold prospect. Why not use them? Top sales performers ask tough questions. Non-performers have a tendency to be afraid of asking tough questions, or of asking anything of their customers—questions about budgets, questions about your customer's career objectives, questions about the decision process, and in this case, questions about referrals.

Keep in mind that the tough questions are the most professional ones. Your customers understand that you have a job. If they like you, and you have done a good job for them, there is a good chance they will want to help you. Your goal with a referral is to enter into a sales cycle with a new customer having a great sense of trust with you. However, do not let this goal damage the trust you have built with the customer who gave you the referral. Do not hound the referrals your customers give you. You don't want to get a prospect upset enough to call your customer and ask, "Why did you refer me to [insert your name]? He will not leave me alone!"

As mentioned in the discussion of the trust cycle, one of the most important aspects of trust is measuring results. If you show up after the sale and implementation to measure the results you discussed in the evaluation, you can prove that you brought value to your customer. You also increase the intent, capability, and dedication elements of trust. If you can show you delivered value, it is a great time to ask for referrals.

Sometimes customers are reluctant to give out names of other people. Their fear is that you are going to hound their colleague or friend. You must put this fear to rest. Assure them that you will contact their referral only one time. You should leave a message like this one:

> Hello Steve, I got your name from Doug Miller. My name is Karen Mallory, and I'm with Acme Company, 999-555-1212. I currently work with Doug, where we have increased his company's throughput time by 30% in less than a year. He felt you might benefit from our services. I promised Doug I would only call you one time. I will honor that promise. However, I will follow up this voicemail with an e-mail that will contain a bit more detail and my contact information. I would like the chance to meet with and better understand your needs. Again, this is Karen, 999-555-1212.

Honor the promise of one contact with the prospect. It will help you in two areas. First, Doug is more likely to offer referrals in the future. Second, if you start doing business with Steve, you will have his trust to treat the referrals he gives you with the same respect.

The other difficulty you will have in getting good referrals is that your customers might not know what your ideal customer looks like. So, help them with possible prospects. These include internal referrals; other divisions within their company; companies they used to work for; professional groups they belong to; and my new favorite, which is to ask to sit down and quickly scroll through their LinkedIn contacts with them.

This list might be different for your particular area of sales, but have a list ready to help jog your customer's memory.

Let's sum up the mechanics of pursuing a referral.

- Customers will want to help you.
- You must assure customers that you will respect the referral's time.
- You must help customers jog their memories.

LinkedIn

LinkedIn is another great source of potential customers. You can of course scour LinkedIn for potential targets, but I have discovered an easier method.

I almost do not want to admit this next point, since I have talked so much about trust, but it is just too much fun not to share. Are you connected to your competition? LinkedIn leaves a trail of their customers to follow. Not only will it show you the companies, but it will also provide you with the contact information of their contacts. I know this is kind of sneaky, but if the information is readily available, why not use it?! This is a two-way street, so use this method with discretion.

Local Business Journals

Almost every region has local business news, which used to come out once a month. Today, you can get daily alerts to local business events, such as customer expansion plans, consolidation plans, new companies moving into a region, and updates as people switch jobs. These are all great potential customers. You developed your ideal customer profile. Are there trigger events that you look for when selling your product or service? Are these trigger events newsworthy?

This is an example from business-to-consumer sales. Whenever a neighborhood has a break-in, every home security company has salespeople canvas the neighborhood within a day or two. They know emotions are high throughout the neighborhood. I am sure that these companies are on the Internet every morning checking police logs, and reading the newspaper.

In business-to-business sales, newsworthy events include things like Company X is looking to hire 350 new people by the end of the year, or Company Y is looking to source more parts from domestic suppliers.

It is a great idea to stay up to date in your industry and with happenings in your territory. These news outlets are a great source of leads, as well as conversation topics with existing customers.

Networking: Lead Sharing

Networking is a sale in itself. Give to get. I want to start this section with an experiment that was conducted at Cornell University in 1971. (The details of this experiment are detailed, among other places, in the book *Influence* by Robert Cialdini.) In this experiment, candidates were asked to rate some artwork in an art appreciation study. Two people sat side by side to rate this art. One of the raters was actually an assistant to the experiment. During a break, the assistant asked the experiment conductor if he could get a drink. In one test group, the assistant returned with two sodas, one for himself and one for the other rater. He simply said, "I asked the conductor of the experiment if I could get a drink, he said okay, so I brought one back for you."

In the second group, the assistant asked if he could go get a drink. He left the room, but this time he returned empty handed.

At the end of the sessions of rating art, the assistant asked each group of participants if they would be willing to purchase raffle tickets. The request was followed by, "Any help is appreciated, but the more the better." The group that received the soda purchased twice as many raffle tickets.

This story shows that there is a sense of obligation to reciprocate when a gift is received.

With your partners and with individuals you network with, remember the motto, "give to receive."

How do you build a network of people to share leads? The best leads come from other salespeople calling in the same market who sell complementary products or services. A great place to meet these people is at trade shows and seminars. The tendency for most salespeople is to gravitate to the people they know. Or, they stay at their booth in their comfort zone. Your time is best spent getting to know the other salespeople, rather than customers. Customers in attendance at these events will be focused on talking to vendors who can solve problems or pains they are already aware of. Typically, it's too late for you to be the front-runner with such opportunities. Other salespeople can provide you with ongoing intelligence in the market place.

With the mindset of giving to get, focus on the people you meet. What do they sell? What are their customers' needs? What are their compelling events? This is "Great Conversation 101." Allow other people to talk about their jobs. Focus on them. Try to determine what constitutes a great lead for this person. You are looking for companies, products, and services that you do not compete with, but may help one of your new or existing customers if they have a need. That way, when you are prospecting and in front of customers, and they mention a pain, you might be able to make a recommendation or refer a network partner. Your trust quotient goes up with the customer. You just helped them with something that you don't sell, which shows great intent. Plus, now this network partner "owes you one." And, it will be more than a soda. I explore this concept in more detail in the qualifying chapters.

Give to get. What goes around comes around. You scratch my back and I'll scratch yours. Sow the seeds you'd like to reap. All these clichés tell the same tale that is firmly rooted in reality. People feel an obligation to help you when you help them.

Example

Chapter 2 talked about the issue of the habitual buyer. The dentist in the example automatically sent orders to Chris, his "guy." A new salesperson from a different organization, Sara, is trying to win this dentist's business. How can she develop trust when the dentist will not give her the time of day? The incumbent, Chris, you'll remember, is just taking orders, but over time his trust meter is depleting. He has the business but has not maintained trust. The new salesperson understands this and develops a strategy to win the dentist's attention, trust, and business.

Sara knows this is a qualified the account. It is a growing practice, and she knows her company can provide better service. Without access to the decision maker, however, she develops a trusting relationship with the office manager. She does not have a high score in any of the trust elements. But she has access.

Over the course of months, she has casual conversations with the office manager to understand the dentist more. What she learns is that the dentist feels overworked and stressed, and he complains about bad backs and headaches. She thinks through her product list and draws a blank on how she can help. However, she remembers talking to an office supply salesperson when she started her new job. She remembers this person talking about an amazing new fully adjustable office/lab chair. So, she makes a recommendation to the office manager: If your boss is having physical issues, maybe you should call this office supply person and have him look at this new chair.

A few weeks later, she gets a call from the office manager. The dentist wants to meet with her. Sara asks, "Really? Why?!"

The office manager says, "Well, he really likes his new chair. And, he has been in a much better mood. He asked me how I found out about this new product. I told him you made the suggestion."

What went right in this example?

1. She qualified the customer and knew he would be a good customer to spend time with.

2. She developed a relationship that kept her in touch with the customer.

3. She learned about the pains of the decision maker.

4. She understood that she needed to earn trust.

5. She found an issue that she knew could be solved by someone else.

6. She made an introduction from her professional network.

Even better, a year later the salesman she referred to the dentist gave her a lead that turned into a major account.

Partners

Some industries have a complete supply chain: vendors, resellers, and distributors. In the IT industry, counterparts in the supply chain are typically the best source of information. For example, if you are a reseller trying to break into an account, you can reach out to the vendors who are doing business with that account. They may help you with contact information, understand the customer environment better, know who the players are, and know who your competition is at each account. If the vendor is already partnered with another reseller at the account, they may be reluctant to share information about the specific business. However, I find they will share information freely about other parts of the customer environment.

More specifically, the backup software vendor, if partnered with another reseller, might not share information about the customer backup environment, but is willing to share information about any other part of the customer environment. So, if you are looking for information about the backup environment, maybe the best vendor to talk to is the one selling something else to the customer. Expect to reciprocate in these situations, and assume that these same people are sharing this information with your competition.

Take the advice from the previous section. Remember to figure out what your partners perceive as great leads. And reciprocate whenever possible.

Purchased Lists

Your management or marketing people may buy industry customer lists. If not, you might ask them to do so. Some of the companies that provide customer lists and information are Harte-Hanks, Source One, and a great newcomer, RainKing. These companies provide lists of customers, as well as market intelligence. They can provide very detailed information about each customer—revenue, number of employees, contacts, ongoing projects, vendors they currently do business with, and so on. These lists can be a great source of information to fill in your ranking worksheet.

Other companies provide extremely detailed reports about potential customers, ranging from annual reports to which projects they have coming up in the next year. These reports tend to be expensive, but they are worth it. You can get specific about the data you request, so I suggest requesting data points that match your customer profile traits.

The main point is to talk with management and marketing to understand what tools they will provide you in order to help you paint a picture of your territory. It never hurts to ask if your company has these tools.

Summary

The first third of this book has been dedicated to understanding the role that trust plays in sales. So your first major shift in strategy is to allocate as much time to qualified customers as you do to opportunities. A great starting point is to start learning about your territory and use a ranking system to justify where to spend your time. Use the resources around you to learn about your territory, including the customers, partners, referrals, purchased lists, marketing, and management. This is hard work, but a solid foundation can help you execute proper strategy.

You now have a ranked list of customers to start your targeting efforts. The next chapter discusses several methods for gaining initial access.

Getting Across the Threshold

Strategy without tactics is the slowest route to victory. Tactics without strategy is the noise before defeat.

—Sun Tzu, *The Art of War*

13

Cold Calling

It's a Company Effort

If everyone is moving forward together, then success takes care of itself.

—Henry Ford

Do not skip this chapter.

It discusses some powerful cold calling techniques, as well as some very creative marketing ideas that you can employ to aid you in *easily* securing qualified appointments.

There are many schools of thought about cold calling. Some say it is a waste of time, and others say you give up all your power to the customer because you want something from them. Regardless, in most cases you will have to do some cold calling.

There are methods that promise you will never have to cold call again, but those methods address only a very small subset of sales. In this case, and without getting into detail, you must have a product the customer does not buy very often, such as every 7–8 years. The customer perhaps owns a small business, and doesn't have other salespeople calling them every day. If you have this scenario, there are some mass marketing techniques that might work for you. See the references at the back of the book.

While the promise of no more cold calling is tantalizing, the reality is that cold calling will go away only when sales becomes obsolete.

The truth is, you must take a balanced approach to prospecting, networking, online self-promotion, and marketing with other media such as e-mail or postal mail. However, calling the customer to follow up on all these methods is crucial. And, yes you must be willing to roll up your sleeves. Over time, as you get into new accounts and establish yourself with a partner community, you can slowly move away from cold calling and take advantage of the reputation you have built with your relationship-focused approach. However, I am assuming you are starting from scratch, so there is some "heavy lifting" from the start. (I put quotes around heavy lifting, because your phone only weighs five ounces.)

Call Reluctance

We have all been there. The phone feels like it's 100 pounds. But, why is that? Why is it so hard sometimes to cold call? I have seen this several times on call blitz days. (I don't believe in blitz days for a few reasons, as you'll see.) I watch reluctant sales reps get coffee, go to the restroom, check e-mail, print something, and do anything they can do to look busy. At the end of a calling session, we all gather in a room to report results, and the person who you know did not pick up the phone once says he made 20 calls and booked 3 appointments.

This person not only has convinced himself that cold calling is hard, but he goes so far as to lie to his boss and teammates. Why?

It Comes Down to Psychology

Sometimes, ideas or thoughts are repeated so many times that we start to believe them. There is a great book by Richard Brodie called *Virus of the Mind*. The premise of the book is simple: a virus of the mind is an idea that is planted in your mind by a parent, a coworker, a friend, or society. The idea then spreads from person to person. And it is repeated endlessly in your own mind until it becomes a truth to you. An example can be as simple as the old "truth" that you can't teach an old dog new tricks. Everyone has heard this saying; it spread from person to person. You repeat it, and reinforce it in your mind, until it becomes a truth. Now, every time you face a new challenge, you bring out this excuse, and you repeat it to yourself again. "You can't teach an old dog new tricks." The fact is you *can* teach an old dog a new trick. Your mind is lying to you.

Unlike a virus of the body or a computer, the virus of the mind is just a thought. You can change your thinking instantly.

"Cold calling is hard" is a mind virus. It is your ego protecting you. But, from what? Someone being rude to you? Someone saying no? No immediate gratification?

There are simple steps to overcoming any misguided thought or fear that is holding you back from reaching your full potential. A fear is nothing but your ego protecting you from a momentary discomfort.

How do you cure yourself of these mind viruses? First, you must be aware of the conversations you are having with yourself. Research shows that the average person has approximately 65,000 thoughts a day. And 95% of the thoughts we have are not true! You first need to be aware of these conversations. You need to become aware that they are thoughts, and start to question whether they are true, or what consequences they are having on your life. Awareness is your first line of defense.

Once you are aware, you are in the position to ask yourself the first question. "Is the thought I just had true?" Most likely, you can never say any thought you have is an absolute truth.

Continuing with cold calling as an example, here are some mind viruses planted by trainers, coworkers, and yourself: "cold calling is hard," "cold calling is a pain," or "cold calling doesn't produce results." Just the fact that there is a section in this book on call reluctance shows that it can be hard. Now every time you are faced with cold calling, you repeat to yourself, "cold calling is hard," or "cold calling does not produce results." Soon you take these ideas as a truth you planted in your subconscious mind. When the time comes to increase your pipeline or have a cold call blitz, guess what you say to yourself? "Cold calling is hard." So, you don't pick up the phone.

The first step is awareness. Once you are aware of your internal conversations, you can ask yourself one simple question: "Is it true?"

Cold calling is actually easy. What is so hard about it? You pick up the phone and one of three things happens.

- You leave a voicemail.

- You get someone on the phone, and they accept your appointment.

- You get someone on the phone, and they do not accept an appointment. This is the worst that can happen. If you don't make the phone call, you are saying "no" for them.

What is so hard about picking up the phone? You didn't have to take an elevator a mile into the earth and breathe coal dust all day. That is hard work.

"Cold calling is hard" does not stand up to the simple question: "Is it true?"

The next step is to ask yourself what will happen if you don't do what you are seeking to do. "What if I don't make cold calls?" You will have to answer to management as to why your pipeline is weak. When your pipeline is weak, you will cling to deals that you have no chance of closing. You will waste weeks, if not months, of your time working dead ends. Now you miss your number. So, you force yourself to cold call, but now you are even more desperate, which impacts your calling results. Your pipeline is still weak and sales are underperforming for two or more quarters. Now you have to worry about your job.

What is worse—dealing with people saying "no" or having to swallow your pride and collect unemployment? I am being extreme to make a point. Picking up the phone and dialing is much easier than dealing with all the hassles of unemployment.

The third step is asking what happens when you do make cold calls, or when you tell yourself cold calling is easy. Your pipeline will increase, and you will close more business. You might even find a massive account. The person on the other end of the line might end up being a great friend. You will reach your long-term goals. Which thoughts would you want to carry around in your head, the thoughts that drive you to unemployment, or the thoughts that drive you to your ultimate financial goals?

The ideas in the previous few paragraphs are an almost unjustifiable over-simplification of two books—*Virus of the Mind* and Dr. Wayne Dyer's book, *Excuses Be Gone*. If you want to change your way of thinking and sell with no excuses, I recommend you read those books and apply them to your sales techniques.

Cold calling is easy. But, it can also be frustrating. Sales is one of the few professions where you put in all the work up front with no guarantees of being paid for your efforts. Cold calling doesn't usually have a tangible component. You might experience instant rejection, but you most likely will not experience instant reward. So, develop an instant reward system for yourself. It is important to find a way to motivate yourself. Find a method that motivates you.

I am going to share some ideas. Some may seem corny, but maybe one will help you. In any case, develop thoughts that motivate you to pick up the phone and call a prospect.

Example 1

For every 500 calls you make, pay yourself $100. This may sound odd, but it makes your effort tangible. The tough part about cold calling is that the payback is typically much further down the road. Paying yourself, or giving yourself a reward for the effort, is positive reinforcement. Let's see what those 500 calls really mean. If you accept the premise that for every 100 people you try to contact, you will do business with two, that means from 500 calls you potentially could do business with 10 people/companies. What is an average revenue for one sale? In my last company, it was in the $60,000 range. So you are looking at $600,000 of revenue in this example. In my company this equated to $13,200 in commission. Work it backward—you are making $26.40 for each of the 500, 15-second phone calls. So, you can afford to pay yourself the $100.

Example 2

Cash is king! There is a simple trick that helps people stop overspending—pay in cash. The value of money is lost today with direct deposit, ATM cards, credit cards, and old-fashioned checks. When you are touching the actual cash, you get a better sense of its value. Think about the last time you saw a dollar bill on the ground. It is kind of like, "wow, I just found a dollar." When was the last time you paid attention, down to the exact dollar amount, of your direct deposit? I bet you can only remember it to the nearest hundred.

So, knowing that your efforts today could eventually earn you $5,000 in commission isn't very tangible. You can make it tangible. I had a colleague who had a fake stack of $100 bills on his desk that added up to $5,000. The money was real enough for his purposes but not real enough to alarm the secret service. It was a prop for him to lean on when he was faced with any menial task he did not feel like doing.

Example 3

Make your goals tangible. If there is something you are aiming for, such as a new house or car, find a picture of it and hang it by your phone. If your goal is to pay for your kids' braces, put a picture of your kids by your phone. Make your work tangible. Know why you are working.

Example 4

This is how I motivate myself—I remember how much work it took me to earn $3,000 when I was a teenager. I worked 16-hour days, 3-4 days a week, all summer, standing over a greasy fryolator, with no air conditioning, to make $3,000. It helps me realize how lucking I am to be in sales, and puts into perspective how easy cold calling is compared to other jobs. The risk is low, and the reward is great.

Lastly, when you have better success calling, you will gain more confidence and cold calling will not seem like such a chore. I have personally used the methods discussed in this chapter. With some I had so much success that cold calling actually became enjoyable. It is rewarding to see your phone ring back just minutes after you leave a message.

How to Get a Response

Voicemail is the primary source of frustration when it comes to cold calling. When you hear "cold calling is hard," I think what most people are referring to is the lack of response back from customers, the lack of reward, and the feeling of rejection. I have stated this several times already; most customers don't want another salesperson in their lives. So, you need to figure out ways to get a potential customer to call you back, or to pick up the phone in the first place. There are many methods for getting past this electronic gatekeeper, and there are several books written on the subject, all claiming to be the silver bullet of cold calling. There is no silver bullet. You must choose a process or method that works for you and that is in your comfort zone. However, these guiding principles of cold calling are common to each method:

- Do not limit your efforts to one person in the target account.

- Aim high within the organization. Even if your eventual target appointment is at a lower level, it is always better to work your way from the top down.

- Cold calling is not a blitz day or a one-day event. It takes a methodical, repetitive approach to work.

- Do not sell on the phone! Your goal is an appointment.

- Mystery—there needs to be an element of mystery in your voicemail to get the person to call you back.

- The most successful cold calling is a team effort. Some of the techniques I will discuss require help from management or marketing.

The first item (targeting only one person at an organization) might seem obvious, but I think it's the number one mistake most salespeople make. This mistake is actually made in a few places in territory management, but it's great to introduce here. Salespeople get myopic. They focus on one opportunity or one person. Being myopic when cold calling means you make the customer about one person. "I can't get into Customer X because Ms. Target will not accept an appointment." Your goal is to get into the company, not necessarily sell only to Ms. Target. That leads to the first rule.

Target at Least Four People per Customer

This does a few things for you. It increases your chances by 400% for getting into the company. It does not limit access to others once you reach Ms. Target. Ultimately, you need to get to the person who makes the purchasing decisions. When you aim low, and get "the one" person you have been targeting, they will sometimes limit your ability to get to the person in power, or your ability to talk to others in the company. You end up asking permission to talk to others. Your contact can sometimes feel threatened that you are trying to get around them, so they make it difficult.

If you start high, or start in multiple departments, you don't have to ask permission. That's because you already had contact, even if it was just with an e-mail or voicemail.

Finding company employees is simple with the Internet. Go to www.data.com (formerly jigsaw.com). At this site you can look up information for free— company names by region, industry, as well as individual employees, including title. If you have the main number of the account, you can get to the person. You can typically guess at the e-mail address too. There are only a few formats. If you want contact information, you can use their free point system. If you give information, you get points you can use to get detailed contact information. They have a paid service, too, if you don't want the hassles. If you want more detailed information, your company's CRM system might have some. Your company might subscribe to purchased lists like Harte Hanks or Source One. Each of these companies provides much more detail about your targets. The point I am making is that there is no shortage of information. Finding at least four people at any account is simple.

Aim High

There are several reasons to start high when you're trying to get into an organization. Remember the fundamentals needed to win an order. Power is defined by someone who has the power to make a purchasing decision. If you are working at this level, the purchasing cycle is greatly reduced. The criteria for purchasing decisions are much clearer. What you do not want is to have to ask for permission to speak to the people in power.

If you start low, you need to bargain your way up to power, or go around the people you have worked with in the earlier parts of the sales cycle. If you start with power, and they send you down the organization, when the time comes for a decision, you do not need permission from people you are dealing with on a daily basis. If you have been pushed down an organization, simply copy the people who pushed you to a lower title via e-mail with important aspects during the sales cycle. When it is time to get power involved in the decision process, you can simply call them without permission.

This applies to the first rule as well. You can call around to other people in the organization if you have targeted more than one person, even if the interaction was only voicemail. The same sort of logic applies. If you have already tried to contact these people at the same time you contacted your champion, you do not need permission or have to worry about talking to others in the account. When you learn about qualifying opportunities, this will become very important.

New salespeople, young or old, seem to be most intimidated by this concept of aiming high. Again, the excuses, the "viruses of the mind" start to come into play here. What if you actually have to talk to someone? What do you say? This person might embarrass you. You feel too young to talk to someone with such power.

In the IT industry, I find this ironic. We sometimes have hundreds of technical products and concepts, about which we probably know 5%. Yet we constantly aim at the IT Director or lower. These are the very people who will want to know every detail about our products. They sometimes want to embarrass salespeople by asking them technical questions. The CIO, on the other hand, is concerned with satisfying the business by driving down cost, increasing revenue, and reducing risk. These are simple conversations to have because it is mainly about asking a CIO about their objectives. Also, as you go up in an organization, you will find the people are more "people people." They rise through the ranks based on people skills. They are better conversationalists. Aiming high should not be intimidating. Yes, they might be busy and push you down to someone else, but that is a good thing. So, even if your goal is to deal with someone at your comfort level, start as high as you can in the organization. That brings up the next rule.

Cold Calling Is Not a Blitz Day

Way too many salespeople wait for a blitz day to do their cold calling. Cold calling takes a systematic, repetitive approach to get results. It is not making one call and hoping the prospect calls you back. Some of the methods discussed here can be used only once, so you may use a combination of approaches depending on your comfort level, prospect type, and how much your company will help you. In any case, a typical cycle of calling should be four targets and eight touch points in ten days.

Put another way, you should call each target four times in ten days, each time following up with an e-mail. That is eight touch points per person, and because you are targeting four people in each company, that leads to 32 contacts with the customer.

Do Not Sell on the Phone—Get an Appointment

The structure of most blitz days also works against you. Let's walk through a typical blitz day. Everyone is called into the office around 8 a.m. Someone brings donuts and coffee. The sales team doesn't see each other very often, so there is some catching up to do. A late start is inevitable. Next, you get the product training de jour. Then you hit the phones. What is logically wrong with this process? It is the product training just before hitting the phones. Your goal is to get an appointment.

So, you fill up on product knowledge for an hour. Then you are asked not to sell on the phone. If you are lucky and get someone on the phone, you are inclined to do what you were taught—talk about the product you were just trained on. Do not sell on the phone. Get an appointment.

Curiosity Will Get Your Customer to Call You Back

A touch of mystery goes a long way. Create curiosity and the person will call you back.

I got input from many sources for this book. I read several books on cold calling, and they all pretty much say the same things. I will share some of the ideas in those books in the pages that follow. The one common element with each method is mystery. However, I also talked to several salespeople who were successful, and the phone was their only tool. I asked one of the more successful people I have seen about her methods. How did she get so many people on the phone? Her response was so simple it was scary. She creates mystery before she leaves a voicemail. This falls into the category of, "Why didn't I think of this?" What does she do? *She dials the phone, and if there is no answer, she hangs up and calls right back. Customers pick up the second time!*

It's so simple! No voicemails to script, no metrics to track. It's just as simple little trick. Why does it work? It's mystery. "Why is this person calling twice? Is it important?" The customer picks up! I like to call this "double tap dialing."

If no one answers the second dial, she does leave a voicemail, so let's move on to effective voicemails.

Leave an Effective Voicemail

The industry standard voicemail is something like:

> Hi, this is Jeff Cooper with Acme Corporation. We specialize in helping customers optimize the workflow space of their branch offices. I would like to set up a time to meet you to show you how we can help optimize your work spaces. Again this is Jeff with Acme; please call me back at 999-555-4141, again 999-555-4141.

Does this seem similar to what you leave? This is the script that management and marketing told you to use. Have you been told to sound like you are smiling, and to stand up when you leave a voicemail because this projects more energy and enthusiasm?

I will guarantee if you leave this type of message you will have almost no results. You will sound like a salesperson, and I have stated several times that the last thing any customer wants is another salesperson. The only way this method works is by leaving a voicemail so many times that you annoy the person into calling you back. But that won't improve your rate of success. Here is how your customer hears this message:

"Hi, this is Jeff Cooper, with Acme Corporation. We specialize in—" DELETE.

If you insist on using this method, at least get the messaging right.

- Keep it short
- Give your name, phone number, and, after a pause, your company's name
- Explain why you are calling
- Say what you do
- Close for a decision
- Provide your name and number again

Your customers might have several voicemails to get through so you must capture their attention quickly; without attention they will not even listen. Start with your name and number. Do not use your company name yet. Stating just your name and number will create a touch of mystery, and you hope they write it down. Then leave your company name and the reason you are calling. Ultimately, you wanted to talk to the customer, not leave a voicemail. So, your goal when talking to the customer was to gain their attention. So, "I was hoping to get a few seconds of your time."

The next element of the voicemail is what you do. Get this down to 10–15 seconds. You just told them you only wanted a few seconds. This is a perfect place for the elevator hook—you turn them into statements. For example, here are the hooks as questions:

- "Do you have issues with spending too much on paper copies?"
- "Do you have issues with explosive data growth?"
- "Does the introduction of mobile devices by your employees onto your network cause you problems?"

- "Are your facilities secured properly?"

- "Are your receivables at the level you would like?"

- "Do you know how hard it is to accurately forecast 90 days out?"

During the voicemail, you turn these questions into statements:

- We help reduce the cost of paper copies.

- We help organizations with explosive data growth.

- We help you manage mobile devices on your network.

- We help simplify facility security.

- We improve receivable rates.

- We help you achieve better forecast accuracy.

Close for a decision. "I would like to know if you are the person responsible for this." This tells the customer that it is okay if they are not the right person. You respected their time, and you were quick. Maybe they will extend the professional courtesy of calling you back. Or, when they see your number pop up next time, they will know you are not going to waste their time.

Put it all together like this:

> This is Aaron Smith, 999-555-1212, again 999-555-1212. I am with Acme Technologies. I was hoping to get a few seconds of your time. We help customers contain their explosive data growth. I am looking for the person with the focus on this issue. I look forward to talk with you. Aaron, 999-555-1212.

This takes no more than 15 seconds. With this method, you definitely want to use the four targets, eight touches (half voicemail and half e-mail), ten days approach. Assume that sending each e-mail takes 30 seconds, and each voice-mail takes 15 seconds. Your total time spent trying to break into this account is 12 minutes.

Simple Mystery Approach

If you are just not comfortable using this approach, leave some mystery. For example:

"Hi, this is Dave. Please call me back at 999-555-4141."

If you are taking a territory over from someone else, say Jennifer, use this approach:

"Hi, this is Dave. I am calling regarding Jennifer. Please call me back at 999-555-4141."

This approach is simple, and the voicemails are short. They elicit curiosity.

Most Powerful Method: Market Your Way to Call Success

If you want to compound your success on the phone, you need the help of your marketing department. Share these methods with management. They are powerful and effective. These methods require a budget, so help from your company is necessary.

I personally used the following method during one my first sales jobs, which was cold calling every day, all day. I had a job setting appointments for the field sales team. My goal was 15 appointments a month. In my second month, I already had 100 appointments set. We were paid per appointment and per close rate of the business. I had the highest number of appointments and the highest close rate by far. As a cold caller, I was one of the highest paid people at the company—until they adjusted my commission plan.

Marketing has in general changed since I used this method. But, I will share exactly what I did. Then I will adapt it to today's technology. The method is based on the principle of reciprocity. Give to get.

In the days of magazine advertising, my company ran ads in *CIO* magazine. As part of the ad, we had a giveaway item, a T-shirt. The readers of the magazine, CIOs and IT directors, would fill out the "bingo cards," also called response cards. These are the post cards that fall out of every magazine. Well, they would come back to the company by the hundreds. I started off like everyone else, leaving a simple "please call me back" voicemail. After two to three days of this, I was already hating my job. The response was dismal. As luck would have it, a bingo card came across my desk that I had trouble reading. Here is the voicemail I left:

> Hello, Bob, I am with Acme Technologies, and recently you filled out a response card in *CIO* magazine to receive a free T-shirt. I would like to send you this shirt, but I am having some trouble reading the card. Please call so we can send you your T-shirt.

I got called back in five minutes!

Being the genius I am, I went back to the old message the rest of the day. As I was leaving, I was frustrated, and was thinking to myself, "The only person who called me back wanted their free T-shirt." Ding, ding, ding! That night all I thought about was how to adapt this concept to every call. Then I decided to just use the same message. Over the course of a couple of weeks, I tweaked the message based on the response rates from the customers:

> Hello, Bob, I am with Acme Technologies, and recently you filled out a response card in *CIO* magazine to receive a free T-shirt. I would like to send you this shirt, but part of your address was smudged in the mail. Please call so we can send you your T-shirt.

It amazed me how many CIOs called back for a free T-shirt. The key was to be ready when they called back. I would have their address on hand and say, "Your ZIP code was smudged. I can't tell if this is a 4 or a 9. They would say, "9." I would say, "Thank you, I will send you that T-shirt."

When the idea of a gift is in the air, you have to give to get, so I would ask, "Do you mind if I ask you a few questions?" What were they going to say—thanks for the shirt and hang up? No, almost every time the customer would engage in a conversation.

Since I had so many people calling me back I could afford to be selective and truly qualify the customer's needs. I only scheduled appointments that were true opportunities. My close rate was higher, and I saved the company thousands of dollars in travel costs. The other salespeople got so few people on the phone that they would schedule anything.

There have been popular variations of this method over the years. A large manufacturer did an executive "door opener," where they sent out large remote control cars. In order to get the remote control for the car, the customer needed to agree to an appointment. I personally think this concept is expensive and generates worse results. They are mailing expensive items to people who might not even want them. In this scenario, the customer already received an item. Second, they sent salespeople out to customers who were not qualified. Third, they were asking for an appointment in exchange for the remote, so there was no sense of obligation. In the T-shirt scenario, I gave before I asked for anything.

The Whitepaper Giveaway

The magazine "bingo" card is all but extinct. But this method can be adapted for the primary forms of advertising used today, which involves e-mail, the web, and seminars. Provide giveaways via e-mail, via the web, and at seminars. Keep the giveaways simple and inexpensive. The best part about this method is that you test interest before you send out anything. A classic example: how many people give away whitepapers on certain subjects via the web?

I download at least 10 a month to keep my skills sharp. Sometimes the whitepapers are on technology and sometimes from other sales training professionals. I enter my contact information and download the whitepaper. I have some sort of interest in their offering because I am willing to read 10 pages of information. You might be thinking, "We gave them a whitepaper, which doesn't cost anything, they have interest, and we have their contact information . . . great! Why change the way we do it today?"

Enter enemy stage right, voicemail. You still have to get past their voicemail, or the e-mail filters, when you follow up. They have no reason to call you back.

Take the giveaway to the next level, like the *CIO* magazine example. The customer still needs a reason to call you back. Have one more check box, to receive a gift. It's that simple. The gift could be a DVD, a T-shirt, or another whitepaper. It should be an item that has to be physically delivered. Now, you are set up exactly like the *CIO* magazine scenario. "Ms. Customer, we got your request online for a free T-shirt, but our database administrator forgot to capture a portion of the shipping information. Could you call me back at 999-555-1212?" The words are chosen carefully, "portion of the shipping information." Don't be specific about the exact information you are missing. This decreases the chance that they'll just leave the missing information if they happen to get your voicemail. If you say, "We don't have your ZIP code," they can leave just their ZIP code if they get your voicemail.

When they call back to provide the missing shipping information, you say, "Thank you, we will send that right out. Would you mind if I ask you a couple of questions?" Now, qualify!

The Seminar Giveaway

The seminar or trade show scenario is almost the same as the previous example. Every trade show booth has a drop box for business cards. A very nice giveaway is typically used as an enticement for the seminar attendees to drop their card. The typical mistake companies make is to have a drawing for *one* big item. You have a drawing, or the item is already earmarked for your top customer. Only one person you're calling is getting a gift, out of the hundreds who left their cards. The gift is presented with absolutely no excitement to the mass of people. Say you give away a small laptop worth $500. You just paid $500 for a lousy cold call list. Because that's what you have: a bunch of people on a list that you now must cold call. There is absolutely no incentive for them to call you back. You can't even use one of the mystery methods because you need to say how you got their name. "Hi, this is Larry from Acme Technologies. You stopped by our booth at Tech Event 2013. We would like to talk to you about X, please call me at 999-555-1212." They probably only dropped their card for the free laptop anyway.

A modified method produces much greater results. Set up everything exactly the same, but in addition to the grand prize of X, everyone else gets Y. They drop their cards. Now when you go to call them back, it's as simple as, "You placed your card in our drawing, and you won a prize. We need to verify some information in order to send out your prize. Please call us back." Now the person has a reason to call you back. You reach out to everyone with this method, not just the one person who won the grand prize. With so many people calling you back, you now have the luxury of qualifying the freebie seekers out. This may sound expensive, but it is actually much less so.

In the first scenario, you have 200 people stop by your booth and drop cards in the bowl to win a $500 laptop. You call the winner of the laptop back and they accept an appointment to receive the prize. Now you cold call the other 200 people. Say on average you get 5% of the people to call you back, or 10 people. You are so happy that some of these "prospects" actually called you back that you try to secure an appointment with every one of them. You are great at it and get eight appointments. I will be generous and say that four of the appointments are qualified. I will even give you the appointment with the laptop as a qualified appointment, for a total of five good appointments. What is the cost of this method? You have the gift at $500, but in this method you also have the cost of the four appointments that were not qualified. A conservative estimate for each appointment, with mileage and time out of the office, is about $150. This does not include missed opportunity cost. Including the prize and the non-qualified appointments, your costs are $1,100. I am not going to include the time you wasted trying to call the other 191 people on the list. The cost per qualified appointment is $220.

With the adapted method, you have the same $500 laptop plus $15 T-shirts for everyone who calls you back. In this scenario, say 100 people call back for the free gift. Now you have the luxury of qualifying the callbacks because you have so many to select from. To be conservative, say you qualify half the percentage of scenario number one, because you will get more freebie seekers calling you back. But this is 25%, or 25 qualified customer appointments. In this method, your costs are $500 for the laptop and $1,500 for T-shirts, or $2,000. You do not have the cost of salespeople going on non-qualified appointments. The math now works out to $80 per qualified appointment. The results are five times the number of qualified appointments, and 63% less per appointment.

It doesn't take much thought to design a marketing method that will result in prospects calling you who you can then qualify. You get better prospects, and more of them. Lay out the math for management, and they should be willing to fund your bright ideas.

Summary

While this chapter does not advance levels of trust, the methods described here can help you gain access to your targets without compromising trust. If you are starting cold, you need to be creative in gaining access. Even if you get called on some of the fringe practices, these methods leave you with a defensible position. It really does not matter if you have some negative experiences with people you probably would not do business anyway. You need to have people call you back. Once you get them on the phone, you can start to establish trust in capability and intent by the approach you use, which you learn about in the next chapter.

On the Phone for the First Time

Objective: A Qualified Appointment

The key to confidence is preparation.

—Unknown

What do you do if you actually get someone on the phone? Whether it's a returned phone call from a voicemail you left, or the prospect picks up the phone when you make a cold call you must be prepared. It is amazing how unprepared most salespeople are for a simple phone conversation. If you listen in on these conversations, you would think that some customers just give them appointments out of pity, or to make the embarrassing moment stop. Preparation has a secondary effect: it gives you confidence, and that confidence will help you pick up the phone and make calls.

In order to avoid being awkward on the phone:

- Be prepared
- Do not sell over the phone
- Respect the customer's time
- Get the customers attention
- Start a conversation
- Qualify

The first three items are more important than you think.

Be prepared. I spent two chapters on planning and being prepared. First, understand your customer and her industry and second, be as educated as possible about your own industry. While you will not sell over the phone, preparation will give you the confidence to handle any question or objection. This chapter serves as a guide in learning how to control the conversation, so ultimately you can secure the qualified appointment you seek.

Do not sell over the phone. The last thing you want to do is instantly show your intent as wanting to sell something. The customer knows you are selling, but do not reinforce the idea by selling over the phone. This is most customers' biggest fear when dealing with salespeople. They do not want to listen to a monologue about how your product is the greatest.

Respect your customer's time. This could also be lumped into "get your customer's attention." You have no idea how you caught this person. If they called you back, you have a slight advantage because they consciously picked up the phone when they had time. When they answer your call, for all you know, they just blindly picked up the phone. As soon you start to talk, they think, "Why did I just pick up the phone?" They might have people in their office. They might be in the middle writing an e-mail or conducting training; you have no idea. So, first youmust ensure you have their attention by starting a conversation with the simple elevator hook question you should already have developed. If you launch into a monologue, you have no shot at a qualified appointment. You must engage in a conversation with the customer. A conversation will hold their attention. The monologue will just cause the customer to think, "Ugh." How do you do this? In the next section, I cover the flow of a call, which will help you capture the customer's attention, start a conversation, and begin to qualify the customer.

Design the Call

Don't sell over the phone. You want to leave a bit of mystery. If you tell them everything you can do on the phone, there is no reason for them to agree to a face-to-face appointment. I believe when you get someone on the phone you should simply ask for the appointment. Most likely, you do not have their full attention. The last thing they want to hear is another value proposition. This method is a variation of the quick voicemail you developed for cold calling.

1. Introduce yourself

2. Ask for a few seconds of their time

3. Use your elevator hook

4. Ask if they are responsible for this area

5. Offer a value statement

6. Ask for an appointment

7. Handle objections

You need to practice this approach so that it does not sound scripted. The opening statement takes care of the introduction and the request for time.

"Hello, I am Jennifer with Acme Medical. I am hoping I can have 10–15 seconds of your time to explain why I am calling."

This should elicit a response. Almost 100 percent of the time you will get a, "Yes, that's fine." The importance of this is that you did not immediately launch into a monologue. You actually get the customers to talk, and now they are more engaged.

At this point, you have two options for the elevator hook. If you are certain that the person you are talking to is the person you *need* to talk to, you can lead with the elevator hook. "Do you know how hard it is to X?" Ask the question. When they answer, you simply say, "We help with that."

If you are not certain that this is the right person, use the statement from the question. "We help customers do X." Then you follow up with, "Are you personally focused on this?"

In either case, you now follow up by checking for interest. "If we could [save you X, improve your Y], would that get your attention?"

Then ask for the appointment.

What If They Object?

This process assumes you get a "yes" at each juncture. Here is how to handle a "no."

If the request for 10 seconds of the person's time is met with a "no," your response should be, "I am sorry I caught you at a bad time. Have a great day." You call this person back in a few weeks, and now open the conversation with, "This is Jennifer with Acme Medical. I called a few weeks back requesting a few seconds or your time. I hope I did not make the same mistake twice. Do you have 10–15 seconds now?"

The next possible "no" comes when you ask if the person is responsible for what you can help with. This "no" can be subject to some interpretation. Is this person saying no because they don't want to be sold over the phone? Or, are they not the right person?

Framing your response is crucial, "I must be a little lost; could you help me? Can you point me in the right direction?" Ask for help. Do not ask for another contact name.

If the customer is just trying to blow you off, most likely they will get lost in their response. If you get the sense that they are just trying to blow you off, you can say, "I promise I am not going to sell you over the phone, or launch into a long, boring product pitch. Do you mind if I ask you a few questions?" The reason not to simply ask for the right person is that the customer does not want you to use their name when you call someone else in the organization. When you ask for a contact name, you'll get more negative responses.

The last possible "no" comes when asking for an appointment. At this point, you might get many different forms of "no."

Method One for Dealing with Objections

Any objection you get when asking for an appointment can be handled with one simple sentence: "That's what most of my existing clients said until they had a chance to meet with me." Ask for the appointment again.

Let's look at some common objections.

- "I don't have the time to meet with new vendors."

- "We are actually in the process of a vendor consolidation."

- "We are not in the market for this." (This is hard for the customer to say if you leave some mystery in what you do.)

- "We don't have the budget for anything new."

- "We have someone for that."

Your response is always as simple as, "Most of my existing customers said exactly the same thing, until we met and showed X."

X is the homework you have to do about your industry. For each of these objections, you need a quick value proposition. The first part of the response gives you a few seconds to gather what you are going to insert for X.

"Most of my existing customers said exactly the same thing, until we showed them that by doing _____, they were able to . . ."

If the objection is because they have no time, you say that you can save them time in the long run. If it is about money, you say that you can reduce their costs. If the objection is about reducing vendors, talk about how your customer saw value in your company. Practice this simple statement. Try to think of every possible objection and practice handling them with that statement.

Method Two for Handling Objections: The Encore

Remember, you have not established trust with this customer. Hopefully, by asking for a small amount of time, you lower the customer's guard to the point where they know your intent is not to sell them something over the phone. However, they will still be guarded just because they are on the phone with a salesperson. You need to lower their guard. When they give you an objection, your response should be, "Thank you for your time..." pause like you are leaving the call (the stage). The customer will be a bit relieved, and their guard will come down. You then say, "Do you mind if I ask you one more question?" That is the encore.

When handling an objection, be courteous but persistent. One of the hardest parts of cold calling is getting someone on the phone. So, do not hang up until they become irritated or they give you to someone else who might be a better fit. Always fight to stay on the phone.

"Can You Send Me Some Literature?"

I point this out as an objection because sometimes this response gets lost in the mix. New salespeople see this response as a door that's still open. However, in most cases, customers use this programmed response because they know it will get you off the phone. Step one is to recognize this as a blow off. Step two is say, "I would be glad to send you some literature. When I do, what is the next step?" No matter their response, make sure you keep handling objections with one the previous methods.

Qualify the First Appointment

Once the customer has made a commitment for an appointment, you can ask qualifying questions. If you are in a high-transaction business that does not require a deep relationship, you can qualify for opportunity. Do they have money? Do they have a compelling event? Are you talking to "power"? If you do not have an ideal situation, it's probably best not to pursue this customer at the moment.

HIGH-TRANSACTION STRATEGIES

High-transaction businesses typically require many deals with many customers. You must manage your time effectively. With many customers, you cannot spend an inordinate amount of time with customers who do not show potential to purchase. You have to ask yourself, "With no elements of a potential deal present, is it worth my time to hop in a car, drive across town, meet with a customer who most likely will not buy, and drive back to the office?" Or, is it better to use those hours on the phone finding two more customers who have a real need, money, and the power to make a decision? In a high-transaction environment, it is okay to qualify out, which means it is okay to move on to the next customer. You can simply tell the customer that this may not be an effective use of time for either of you.

If you are in more of a relationship type of business and make your living with fewer accounts, it's better not to qualify out. You need to visit customers to qualify them against your ideal profile, as well as for personal fit. Relationship is more important than opportunity, so it does not make sense to qualify for opportunity before you meet with customers. If you have done a good job prequalifying the customers against your ideal profile, there is no need to qualify them on the phone. Even if they are not the right person to talk to, you are much better off meeting face-to-face to get a better understanding of the company. You can learn more, and find out who the right players are.

Recognizing the Golden Ticket

If you have seen the movie *Willy Wonka and the Chocolate Factory,* you can't help but tear up when Charlie opens the chocolate bar and unveils a golden ticket. If you have not seen the movie, the golden ticket is the coveted invitation to tour the reclusive chocolate factory. There were only five tickets in millions of chocolate bars sold—a needle in the haystack. You should feel the same way when you get lucky and stumble upon an opportunity with perfect timing; they don't come around very often.

Whether you are in transactional or relationship sales, good timing can be better than any strategy. When doing the math to show that relationship is more important than opportunity, there's a natural cycle of procurement for most purchases. If the company is in a 48-month purchase cycle, it might seem lucky when you find a customer just entering the decision process. But this can be a huge time waste of time as the incumbent has a huge lead in this case. Perfect timing is when you find a customer who needs something, but has not yet decided to enter the market.

Perfect timing isn't stumbling on an opportunity. Perfect timing is stumbling on a need before a company has decided to make it an "opportunity."

If the customer has been living with a pain, like the homeowner with the long commute, you have found a customer who is one compelling event away from a need. This is great timing, because they have a need, but have not acted on it. They probably haven't actively talked to other vendors about the issue, either.

When you are new to the customer, and they are not actively looking for a solution, they will not take the time to share with you their pains. They are not going to come right out and say, "This is the problem we have, and you are the first person I have told this to." The statements that should cause your ears to perk up are, "Call me back in six weeks," or "Call me back next month." When you hear this, you should smile ear to ear, on the inside. Your timing could not be more perfect.

What they are saying is that they are not quite in the market for what you are selling. They are living with some pain, and know they will eventually address the need. They will enter that market when a compelling event happens. The catch is that once they enter the market, their first call will be to the incumbent, or to a vendor they already have a relationship with. When you hear, "Call me back in X time," find any excuse to get in front of them sooner. You want to engage them just before they enter the market. You want to start establishing trust.

I speak from personal experience. It only happened to me six or seven times before I learned my lesson. I am a quick study! (Don't miss the sarcasm in that statement.) You hear, "Call me back in six weeks," and you are excited. You did not get a full rejection. So, you put on your calendar to call the customer back in six weeks. Worse yet, you put a placeholder in your forecast: "Acme, Product X, 90 days out."

The six weeks are up. The customer is expecting your call, great. You get the customer on the phone. "Hi, this is Dave. We spoke six weeks ago and you asked me to call you back in six weeks. How are you doing today?"

Customer: "Yes, how are you doing Dave?"

Dave: "Great, I was calling to set up an appointment regarding X, and you said this would be a better time."

Customer: "I did ask you to call me back, but unfortunately we just signed a deal for the purchase of X."

Dave (silently to himself): *"Damn, what the..."*

When you hear, "Call me back," let that be music to your ears. But do not wait! Find any reason to get in front of the customer sooner. Use the strategies in Chapter 16, "Sales Strategies," to start building trust.

Summary

Keep it simple. First be educated about the customer, your product, and your industry. You are not going to sell over the phone, but having that knowledge behind you will give you confidence. Your customer is busy, so keep your message short, engage in a conversation, and ask for an appointment. Pick one of the two methods for handling objections, and practice it. Each method is very simple. If you follow the rules of this chapter, you'll be prepared and will have the confidence to talk on the phone to any person with any title. Before I dive into selling in front of the customer, I need to point out simple comments or acts that have the potential to sabotage your sales efforts. The next chapter is simple, short, and powerful (pun intended).

Executing the Strategy

Guessing what the pitcher is going to throw is 80% of being a successful hitter. The other 20% is just execution.

—Hank Aaron

Power in Sales

Don't Give It Away

Wherever there is a man who exercises authority, there is a man who will follow it.

—Unknown

There is sure fire way to cut your sales in half with the very first sentence out of your mouth. I'll get to that in a moment. But first let me say that I included this chapter because there are a few simple behaviors that you might not be aware of that can sabotage your results. And there are, likewise, a few things you can do to multiply your results.

Power, or authority, is required if you want to join the ranks of the best salespeople. The salespeople who take control of the sales cycle are most likely to win any given deal. There are many reasons this is true. In Chapter 5, "Trust," for example, you learned about the elements of trust. Each of those elements leads to a position of power over the customer.

There's more. Whenever you meet with customers, you should adopt a mentality that you are the most powerful person in the room. After all, you are there to help, educate, and ultimately allow the customer to execute the company's business more efficiently. You bring insight from the entire industry, as well as insight from other customers who have dealt with similar situations.

Your customers not only respond to the power you bring, but they crave it. The last thing you want to be is a burden to your customer; instead, be someone they want to hear from. That someone has power and isn't afraid to use it.

Milgram Experiment

Adolf Eichmann, a high-ranking Nazi official, was tried for World War II war crimes in 1961. He was the architect of the "Final Solution," the extermination of Jews in German-occupied territories. The main theme of his defense was that he was simply following orders. Further, he believed that orders from authority are not to be ignored; they are to be obeyed.

Shortly after the trial, Stanley Milgram conducted an experiment to see if subjects would follow the orders of an authority figure, even when those orders were morally questionable. Milgram set up an experiment where the participant was seated at a panel that controlled a generator that would shock one of the experiment's assistants in an adjoining room. The panel was set up with different levels of voltage to be delivered to the assistant. The buttons started at 30 volts and worked their way up to 450 volts in 15-volt increments. There was one final button that was labeled *XXX*. The participants did not know that the buttons did not actually shock the assistant.

The participant was told to ask the assistant in the next room a series of questions. If the person got the question wrong, the participant was to deliver a shock to the assistant. With each wrong answer, the participant was instructed to increase the voltage by 15 volts. As the experiment started, the participant started to ask questions, and as planned, the assistant would answer each question wrong. When a false shock was delivered, the assistant would act as though he or she was in pain. As the voltage increased, the assistant would increase their pleas to stop the shocks, and would feign a heart condition. As the voltage continued to increase, the assistant would beg even harder to be released from the experiment. The acting would increase to the point where the assistant would pretend to pass out or go unconscious.

Most participants became very uneasy with the experiment, and would ask one of the experiment's conductors if they could stop, or if they should continue to deliver shocks. The experimenter simply would tell the participant one of four lines. "Please continue." "The experiment requires that you continue." "It is absolutely essential that you continue." And finally, "You have no other choice; you must continue." Out of 40 participants, 26 of them delivered the maximum shock. Only 14 stopped short of the highest voltage levels. Although most of the participants questioned the practices, when ordered by the experimenter to continue, most proceeded.

The experiment itself was considered cruel to the participants, not the assistants. There are many conclusions and interpretations of this experiment. And, the experiment has been conducted many times and in slightly different fashions, but all with similar results.

The main conclusion is that people will follow authority figures. If people are willing to torture other people just because they are persuaded to do so by an authority figure, it is clear that a customer will buy from an authority figure.

There are hundreds of books on projecting power to clients. Some of the ideas—about how to stand, how firm the handshake must be, and how to stare a person down—are worthy and some are simply gimmicky and ill advised. I will not discuss such elements in this book, but instead come at the issue of power from a different angle. I want to address the simple things I see many salespeople do that simply deplete their power.

Killing Power with One Line

It is amazing how many salespeople do not take pride in their sales careers. You can spot them within the first five seconds of a meeting, because they start with something like:

- "I am just the sales guy."
- "My job is to bring the smart people into the room."
- "I am just the guy who buys lunch."
- "I will be your cruise director during this meeting."
- "Don't pay attention to me; I am only the salesperson."
- "Let me stop and let the smart people talk."
- "I am just a facilitator."
- "I am just the person who schedules the resources."

These type of behaviors are even more prevalent in technical sales, where salespeople work with a team of product experts. It is okay to let your customer know that, for the technical details, you will defer to the technical experts. But, do not downplay your value in a wholesale way with sweeping statements like those.

You must think of yourself as a doctor. You are there to help diagnose issues and solve problems. How would you feel if your doctor walked into the room and said, "I am not an expert in this, but let's get started."? The doctor may not be a specialist in cardiology for example, but he can still listen to the heart and recommend that the patient see a specialist after the exam. However, if he starts with, "I am not a specialist," then the patient will think, *"Then why are you even listening to my heart?"*

The same holds true for salespeople. It is okay not to be a technical expert. However, everything you sell should bring business value. You are the *business* expert in the room, so project that confidence.

Your Time Is Important

Making the best use of your time is an important mantra for you to practice from day one. It is also important that your customer sees that your time is important. Powerful people have busy schedules. If you allow yourself to let your customers dictate your schedule, your customers will sense that you do not have power. Statements like, "I am open all next week," "I will rearrange my schedule to accommodate you," and "Pick a time, I will make it work" are all examples of how a simple statement can diminish your power, thus reducing the trust your customer has. When scheduling, be specific about your available times. "I have an opening on Friday at 10:00, or next Wednesday at 1:30." Even if your calendar is wide open, show your customer that your time is valuable.

It will help you set a precedent with your customer that you are important, and that your time is precious. If they sense your time is free, the customer will be more apt to make you jump through hoops. "We need this," "Can you be here next week?," "We have a an urgent request," or "We need you here tomorrow!" Once you start falling into these traps, they are hard to get out of. Once customers start giving you hoops to jump through, you know they either don't respect your power, or are testing it.

Example

I had just hired Kevin, whom I had known for years. I was more than happy to have him on my team. He was very well respected, and had a proven track record, as he has been in our industry for over 20 years.

We were meeting with a junior engineer barely out of college. We entered our names on the sign-in sheet that every customer has, got our badges, and sat down to wait for the person to come escort us to the meeting room. We reviewed our objectives for the call one more time. I was impressed with the agenda Kevin had for the meeting. Everything was looking professional, and I was feeling more confident in my decision to hire him. My only concern was this was a pretty low-level engineer we were about to meet. A few minutes passed, and the junior engineer came out to greet us. I extended my hand and said, "It's nice to meet you; I am Dave."

Kevin extended his hand and said with a sweet-as-molasses tone, "I am Kevin, and thank you so much for your time; thank you."

As we walked down the hallway toward the meeting room, there was some idle conversation, and Kevin slipped in another, "Thank you so much for meeting us." We arrived at the meeting room, and as we sat down, Kevin again said, "Thank you; Thank you for your time." I was glaring at Kevin trying to will him to stop!

I teased Kevin for years about this, because I wanted him to stop this way-too-nice behavior, especially when it came to time. He was giving up all his power to an administrative engineer. What I wanted to convey was that a salesperson's time is more important than a customer's. Most of your customers are getting paid whether they sit there or not. You get paid for what you sell. You could be in front of more important people, making more money. Your time is valuable.

Respect your customer's time, but don't put it on a pedestal. Your time is actually more valuable, because you get paid only for performance.

Jumping Through Hoops

Again, you must show that your time is important. You need to convey that you are willing to help your customers, but they have to put as much skin in the game as you do. Do not blindly jump through hoops. Especially be aware of hoops that are meant to blow you off, like the "Please send me some literature" hoop.

I believe that sales is a profession in which you help and educate customers. This does not mean being subservient. Your customers will request administrative items from you, such as proofs of concept, new quotes, more quotes, and answers to RFPs. Sometimes customers don't know the effort some of these tasks require. It is okay to push back some and to ask for clarification as to why they are requesting something from you. It is also okay to negotiate with the customer. Give into the request reluctantly, and for something in return. At a minimum, put the task on your timetable.

If you have been in sales long enough, you will recognize the salesperson who runs around like a chicken with its head cut off. "I need to get this quote to the customer yesterday, and you need to drop everything you are doing to help me." This is a salesperson who is not in control of the sales cycle; they have given up all their power to the customer. Do not assume your customers need everything immediately. It is okay to tell the customer that her request will take a certain amount of time. Set the expectation that your time is important.

Summary

There are many techniques for establishing power with customers, including the way you hold your hands, how you enter a room, how you stand, how you shake hands, and so on. This chapter was not about techniques you can use to project power. The point here was to point out simple mistakes that many salespeople make that are very easy to avoid. You are working hard to establish trust with your customer, so do not let your power wane with seemingly harmless statements. I am not asking you to change your personality or use gimmicks to get power, but just be aware of the self-worth you project to your customers.

You are two-thirds the way through the book, and finally you get to meet with the customer in the next chapter. I will cover some selling skills and strategies, and discuss a small shift in focus from opportunity qualification to qualifying the customer as someone with the potential to become a long-term buyer of your products or services.

CHAPTER

16

Selling Strategies

Sales 101

People don't care how much you know until they know how much you care.

—John C. Maxwell

No matter how much strategy you have, you still must be able to pull the trigger and execute. Selling skills are your number one tool in developing the element of trust. Like with many things, selling skills are not the only thing you need, but without them you face an uphill challenge.

Selling is simple. Listen to the customer. Ask questions. Push the focus back on the customer at all times. If every salesperson could do these simple tasks, it would put every sales author and trainer out of business.

Why are questions so important? You ask questions for two reasons.

- They enable you to dive into the heart of the issue. You can expand the issue to the point where the customer says, "I have to fix this problem."

- They show that you care. As John Maxwell said, "People don't care how much you know until they know how much you care." This is the quote at the beginning of the chapter, but it is worth repeating. Showing you care will win you more trust than any strategy you employ. Without proper intent from the beginning, you will have difficulty advancing the sales cycle.

I just saved you hundreds of dollars on sales books. It really is that simple. The problem is that for most people, the 80% crowd, this is hard to do. I am no exception. I teach sales skills, yet I still have to constantly remind myself, "Shut up, focus back on the customer, and don't talk so much about what I can do or my strategies." I like to hear myself talk, but I am at least to the point where I am aware when I am boring a customer.

Questions!

I was just reading an article that said questions are becoming a passé concept as a sales tool; conversations are the way to go. I agree that conversations are most important. However, questions are the tool of choice to guide conversations. The easiest way to start a conversation or keep a conversation going is with questions. I think the article was referring to the old questions like, "What keeps you up at night?," "What's the stone in your shoe?," or "If you could fix one thing, what would it be?"

I believe canned questions like these are past their prime. First, everyone uses them, so they sound insincere. Second, as a salesperson new to the account, you have not earned the trust to ask personal questions yet. No one is going to dump their troubles, business or personal, on someone they have no trust in. This chapter helps you better understand why questions are important, why you need to build toward tougher questions, and how to use questions effectively so you become a conversationalist without sounding like an interrogator.

Overused word alert: I will use the word "question" in some form 121 times in this chapter. (I counted.) I overuse the word to drive home the importance of questions.

Example

Why is something as simple as asking questions so hard for salespeople? For 80% of salespeople, their comfort zone is in talking about their products. I see it with new salespeople, regional managers, and VPs of sales; they like to talk about what they can do for the customer. They like to talk about their products, their company, and themselves. I could share with you several stories about bad sales behavior, or salespeople with long monologues, but this example best exemplifies the challenge of staying focused on the customer and asking questions.

I have had the chance to interview many sales candidates over the years. During the interview, I spend half the time on an exercise with the candidate. My goal is to determine if they can keep asking questions. From the quality of their questions, I can get a great sense of how technical or business savvy they are. Here is how I set up the role-play.

> This is *not* a sales call. You have a customer who has just awarded you a deal to help them implement a project. I will play the customer, and all I want you to do is ask me questions about the project. I want you to understand the business goals, the technical environment, the timelines of the project, and the technical objectives. Understand the timeframes, budgets, and how this project affects the business. Again, just find out as much as you can about this project. *Do not sell to me.* Listen to my answers; they will help you form your next question.

I have set them up to exhibit the proper sales behavior, asking questions. I even tell them the exact information they need to get from me. In the interview, there are a few check boxes I am looking for.

- Does the candidate keep asking questions?
- Are they asking business questions?
- Are they asking technical questions?
- Are they asking personal or pain questions?
- What caliber of questions do they ask?
- What depth of knowledge is demonstrated?
- Are they carrying on a conversation?

The results are typical. Nearly 80% of the time, the candidates ask two, maybe three, questions, and then start making statements about how they can help. They think since it's a sales interview that they need to sell. What I want to see is proper selling behavior, which consists of asking questions. When they start selling, I think, *"They just stopped selling. Now I am getting a monologue."* I stop them, and tell them once again, "Just ask questions to understand this project." Still, 80%–90% of candidates find an opening in the conversation to deliver a monologue. The true indication of the depth of the problem is the fact that these candidates are making up their monologue. They know very little about what the company does, but they proceed to "wing it" and make up value propositions on the fly.

I cannot resist this next anecdote. The worst case of this happened when I was forced by circumstances to phone-interview a candidate. I was traveling with one of my sales reps in the mountains of North Carolina. The mobile phone reception was lousy. We agreed he would call me. I received the call from the candidate right on time. Since it was so rural, the call did not come through with caller ID. We started the interview, and shortly thereafter the call dropped. The candidate called me right back. I was thankful for that because I didn't have his number.

We then got to the exercise part of the interview, and as usual, he asked a couple of questions and then started in on how our company can help the customer. About 30 seconds in, the call dropped. Again, I was thankful, but for a different reason: he was already boring me. I waited for him to call me back. I waited, and I waited some more. I was frustrated since I couldn't call him back. Finally, after 20 minutes my phone rings again, and it was the candidate. "We must have dropped. How much of my answer did you hear?" I asked right back, "Well, I am not sure; how long did it take for you to get me back on the phone?"

"Well, the call just dropped a minute ago, and I dialed right back."

He had talked for 20 minutes, without one ounce of feedback. He was talking to a silent phone for 20 minutes. He had no idea how long he had talked without feedback. To give him the benefit of the doubt, he did not have my body language giving him negative feedback, but still, 20 minutes?

He didn't get the job.

As stated, selling is simple, but hard for most salespeople to execute. I believe the disconnection lies in how each person's selling style is ingrained in their personality, which is difficult to change.

What is easy to change is strategy. Strategy can be done with management, in the car, in the parking lot, and in a conference room. When strategizing, you do not have the pressure of the customer in front of you. There are no repercussions for missteps. Setting a strategy is easy. The proper strategy will keep you aligned with the skills you need to employ. You cannot execute the strategies in this book without asking questions. Questions force you to exhibit the proper skills. And the answers to your questions can be used to further refine your sales strategy and make it more effective.

One of the major strategies discussed is qualifying customers. You must spend your time developing trust with customers before an opportunity cycle. You cannot qualify without asking questions.

Even if you ignore the advice of building trust before you enter into an opportunity cycle, you cannot learn about the opportunity without asking questions. How else will you learn these elements in the sales equation?

$$CE \times V \times P \times DP \times (D+I+C+R)^2 = Sale$$

- Pain/compelling event (CE)
- Value/budget (V)
- Access to power (P)
- Decision/purchase process (DP)
- Your relative trust strength $(D+I+C+R)^2$

No matter how smart you are, or how well you position your products, you cannot qualify the customer or the opportunity without asking the right questions. Using the hunter analogy, your skills are your ability to aim and shoot. Questions are your gun. Questions are your sales weapon of choice. When asking questions, you give the customer a chance to talk. This is a conversation. No matter how well you think a sales call went, the next time you get out of an appointment, stop and think, "Who did all the talking?"

In your first few encounters with new customers, your focus should be on raising trust levels. This is as easy as asking questions. Ask questions; ask questions. Why?

Intent. If you stay focused on the customers by asking them in detail about their issues, you show that you care about them. They may even forget they are in a sales meeting.

Results. This one is hard to earn from the beginning. However, you must ask questions about their goals. Understand where they are, and where they want to be. Have them tell you what a successful solution looks like.

Dedication. In the early stages of the sales/buyer relationship, your dedication is closely tied to your intent in the customer's mind.

Capability. You are better off showing capability through intelligent questions rather than telling what you can do for them.

I was once in your shoes and wanted to prove that, even though I was a "sales guy," I could hang with the customer's engineers. I could. It took me 10 years to realize that the engineers dismissed what I was saying, just because I was the salesperson. I was not doing myself any favors. I eventually learned that the quality of my questions could demonstrate my capabilities. I now have a goal with every sales call: to hear the words, "great question." The more "great question" responses I get, the more comfortable the customer is about my abilities. As trust grows, they open up even more.

ASK TOUGH QUESTIONS

The tough questions you are afraid to ask are the most professional ones. Questions about the decision process, budgets, time frames, goals, how the business is affected if they don't do something, or the advantage the customer will have if they do move forward, will show you are the business consultant they are looking for. The interview process I described earlier in this chapter had this very goal—to determine the quality of questions asked by the interviewee. I wanted to know if they asked technical, project, or business-related questions. I wanted to know how detailed, or how in depth they could go in any one subject. Your customers want to know the same things. You will impress them with great—and sometimes difficult—questions, and you will annoy them with the answers you provide unsolicited.

A Study on

A large manufacturing company noticed a trend with their sales teams. After two years in a sales position, most salespeople started to lose momentum. Morale would decrease, and their sales results would diminish to the point of disrepair. (See Figure 16-1.)

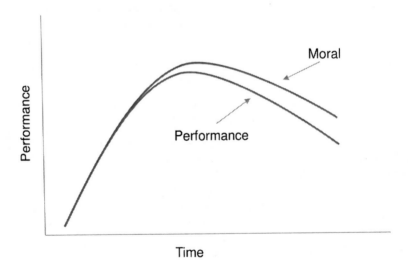

Figure 16-1. Declining sales performance over time

The two curves show morale and productivity. When starting in a new territory, you are working hard, and you are probably insecure because you do not know your customer, market, or products very well. However, as you gain experience, your morale and performance pick up. At about the two-year mark, your morale and performance are at an all-time high. So why does the curve start to go down at that point? This seems like a huge contradiction.

It's called the "double E effect." Experience and enthusiasm kill sales. Wait! You probably have read some place that one of the key qualities of any salesperson is passion. Isn't enthusiasm another word for passion? Why would experience play a role in causing sales to decline? The answer is simple. Once a salesperson masters her product or services, she stops asking questions. She is now an expert in what she is selling. She has great intent and has helped many customers produce results. She is eager (enthusiastic) to help the next customer. With the two Es, she starts telling the customers how she can help. She stops asking questions! Think about an uncomfortable conversation, or an early sales call, where you knew little about the product. Your defense mechanism was to ask questions and get your customer to talk, which is great selling. It is simple to see from the outside looking in, but hard to recognize when you are actually on the sales side of the call.

Example

During sales training, I do an exercise where I ask one of the participants in the class to role-play with me. This kind of role-play demonstrates behavior, rather than sales training-type role-play that is meant to ingrain specific memorized wordings. The first thing I do is put the salesperson on a sales call where they know *nothing* about their product. The example I use is a vacuum salesperson (I like the stereotype) going to a potential customer's home. It's this person's first day on the job and he was going only to observe the senior salesperson. The new person shows up in the driveway and is waiting for his partner. The phone rings. The partner is stuck in traffic, "You have to cover this call for me."

Since the participants know very little about vacuums, they are typically very nervous, so I tell them to just ask me questions. They hesitate, thinking of questions, and then they come out. Why did you agree to an appointment today? What is your old vacuum? How does it work? Is there anything you don't like about it? Are there features you wish it had? How often do you vacuum? Do you have kids or pets? Questions, plain and simple. The participant looks very awkward. So I let them off the hook. I say, "Great job. I know you are nervous. Let me make it easier on you. Let's role-play a sales call within your industry." You see the person's mood and morale instantly improve. They are back in their comfort zone.

Jeff, the participant in this case, is eager to get another try, this time with a product he knows something about.

I say, "Jeff, welcome; thank you for coming in, we would like to talk about x today." Jeff starts with some pleasantries. Then he asks a couple of questions about what the customer would like to hear about. Then Jeff starts to "sell." He says how great the company is; how their product is better and why. On and on.

After teaching on my feet all morning, I feel like letting him go on all afternoon, so I can rest. However, I am nice and I cut him off after three minutes or so. "Good job Jeff; please take a seat."

Jeff proudly walks back to his seat, since he just did a great job selling. He did do a great job selling, but it's not in the scenario he thinks. I poll the class, "Which was a better sales call?" Almost unanimously, the class votes for the vacuum sales call. Everyone can see that the call was smoother, the customer was more engaged in answering questions, and Jeff got a ton of information from the customer.

When you are in the middle of the "sale," you need to be an outside observer, like the class, and start to be aware of what's going on. Are you sounding like a bore? Is the customer engaged? Are you asking questions?

Objectively, when I look back at people I have worked with, or for, one great salesperson stands out in my mind. At the time I thought he was average, but over time, I gained new respect for his abilities. I wish he had taught me more. I was a beginner who was slowly becoming an expert, and he was an expert. I liked to prove I was as smart as the engineers, so I talked about products. I had the answers to the customer's problem; I had quick answers to their questions.

He acted like he didn't know a thing. He would just ask simple questions that I knew he knew the answers to. I would ask him, "Why are you asking so many simple questions?" He would just smile. I didn't get it 20 years ago, but today I do. He did not let his enthusiasm and experience stop him from asking questions. He was an expert acting like a beginner. He was a professional.

Example

Let's go back to Susan from Chapter 2, the woman who had access to 20 CIOs in her territory. When we analyzed what was going on, we realized the weak link was the sales manager. She had an enthusiastic sales manager who was overjoyed with the fact that Susan had C-level access at 20 accounts.

In the first three months of her being on board, Susan introduced her boss to each of her previous customers. After six months, there were no measurable results in Susan's territory.

At the quarterly business review, the VP of sales analyzes the situation. The VP asks the regional manager, "So, how are things going?"

He replies, "Great. It's just a matter of time before we can take advantage of Susan's relationships."

VP: "What activity has occurred?"

The enthusiastic regional manager: "It's been awesome. Susan has brought us into about 20 accounts, at the C-Level. We've had the chance to tell our story to 20 new customers!"

The VP's response was not so enthusiastic: "What the [****] do you mean?"

Confused, the regional manager asks: "What do you mean?"

Ignoring the question, the VP suggests, "Let's go down the list of these customers and understand what next steps we have with each. I want to know what issues they have. Customer number one, what are their main initiatives for the year?"

Silence.

"Customer number 2, what are their main initiatives for the year?"

Silence.

VP: "You told our story? How long did you take in telling our story?"

Regional manager: "Well you know our slide deck, 30 minutes or so."

VP: "Did you bother asking the customer anything about their business?"

Regional manager: "In most cases with the C-level they only had 45 minutes. So, we didn't have much time for that."

VP: "[****]!"

This is typical. The regional manager was excited to have Susan's access to the C-level contacts and took for granted her relationship with the customer. He thought with her relationship, all he needed to do was tell the customer how great her new company was and orders would flow in.

What happened?

- He forgot sales 101, which is to ask questions.
- He forgot about the incumbent.
- He forgot about qualifying the customer.
- He bored the customers.

The customers dismissed the new vendor, because Susan and the regional manager did not take time to establish a trusting relationship. They did not show intent by taking the time to ask about their customer issues. Susan didn't improve upon the trust she had built through her previous job, and she underestimated the trust the incumbent had built. She lost these sales as a result.

Questioning Skills

Here are the basics for questioning prospects.

- Listening will help you develop your best questions.

- Focus on the basics—who, what, where, why, and how (how many, how much),

- Asking "why" three times will lead to the real reason the customer has discussed an issue.

Let's consider each of these points in detail.

Listening

The number one mistake you see with sales reps who are trying to question is that they do not listen to the answers. They ask a question, wait for the answer, and then move on to the next question on the list. The best questions feed off the customer's responses. In sales, questions are your weapon. In hunting, your rifle is your weapon. The best sharpshooters in the word have an extra set of eyes on the target; they have spotters. The spotters tell the shooter where to aim. The shooter fires one round, and the spotter tells the shooter, "You were down six inches to the left." The shooter adjusts the weapon, or the scope on the weapon, to accommodate for the errant shot. The same goes with questions. Look for feedback from the customer in the form of their answers. Your next question should build off their answer, and probe for deeper understanding.

Example

A couple is on their first date. The guy has just read somewhere to stay focused on his date and ask questions. So, he starts with, "Where did you grow up?"

She replies, "Ohio."

"Oh really, what do you do for work?"

She replies, "I am a lawyer."

"Wow that's impressive. What kind of music do you like?"

At this point she is thinking, "*What is this, a game show?*"

Here is how the conversation should go:

"Where did you grow up?"

Her reply, "Ohio."

"Really? What town in Ohio?"

"Cleveland; it was great."

"What did you like most about it? Why was it great?"

Can you see the difference? One is disjointed and uncomfortable; the other flows, and she can tell her date is actually listening.

This is no different in sales. When you ask a customer about her computer and she tells you she has a Dell, you should not then ask, "What kind of network do you have?" Proper follow-up questions relate to the Dell computer. How many, how old, and when was the last time you upgraded? Who owns the responsibility for your servers, or for your desktops? Have you looked at other vendors?

Sounding Like an Expert with Basic Questions

So the first principle is to listen and feed off the answers. How do you do this? Use the basic questions—who, where, what, when, why, and how. These questions will make you seem like an expert on any subject.

In the earlier example, Jeff was in front of the class asking questions to his potential vacuum customer. He must ask questions out of necessity. I call Jeff back to the front of the room and give him the instructions to listen to my answers and then follow up with the what, who, how many, and why questions. Here is how the conversation goes.

Jeff rings the doorbell and I welcome him in.

Jeff: "I understand you are in the market for a vacuum?"

Customer: "Yes I am."

Jeff: "Why are you looking for a new vacuum?"

Customer: "Well, I don't think the one we have works all that well."

Jeff: "What doesn't work well? Is there a function you are looking for, or are your floors not as clean as you would like?"

Customer: "A little of both. I think my current vacuum is heavy, and it's hard getting the stairs clean. But mainly, the carpets don't look as good as they used to."

Jeff: "Can you show me the stairs? Where are they dirty?"

Customer: "See the edges and corners? I don't have an attachment for those."

Jeff: "So, it's heavy and doesn't have some features? How often do you vacuum the stairs?"

Customer: "I vacuum all the time. My kids are always dragging in grass clippings."

Jeff: "How many kids do you have?"

This can go on forever, but you can see that this is a much smoother conversation. He asked how, what, who, and why questions. He listened and molded his next question based on the customer's answers. Does Jeff know anything more about vacuums than he did 10 minutes before, when he was up in front of the class? No. But with some guidelines, he comes across as confident and knowledgeable. And, by asking deeper questions, he shows he cares. The trust is building. Luckily for Jeff, he knew nothing about the vacuum he was selling. If he had, he would have had the urge to start talking about the company's new "Featherweight Series," or something like that. Fight the urge to start talking about the solution right when the customer opens the door, and keep on feeding off their answers.

You can use the questioning method anywhere—in sales or even at parties. You will be amazed at the conversations you can hold without knowing a thing about a topic.

Get to the Heart of the Matter

If you ask "why" three times, you will get to the heart of the matter. You will get to the real reason that someone wants to make a change, fix a problem, or buy something new. Looking back at the vacuum scenario, the conversation could just as easily gone like this.

Jeff: "I understand you are in the market for a vacuum?"

Customer: "Yes I am."

Jeff: "Why are you looking for a new vacuum?"

Customer: "Well, I don't think the one we have works all that well."

Jeff: "Why do you say that? Is there a function you are looking for, or are you floors not as clean as you like?"

Customer: "A little of both. I think my current vacuum is heavy; it's hard getting the stairs clean. But, mainly the carpets don't look as good as they used to."

Jeff:"Can you show me what you mean?"

Customer:"See this area? It doesn't look like stain; it just seems dirty."

Jeff:"It doesn't seem too bad; why does it bother you?"

Customer:"My mother in-law had fun pointing that out."

Jeff, smiling:"Mother in-law? Is she here often?"

Customer:"Too often; I always feel my house has to be spotless."

These questions are not exactly why, why, why, but variations of "why" are woven through each question. The real reason this customer wants a new vacuum is to impress her mother in-law. This is a much more powerful motivator than a dirty carpet.

This applies even more so to B2B sales. I have talked about how each title within a company has different goals. It is critical that you determine the real reason why someone is contemplating working on a new project or purchasing something new. Let me clue you in. Most people do not want to work harder. They want their lives to be easier. So the real reason they are willing to make a change has to be personal. Asking "why" three times will get you to the personal reason. Once you figure out the personal reason, your trust score goes through the roof. Your intentions become about helping them personally. The results you will show have an impact on their life or their career.

Salesperson:"So Bob, you are looking at buying some more storage; why?"

Bob: "The current system does not have the horsepower we are looking for."

Salesperson:"Horsepower, meaning . . .?"

Bob: "Recently, we changed the backup of our major systems over from tape to our storage system. That was supposed to improve performance."

Salesperson:"Supposed to?"

Bob:"Yes, it helped a little, but our backups are still taking hours."

Salesperson:"Why is that a problem?"

Bob:"I am not allowed to leave work until the backups are completed."

Salesperson:"Wow, that's a bummer. How late have you been staying lately?"

Bob:"Well, I can't play in our softball league anymore."

The reason Bob wants a new storage system is because he wants to play softball!!! Nowhere in any cost justification, or ROI presentation, will it ever mention softball. But now that you know why Bob wants it so bad, you have an ally.

However, Bob's boss will have a whole different reason why she wants new storage.

Salesperson:"Bob tells me you are looking at some new storage."

Karen:"Yes, our backups are not running as fast as we would like."

Salesperson:"Why does this bother you—is it causing a problem?"

Karen:"About a month ago, a large database was corrupted, and Finance was unable to run an end-of-quarter report. They were late in getting their quarterly earnings report to the CEO."

Salesperson:"How will faster backups help with that?"

Karen: "It didn't have any direct effect, but it put a spotlight on our slow backup process."

Salesperson:"Are tasked with solving this issue?"

Karen:"Yes, my next quarter MBOs are all based on this project."

By asking Susan enough questions, you finally get the real reason that Bob's boss wants new storage; she is financially incented.

Summary

Remember the true reasons for asking questions:

- To uncover enough information about the situation to the point the customer is saying to themselves, "We have to fix this issue."

- To show that you care.

Questions, questions, questions. You can see how customers will open up to questions. If you want to sum up sales skills, think questions, questions, questions. You can't hunt without a gun. You can't sell without asking questions.

Even though this book is about strategy that anyone can use regardless of skill level, it's important to include on chapter about sales skills. To change your personality is a long process. The process starts with awareness. Be aware of the conversations you have with customers. After each sales call, ask yourself who did all the talking.

With this crash course in selling, you are now in a position to ask questions and listen to the customer. It is now that you start truly executing your strategy. In the next chapter, you learn more about qualifying customers to determine if they are worth your continued sales efforts.

Qualify the Customer

The Quickest Path to Sales Success

"Time is the scarcest resource, and unless it is managed nothing else can be managed."

—Peter Drucker

Now that you are armed (with questions), where do you point the gun?

The last chapter was about asking questions and starting to drive the most important aspect of an opportunity, which is the compelling event or pain. However, your initial meetings with a new customer are more about qualifying the customer against your ideal profile. This chapter is therefore an expansion of Chapter 11, "Rich Hunting Grounds."

Develop Your Ideal Customer Profile

During the planning stage, it's important to develop the ideal customer profile. Prior to your initial engagement with the customer, the data points in the ranking system come from assumptions and from third-party sources. At this point in the sales cycle, you want to start filling in the gaps of information and validating the data you have.

Gathering information to qualify your customers is the most crucial step in managing your territory. It guides where you'll spend your sales time. The goal is to rank customers first as targets, and then as potential customers. The elements of your ranking system should direct your questions, and you should learn as much as you can about this customer from the start.

While some of these items might overlap with the characteristics in your ranking profile, this information will help you start doing business with the customer.

Outside of an opportunity, you can start to learn about the requirements of the sales equation (see Chapter 8, "The Sales Equation").

$$CE \times V \times P \times DP \times (TR)^2 = Sale$$

Some of those elements are universal to every deal. This includes the decision and purchase processes, who is who in the account, who the power decision makers are, and the budget cycles. It is good to know whether your customer has to send every quote out for bid, because it will help you determine if this is the type of customer you want to pursue as well as help you set initial and long-term strategies. Do they have a preferred vendor list? If so, what is the process for getting on it?

While you might find opportunity right away, the true goal is to build trust first. Be on the lookout for opportunities that are not so immediate. You can do this by discussing any long-term business initiatives or challenges the customer is facing. If you sell technical items, make an effort to understand the technical environments in more detail.

Lastly, you want to start to learn who your competition is. As you get to know the market competition, including their strengths and weaknesses, you can start to develop messaging that markets your solutions against their weaker areas. Listen to what your customers say about your competition; they will tell you what they like about them, and what they don't like. If your customer starts to talk negatively about a competitor, resist the urge to jump in and talk negatively as well. Remember your customers are judging you on your character to determine if they can trust you. Even when customers are negative, they want their vendors to be positive and professional.

Personal Relationships

I discussed that a business relationship is crucial, but customers also want to buy from people they like. You must be in tune with your customer's feedback. Being liked will gain you access; providing business value will keep you in the door.

The very moment you step in the door, the customer begins sizing you up. They begin thinking, *"Do I like this person? Can they help me? Can this person be trusted? Is this person a waste of time?"*

You must do the same. Is this customer worth your time? Will you enjoy working with this person? Does this person need help? You have to deal with customers on a day-to-day basis. Make your life easy and select customers you enjoy spending time with. It will lead to lasting business relationships. It will reduce your stress, and it will help you relax around the customer. The customer will experience your good intent and dedication.

When you're starting a new territory, be selective with opportunity. You might not have the luxury of being selective with customers just yet. However, as you grow the territory, customers you don't like doing business with will naturally move down in the ranking system.

Take note of the person's title at accounts you're comfortable dealing with. Are they the decision makers? If not, you must start building a team that can deal at that level. Can you get other people from your company lined up at the proper levels? Over time, with continued success and results, you will build a comfort level with higher titles within your customer base.

Rank and Rerank Customers

With all the information you are gathering, start to populate a ranking system worksheet (Figure 17-1).

Sort by Rank	Gut Feel	Revenue ($ Millions)	Servers (#)	Amount of Storage (TB)	Vertical Market (Rank [1-10])	Trust Built (8 Points)	Company Growing? (Yes/No)			Incumbent Trust (8 Points)	Buys on Price (Yes/No)		Rank
Customer 12	200	400	50	100	6	2				6			323
Customer 15		2,500	350	1,000	8	2	10			7			290
Customer 10		120	20	45	10	8	10			4			258
Customer 14		2,000	500	500	9	7				7			238
Customer 7		5,000	700	1,200	2								236
Customer 6		150	750	1,000	5	5				5	10		211
Customer 3		1,000	175	200	2	2	10			8			185
Customer 11		250	30	50	6		10						178
Customer 1		1,000	150	150	5	2					10		168
Customer 19	-100	1,500	225	1,000	7					2			119
Customer 2		50	100	20	10	4				6			115
Customer 4		2,000	200		7					6			93
Customer 13		650	50	120	7	2				6	10		91
Customer 16		50	200		2								83
Customer 5		100	35		5								71
Customer 8		25	120	20	2								66
Customer 18		45	10		4								27
Customer 9		75			10						10		18
Customer 17		90	25		3					8			1

Figure 17-1. Sorted customer ranking worksheet

Do not be afraid to add or remove characteristics from your ranking sheet. This is a working document; it is your tool. This worksheet will slowly move from being a target to being a list that guides your discussions with your customers. It will force you to ask for missing information. It will also start to be a list of existing customers, where you become an incumbent. As your trust scores grow with certain customers, these customers will rise to the top. The easiest place to win new business is with existing accounts, and you will see the ranking system prove that fact.

Summary

With initial access to your customer, don't just look for immediate opportunity. Remember that immediate opportunity is a trap that is hard to escape. Having a framework to qualify your customers will keep you on track, help you exercise proper selling behavior, and help you determine where you should spend your time. The goal is to build long-lasting, trusted business relationships. With confidence, you can spend time only with qualified customers. There might not be an immediate opportunity, but now is the time to start building trust with these qualified customers.

In Chapter 18, you learn tactics and strategies to solidify trust, which will put you in a position to win current and future opportunities.

Building Trust Before Opportunity

As you go to work, your top responsibility should be to build trust.

—Robert Eckert

Continue to level the playing field. You have established your online presence in order to show capability. You have utilized warm introductions to show capability, intent, and result. None of these is a new concept, but hopefully you have a better understanding of why they are important. The most important strategy discussed so far has been to focus on the customer relationship rather than on the immediate opportunity. This point was driven home with information about improving sales skills, managing opportunities, avoiding becoming column fodder, and handling leads well. You have spent time qualifying and ranking your customers, so now you need to develop their trust. However, what do you do when you are not completely focused on an opportunity?

Why You Can Win an Incumbent's Business

Assume you qualified the customer and you have established some trust with them. You received a warm introduction and you have successfully shown intent by staying focused on them. Your intent is solid, while your capability, dedication, and results are at best, warm. Your trust meter looks like Figure 18-1.

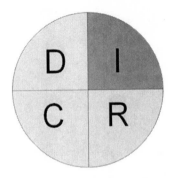

Figure 18-1. Example of building trust before engaging an opportunity

In the trust-ranking system, you have a score of five, but you need at least a six to compete with a fully trusted incumbent. You need to work on capability, dedication, and results.

I want to remind you that it's likely that you're building a trust meter that is actually stronger than the incumbent's. In the incumbent's ideal world, the meter is full, but in reality they have probably taken their customer for granted (Figure 18-2).

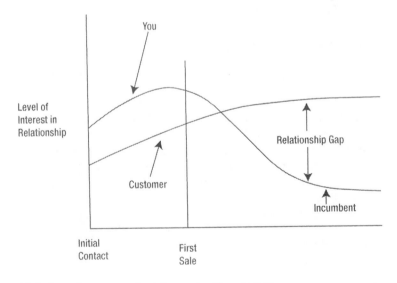

Figure 18-2. Incumbent not maintaining trust with customer

The smart incumbent realizes that the relationship after the sale is important to the customer, and that selling to an existing customer is much easier than finding new ones. However, this graph shows that the typical salesperson moves on to new opportunities after the sale. I guarantee that your focus on bringing value to the customer will be rewarded once an opportunity is presented.

These elements are easy to change when given a chance. However, your customer has been conditioned over the years to engage with salespeople within the confines of a project. You need to be creative in demonstrating dedication, capability, results, and intent without the benefit of a "natural" sales cycle.

Methods to Increase Trust

The ideas shared in this chapter are only suggestions for actions you can take to improve business relationships. These ideas go beyond, "Can I take you to lunch?" or "Would you like to play golf?" While you can develop a friendly relationship with the customer in order to win their business, you must also establish business trust.

The primary strategy is to stay in front of your customer while offering value. If you focus on product presentations or just grill the customer for information over and over, they will stop seeing value in your interactions, and your ability to secure future appointments will dwindle. In everything you do with a customer, you must make sure you are adding business value. The most powerful tools you have are information and concern. You want to keep your customers educated about your solutions, new trends in the industry, news articles, or information that will help them with their careers. The more you understand your customer from the beginning, the more focused the information can be to that customer. The information must complement their concerns. Sharing information can demonstrate your capability.

Capability is established with industry knowledge more so than with product knowledge. Customers are always curious about the latest industry trends.

Phone Call with Follow-Up E-Mail

This one is simple. As you are maintaining your industry knowledge, you will come across information that your customer will benefit from knowing. Call your customer and leave a simple voicemail. "I came across an article today I thought you would be interested in. I am going to mail (or e-mail) it to you. Let me know your thoughts." Make these calls personal and specific to each person. An ideal situation is when you come across information pertaining to a specific issue the customer has mentioned. "You mentioned you had X as an issue; I thought this article would be useful to you." Customers are inundated with blanket marketing e-mails. Make it personal.

The order of calling and then sending the e-mail is important. Do not send a mass e-mail to every prospect. The reason you are calling and then sending the e-mail is to show dedication and dependability. You told the customer you were going to do something for them, and then you followed through. It creates two positive touch points.

You should not do this in reverse order. The information you are sharing is for their benefit. It makes no sense to send an e-mail to the customer and tell them you'll follow up with a phone call.

You phone in hopes of getting the customer. If you don't, leave a voicemail. Then send the e-mail with information that's useful specifically to them. Incidentally, use this tactic only after you have met with the customer, not as part of your cold calling activities.

Lunch and Learn, or the Seminar

The lunch and learn is a different animal than just a lunch. The straight, "Can I take you to lunch?" does not inherently have an agenda. The conversations can go in many directions, and getting around to business can be a challenge. Lunch and learns have built-in agendas. Your goal is to educate the customers and have them view it as an important learning opportunity. The most effective lunch and learns have the following components:

- The lunch is held in a neutral spot—not at the customer site.

- You invite multiple customers at one time.

- You cover elements of industry knowledge transfer, or define a common issue that most customers face.

- You offer a brief description of how your solution can help.

This should not be a product pitch or a 60-minute presentation on your product.

Since the customer is offsite, you create an event feel rather than a disguised sales call. This will have the effect of demonstrating stronger intent, and it will cause customers to lower their guards. You want them out of their offices and away from their computers. Granted, this is harder today, with smartphones. You don't want them to feel that they're being "sold to" in a place where their guard is up.

Having multiple customers at the table is your strongest tool. Subconsciously, to the customer, it's like you were referred to them by these 10 other customers in the room. Chances are, not everyone will meet everyone else. Each attendee has no idea whether they are existing customers or prospects like themselves. Typically, they will assume the others are existing customers. Referrals help strengthen all aspects of trust, and you can multiply that by the number of other customers attending. If you have existing customers at the event, there is a good chance they are there because they already trust your capabilities. There is a natural tendency for customers to network at these events, meaning there is a good chance your existing customers will refer you. You hope your prospect asks, "What has this vendor done for you?" Results!

Your industry knowledge will continue to keep the customers' guards down. They will be thankful it's not just another product pitch. Events that educate people about the latest industry trends are the best attended. The lunch and learns that are product-centric have your customers thinking, "*Will there be dessert?*" Focusing on knowledge transfer will improve your trust meter in the areas of intent and capability.

The follow-up product presentation should be brief, and should be focused on a real-life scenario that highlights a customer's challenge, a brief description about how your solution helped, and the results you delivered for the customer. The goal behind this approach is to show compassion for the customer's issues; this is intent. You show capability in solving the issue, and lastly, you show that you can deliver results. Keeping the how-to portion brief will leave the customer with a touch of mystery. Lunch and learns are similar to cold calling in this aspect; the goal is to leave the customers wanting more. You need customers to talk about their specific issues; obviously they are not going to do this in a group setting. You will need a follow-up appointment. Leaving the customers wanting more increases your odds of securing that follow-up.

The event's topic is the force that drives attendance (a nice venue never hurts either). If you stay with industry trends, or general-knowledge events, customers will attend. You may also want to try some of the cold calling techniques to drive attendance to these events.

Never Bash

When establishing trust with a customer, a huge mistake is to bash your competition, or sow fear, uncertainty, and doubt (FUD) about the incumbent. Customers make emotional decisions for logical reasons. If you bash the incumbent, you are effectively insulting the decisions your customer has made. Build your trust! Do not try to tear down the competition.

It is okay to position your offerings against a competitor's weakness. But never bash! We have all done this in the past. I have done it. I have done it after I was told not to do it. However, now that I am better at reading my customers' reactions, I can see uneasiness in most customers' eyes when this bashing occurs. I can see the walls go up. It's just not effective to bash.

When you bash you are not doing one thing to build your own trust. Your customers are judging *you* more than your product. They want to know if they can trust *you*. Build your own trust.

It is okay to highlight strengths you know your competitor cannot match. This can be done in a positive manner. If you know of a competitive weakness, you can ask the customer if they are having any issues specifically related to that weakness. For example, if I know my competitor's product is much slower than ours, I can simply ask, "Have you been experiencing any performance issues?" You want the customer to highlight their issues. It is okay to guide them to issues they may have with an incumbent.

Never bash!

Give to Get

This is a delicate concept. The next example in this chapter illustrates the psychological value of reciprocity; it shows the value of a gift. In today's world, there are many rules about giving customers gifts; some companies prohibit the use of them; some customers are not allowed to accept gifts. However, when I interviewed customers for this book, there was a sense that they like to see a vendor make an investment in them. So, you must take this concept and turn it into a business value. Instead of tickets to a football game, how do you give the customer something of business value—something that does not infringe upon any employer or legal restrictions?

Example

Recall from Chapter 12 the experiment in which the participant, when given a soda, was two times more likely to buy a raffle ticket. This concept is so important it is worth looking at another example. In the 1970s and 1980s, the Hare Krishnas gained a reputation by hounding passengers at airports across the country for donations. After limited success in gathering the donations they needed, they decided on a new tactic. They would hand the passenger a flower before asking for a donation. It must be noted that most passengers did not want to accept the flower, but when it was extended it was natural for the passengers to reach out and accept it. Sometimes the flower was almost forcefully placed in a passenger's hand.

Upon the introduction of the flower, the rate of donations went up five times. When they were given a gift, the passengers felt a sense of obligation to reciprocate. It did not matter what the gift was. How do we know that the passenger was not just paying for a flower they wanted? It turns out that 70% of the time the passengers would go around the corner and throw out the flower. (Being concerned with profit, the Krishnas retrieved the flowers from the garbage and handed them to the next passenger.) Think about it—five times the donation rate for a flower that was forced on them, all thanks to reciprocity.

You see this tactic every time you go to the grocery store; it's called the free sample. The sample has two purposes. First, they get you to try the product in the hopes you will like it. More importantly, there is a sense of obligation to purchase the item.

During my interviews with customers, none ever came out and said they wanted something for free, or a gift. A majority did want to see a vendor deliver something to them for the cost of doing business. Relating this to the concept of trust, ask yourself how you can show them results and minimize the customer's risk of time and money? You are an unproven vendor, and the customer wants you to stand behind your solution before they have to enter you into their procurement system, seek budget approval, and cut you a PO. They want to see that you can deliver something, and show some results, before they have to jump through their internal hoops.

So what do you give? Like the free sample at the grocery store, your gift should have two purposes. Give the customer a taste for what you can do, and instill a sense of obligation. In order to show value, you need to first put a value on the service or product, rather than present it as free. It does not have to be a large service engagement or an expensive product. With the goal of driving a deeper level of trust, it's best to choose something unique, and something you know you can deliver. Giving shows intent. You are not just out for yourself; you have the customer's best interests at heart.

The next two elements you can address are results and capability. Highlight a solution that will demonstrate your company's—or product's—capabilities and expertise. Lastly, when the customer perceives an initial value, ensure you show results against that initial perception. Trust has to be shown, not told. If you have multiple offerings and you are trying to gain a foothold, do not go to the most competitive offering you have in your bag. Is there an offering you can lead with that will get your foot in the door? Do you have something that is unique versus going head-to-head with a competitor? Think about niche selling earlier in the book. Pick a niche if possible. Initial deals do not have to be large. It's your first step to checking the trust boxes (Figure 18-3), so that you can eventually work toward larger opportunities. Demonstrate and show trust.

☑ Dependability

☑ Intent

☑ Capability

☑ Results

Figure 18-3. Check off each trust element before a major opportunity

Example

A classic example in the IT industry is to deliver a "gift" in the form of a free assessment. Typically, these assessments lead to roadmaps for orders. In other words, the deliverable from the assessment shows the customers their strengths and weaknesses in a specific area of their IT environment. The vendor then uses the findings of the assessment to propose solutions. The assessment is a formal needs analysis, which is part of the sales cycle. To the customer, it seems like a free professional services engagement.

Let's put all the elements of this together. First, there must be a value assigned to the service engagement. If you present to the customer a free assessment, the customer will perceive it as having no value. On the other hand, if you say, "We typically charge X for this type of service, but we are waiving the cost for you," then the perception is one of value; one of getting a "gift." This can be a tremendous asset to the vendor. The cost to the vendor is typically small. You use people you have on staff already. The customer sees your capability and your intent, and you can show results. And, remember the call to action from the assessment is for the customers to buy something to fix a problem.

Another example, which is much softer, comes from my very first sales job when I was in high school. I sold hockey equipment at a skate shop. The customers were typically parents of the kids who were playing hockey. When they had younger kids, the parents were new to the sport, and they were not always the most informed on hockey equipment. New parents would come into the shop to purchase hockey skates, which range greatly in price and quality. Most parents perceived the price of the skate to be the best indication of value. However, the kids who new to the sport were usually five to six years old, and still growing. The expensive features of the more costly skates were wasted on these younger kids. I learned early on that when I told the parent that their child would be better off with a less expensive skate, they would purchase anything I suggested. The way I analyze the situation is almost like the free assessment. First I "gave" them some free advice, which resulted in a gift of less expensive skates. I showed great intention and implied great capability. There was also a sense of obligation. This tactic earned the customer trust, and developed a sense of obligation to purchase more.

Help the Customer Regardless

If you truly want to provide your customers with business value, and you want to show your customers that your intent is to help them, the number one way to do that is to help them with a solution that you do not sell.

As you start to spend time with the customer, she will start to open up about all sorts of problems and issues. Stay tuned to your customer's problems. Don't just have rabbit ears for problems you can solve. As you learn about your industry and build your network, you will have a much bigger set of solutions. Consider your professional network as an extension of your line card, or solutions you can deliver to your customers.

This is exactly like a doctor who has an entire list of specialists that he engages to provide care for his patients. By understanding the compelling events your noncompetitive partners are looking for in the industry, you can help customers. What happens if you hear a customer say, "I really need to solve this problem?" You know you can't help with it, but you network with someone who you know can help. If you have the chance, line up the customer with someone you have networked with. You just strengthened your position with your customer immeasurably.

By the way, the person you brought in to help the customer now "owes you one." Reciprocation!

Your goal is to get into the position to win against an incumbent. How do get into the inner circle, the circle of trust? You are creating a sales cycle with no competition, no close, and where the proof is on your dime (Figure 18-4).

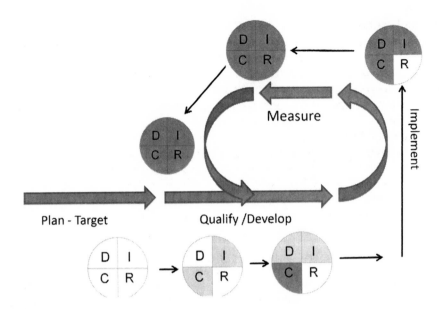

Figure 18-4. By giving, you can implement and measure results, without a sales cycle

With the close and prove stages eliminated, you put yourself in the position to build full trust (Figure 18-5).

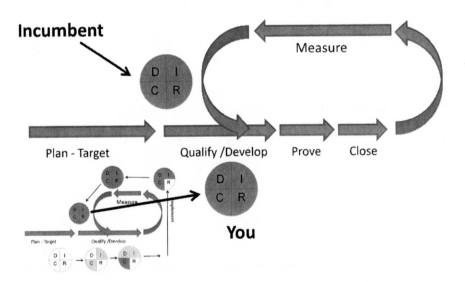

Figure 18-5. Establish trust before you engage the incumbent on a full sales cycle

Adding value in the first stages of an engagement, for even a small deal or proof of concept, will help you develop trust. You can then enter into a larger deal on an equal playing field. By creating a "sales cycle," like the one shown in Figure 18-4, you create trust before you have to compete against an incumbent on a larger deal. See Figure 18-5.

Partnering for Trust

This book was written for the person who owns the primary relationship with the customers. Here are some typical statements that are, however, cast in stone.

- Resellers or distributors typically have closer relationships with their customers than manufacturers do, unless the manufacturer is selling to the customer directly.

- Resellers typically make their living based on strong relationships with fewer accounts. Manufacturers typically need more transactions at more accounts than they can handle.

If you are a manufacturer, you have the "luxury" of not having to develop as deep a trusting relationship. You demonstrate capability of self and product. Then you can partner with an incumbent reseller who has already built the other elements of trust. The reseller should be strong in dedication and intent. They do not need capability; you bring that to the table. Their results are proven, but for other solutions (Figure 18-6).

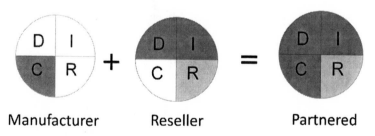

Manufacturer   Reseller   Partnered

Figure 18-6. Partnering to improve trust

The concept of partnering with these accounts, and possibly choosing the incumbent reseller, isn't new, but it's worth pointing out how you enhance your trust.

At the reseller, the opposite holds true. Being new is a lot harder for a reseller. They do not have the ability, most of the time, to partner with an incumbent manufacturer. They are probably partnered with an incumbent reseller. Your strategy for partnering should be to find a niche play (Chapter 10) with the customer, and a niche manufacturer.

By starting a relationship based on understanding and education, you hope to instill some intent and capability. Look for areas where you might not see capability from an incumbent and fill that niche (Figure 18-7).

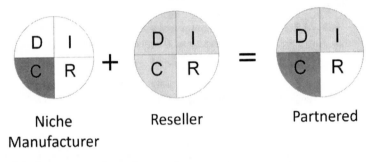

Figure 18-7. Partnering with a niche manufacturer to increase trust

Now you are matched to an incumbent with a trust meter that looks something like those in Figure 18-8. The incumbent may have a full trust meter, but when you have a solution in an area where they have not shown capability or results, their trust is somewhat reduced.

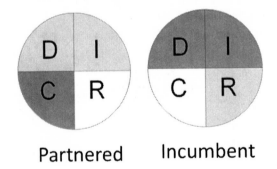

Figure 18-8. Partner to compete against an incumbent

You now have a four or five on the trust meter. This is in the range to compete.

Summary

The ideas in this chapter do not comprise an exact science. The point is to think outside the circle—the incumbent's sales circle. You can engage the customer outside of an opportunity cycle. Your time is critical. First qualify the customers—are they worth spending time with? If they are worth the time, use it wisely. You need to show value. Use the trust elements as a guide to thinking through your strategy with new customers. Use trust to build business value. In the next chapter, you learn how to manage, compete, and win opportunities.

Understanding and Developing Opportunities

A good plan is like a road map: it shows the final destination and usually the best way to get there.

—H. Stanley Judd

Qualifying and Developing Opportunity

However beautiful the strategy, you should occasionally look at the results.

—Winston Churchill

Eventually you will get an opportunity. Whether it is on your first or fifth call, qualifying an opportunity becomes as important as qualifying customers. In order to develop opportunities, start with the end in mind.

Recall the elements required to win a deal:

$CE \times V \times P \times DP \times (D+I+C+R)^2 = Sale$

- You've developed trust on a level playing field with the competition

- There's a compelling event, which is a pain or desire with a time constraint

- You have the money, budget, value, or valid ROI

- You have a yes from power

- You have identified the decision process

When you have trust, qualifying opportunities becomes as simple as validating the other criteria in this list. In the sales cycle, you should not cross into the evaluation stage until you have identified the budget and a compelling event, you have or can gain access to power, and you know all the steps the customer and you will go through to close the deal. Do not waste time on demos or web-ex meetings, or respond to any administrative-type request from customers, unless you have identified these elements.

The good thing about having to identify these elements is that you remain focused on the customer, and on asking questions. This will inherently improve your sales skills. New salespeople often have a hard time asking tough questions about money, timeframes, access to power, and the decision process. These questions become especially hard when your pipeline is not at expected levels. You are almost afraid to ask out of fear you might upset the customer or they might not have the answer you want. Here is the truth:

- The tough questions are the most professional ones.

- It's better to qualify to a "no" than waste time on a deal that has no chance.

Let Go of Poor Opportunities

What do I mean by, *qualify to a no?* It means that it's better to lose early. Simply ask yourself, would you rather lose upfront or after you have spent six months working a deal? If you can't identify the basic components of the deal, most likely you are wasting your time. It is as much of a waste of time as competing against an incumbent without the customer's trust.

If you opt out of an opportunity, that does not mean the customer is forever lost to you. Hopefully, you have already qualified the customer as worth spending time with. It is okay for you to say no to a specific opportunity. The ability to tell a customer that you are not a good fit for a specific deal will instill trust.

It is okay to walk away from some business for which you are not a good fit. It will give you instant credibility. It shows you have the customer's best interests at heart. You are putting their needs above your desire for financial gain.

So many salespeople and sales managers hold onto bad opportunities; they are opportunity hoarders. If you have ever seen the television show *Hoarders*, you have seen the absolute devastation that hoarding can bring to someone's life. Hoarding is a psychological disorder whereby people never throw out anything. They are afraid if they get rid of something that they will lose everything.

Their houses and cars fill up with so much junk that they can't walk through their own homes. It gets to the point where it can be physically dangerous, and the illness ruins their lives.

Do not hoard opportunities. When strategizing with salespeople about specific opportunities, many times it becomes obvious that the deal has no chance. There is no access to power, no money, or no trust. As an impartial outside observer, you can see as plain as day that the right answer is to walk from bad deals. Their forecasts become so cluttered with deals, that the real opportunities are lost in the weeds. The salesperson (and sometimes the sales manager) makes every excuse in the book to hold on to a bad lead or deal, which keeps their pipeline filled with junk. It seriously is like watching hoarders justify why they need keep coupons that are past their expiration dates.

Qualify, qualify, qualify. Do not waste time with deals that are not qualified. Do not fill your pipeline with junk.

Developing Opportunities Is an Art

Disclaimer: Developing opportunities is not the focus of this book, but it is necessary to include at some level, since this book is about developing territories. I keep these strategies to the bare minimum. Volumes of books are written on developing opportunities.

Your job is to facilitate sales and lower the barriers to purchasing. The greatest barriers are the qualifying elements. When qualifying, you are looking for an advantage in each element of the sales equation. Your job is to create that advantage, and to advance the sales cycle.

Let's look at each of the elements needed to develop an opportunity.

Trust

$$\text{Trust: } CE \times V \times P \times DP \times (D+I+C+R)^2 = \text{Sale}$$

I will assume that by now you have developed trust with your customers. If not, go back and read the first 18 chapters of this book. Without trust, you are generally not going to get the sale.

Compelling Event

Compelling Event: $CE \times V \times P \times DP \times (D+I+C+R)^2 = Sale$

Create enough pain for the customers so they need to take ownership of their problem. A compelling event is pain with a time element. For example, if my car breaks down, the pain is immediate and the time element is acute. After all, I need to get to work. If I change jobs and need to move, there is a date I need to sell my home by. The customer might have a project that supports the opening of a new store. That store will have an opening date. Sometimes, the event is more subtle. If you can save the customer with a strong ROI, the longer they wait, the more they lose or the less they gain.

There are three types of pain: latent pain, admitted pain, and actively looking for a solution to the pain. Latent pain is pain customers are living with. They might not even know they have certain issues. Or, they realize that they have an issue, but they do not think there a solution, or a cost effective way to solve the problem. It is up the salesperson to either educate the customer or help the customer realize they have a specific issue.

Again, the IT field offers good examples of customers living with latent pain they do not know they have. The main function of the IT department is to provide computing services to the company, so employees can more efficiently complete their jobs. In IT, customers complain when things change. When they are steady state, or status quo, there is no complaint.

I used to run sales reports all the time, and most of them would take between 20–40 minutes to run. The first time I ran the reports, I asked a colleague if this was normal, and he said it's always been that way. So, I never mentioned the issue to the IT department. If the reports suddenly took over an hour, most likely I would then complain. The latent pain here is that the business is running inefficiently due to poor-performing applications provided by the IT department. One of a few things could be going on here.

1. The IT department is unaware of the reporting issue.

2. They are aware, but do not think there is a solution or a cost-effective solution.

3. They are aware but do not think there is a solution.

The second level of pain is when customers know they have a problem. They know there is a solution, but they are not ready to look for a solution. Remember our home buyer from the sales cycle discussion? This is the type of pain he had. He knew his house was too small, and he knew his commute was too long, but for a variety of reasons he was not ready to look for a new home. Typically, the customer is one compelling event away from taking action.

The last level of pain is when the customer knows of the issue and is actively looking for a solution. You know the customer is at this level when you call them, or they call you, and say, "We are looking to fix that problem as we speak, and we are ready for a solution. Can you quote us, or send us a proposal? Here are the specifications we are looking for."

When you asks most salespeople what is the best type of pain, they usually will answer the latter situation—where customers are looking for a solution. After all, they are ready to buy. However, the best pain you can uncover is latent pain. When you educate a customer on an issue, or a better way of doing something, you are setting the decision criteria for the sale. The window of opportunity is wide open. The second level of pain requires that you have perfect timing: a compelling event happens, and the customer has not discussed it with other venders. The window of opportunity is very narrow. If you engage a customer after they have started to investigate solutions, you most likely are too late. (We will address what to do in this case in Chapter 20, "Are You Winning or Losing?")

The biggest impact you can have is therefore with latent pain.

When you establish trust outside the opportunity, you are increasing your chances of winning opportunities in three ways.

- When there is a real opportunity, you have enough trust to compete against the incumbent.

- You spend time with the customer, broadening the window of opportunity.

- You get the chance to educate the customer and find pains they have not addressed (latent pains).

When developing the sales cycle, I mentioned that customers will live with pain. When you're spending time with the customer, you have the opportunity to expand the pain in a situation until they realize they have to act. When your customer complains about a stubbed toe, you make them feel as if it's more like a broken leg.

Remember the dentist with the sore back a few chapters back? Say you are selling lab or clinical chairs, and you visit a dentist who is leaning over her patients all day. If the dentist says that she is not very comfortable, but can live with it, your goal is expand that pain. The best way is to lead the dentist through questions. Here is the shorthand version. "Your sore back leads to being extra tired at the end of the day, and if the last patient is a difficult case, being tired can lead to a mistake. That mistake can lead to a lawsuit." You're pointing out that a mildly sore back could lead to the dentist losing her practice.

This has been stated before, but it's worth repeating. Your goal is to expand the pain to the point where the customer thinks, *"Wow, this is a big problem. I need to do something about it."*

The second, and maybe even more important, reason to spend time with customers is that when a compelling event happens, you want to be there to capitalize on it. You want to be the first person the customer talks to after they experience this event. You create great timing by spending more time with the customer.

Business pain comes in many forms—high cost, low revenue, or huge risks. Are your customers struggling to generate revenue; do they need to reduce costs; or is there a regulatory issue that needs to be solved? When diving into pain, you want to assign a value to it. What is the cost of not solving the problem at hand, either in lost revenue or low financial efficiency? You should ask "quantity" questions, such as "How much? How many? How often?"

Example

You have a meeting with a doctor, and you are trying to get him to realize how much of a problem he has. Right now, the doctor is in a status quo state. "Everything is great," he says. He's an "if it ain't broke don't fix it" kind of guy. If the salesperson walks into the room and says, "You can save time using our procedure in your office, and the profit is the same," this doctor will not connect all the dots. You need to connect the dots for him. Although the customers must draw their own conclusion that they have a problem they need to solve, it is much more effective if you guide them there.

Consider a different example, where the a salesperson is attempting to sell to a doctor a solution that enables him to perform a procedure in his own office versus the way he is performing the procedure today, in a hospital. This is a classic example of a salesperson pointing out a pain the doctor does not even know he has. It's a latent pain.

The salesperson starts with, "Doctor these procedures we are talking about, how many of these do you do a week?"

"Well let's see. I would say three a week," he replies.

"And are these done in your office?"

"No, they are done under general anesthesia, so we perform them at the hospital."

"How much do you make from each procedure?"

He lists the price and the costs. "Well we charge $2,200 for the procedure, but the cost from the hospital and for the anesthesia is about $1,500, so we make about $700 per procedure."

"Not bad for an hour of work. Can I ask you how long you are actually out of the office per procedure?"

"For this procedure, I try to do these all in one afternoon. So, when I have three, I am out all afternoon on Tuesday."

The salesperson starts doing the math, "So, on average you are making $2,100 per afternoon of surgery. How many office visits can you do in an afternoon?"

"We do about approximately 5-6 clients an hour over four hours, so 20-25 patients in an afternoon."

"At about $90 per visit, plus miscellaneous lab tests, and so on. You are looking at about $150 per visit?"

He replies, "Yes that's about right."

The salesperson says, "So in an afternoon, at 20 patients, you are grossing $3,000?"

The doctor is starting to get the picture that he is actually losing money when operating. He asks the salesperson, "How long does your procedure in the office take?"

Sometimes customers in the status quo stage need to understand that there is a problem. When it comes to the business, it is always about the numbers. However, there is also a personal side to pain.

How does this issue personally affect the person? If you can get to the personal or emotional level, you win.

Example

While training a class on selling 101, I asked if anyone had the chance to bring a customer to personal pain. One person raised her hand, "Yes, I have."

"Well, how did it go?"

The student explained, "I was talking to the customer about software to help them save time. I ask how this person spent their time during the day. The customer started listing all their responsibilities. I then asked him how much time each of these activities took. What happens if they do not get done? I was trying to get to the crucial activities. Without going into detail I was able to get the person to admit they worked more than 60 hours a week. Remembering part of our earlier conversation (he had just moved to the area), I asked him how he found time to meet anyone. Almost in tears, he replied, 'I have no life, I have no time to meet anyone.' At that moment I was his number one salesperson."

I asked, "Well did you get the deal?"

"Within a week!"

"What is a typical sales cycle?"

"Four months at a minimum."

This is an extreme example, but powerful. The salesperson got very quickly to this customer's personal pain. His current way of doing things was ruining his personal life. This leads to the second that reason latent pain is so important. The salesperson makes the customer aware of an issue, and thus becomes a caring, trusted salesperson. Intent levels go through the roof.

Value

$$\text{Value: } CE \times V \times P \times DP \times (D+I+C+R)^2 = \text{Sale}$$

Value is the logic behind the emotional decision. If there is enough pain, the customer will find the money. I don't have a budget for a new car, but if the transmission in my current car suddenly drops out, I'll find that money somewhere. Money can also be thought of as value. If your solution can provide the customer with significant cost savings or generate more revenue than the cost of the solution, the customer will buy. Is there a return on their investment? Once they agree they have an issue, and that your solution can fix that issue, you must show them the value of the investment.

Every company has a concept called the *hurdle rate*. Hurdle rate is the level of ROI at which the company will purchase or develop a project. Ask your customer if they know their company's hurdle rate. The individual might not even know the term. If they don't, explain it to them. The hurdle rate is the required rate of return. It is a more detailed ROI analysis that takes into account cash flow, capital costs, and risk analysis. In layman's terms, it answers the question, "Does it make financial sense to purchase this product?"

It will cause customers to go to their finance departments and ask if they have a hurdle rate. If they do, you may have just opened up a whole new world for your customer. Obviously, you have to believe and demonstrate to the customer that your solution does exceed this hurdle rate. Your trust is then improved around capability and results. You are more than a product person—you are business savvy.

When you're trying to uncover pain, many of the questions you ask are quantity questions, such as with the doctor example. When you ask how much, how many, how long, and so on, you are gathering data to support the value of the solution you will eventually present. Your goal is to figure out how much a problem is costing the customer, as well as how much you can help him save or make. Show customers how much it will cost them if they do not act.

Power

Power: $CE \times V \times \boxed{P} \times DP \times (D+I+C+R)^2 = Sale$

Getting a "yes" from *power*—someone who can make purchasing decisions—requires that the power buyer has enough pain and has the budget to solve the problem. If your solution does not alleviate the power buyer's pain, you do not have a chance.

Remember that everyone has different pains they are trying to ease over. You may be engaged with a person who is trying to solve a problem, like reports are taking too long, and that person is having to work through lunch to get his job done. However, the person that makes the purchasing decision might not care that your contact is working extra hours. She might start to care if the reports are missing critical deadlines to the business. So, you must, at a minimum, understand the pain points of the person(s) making the purchasing decisions. Ideally, you want access to power, so you can uncover the pain first hand, and help expand it for that person.

One of the most difficult challenges is how to get a meeting with the person of power. There are three avenues.

- *Start at power.* We have discussed this concept a few times. If you start at power, you will have easier access to power in the future. Your initial primary point of contact does not need to be power, but it's best to get to your primary point of contact via power.

- *Bargain your way to power.* Along the sales cycle, your customer will ask you for information, for demos, or for evaluations. They will ask for something. Use this as a tool to bargain for access to power. "Yes I will run a demo, or show you a formal ROI, but if I do, can you get me an appointment with_____?"

- *Gain secondhand access.* Unfortunately, the business climate has changed over the last 10 years. Secondhand access to power is becoming more and more common. And, being new, this may be where you operate until you earn more trust. If you do not start with power, your access to power may be blocked. You need to work through your main contact. However, you need to make sure you know what their boss will require in a solution, and what pains they are trying to solve. If you have your contact proposing your solution to power, help them develop the message to their boss.

Decision Process

Decision Process: CE x V x P x (DP) x (D+I+C+R)^2 = Sale

Before you start the evaluation stage, and start jumping through hoops, be sure that you understand the decision process. What do they want to see in a demo, and why? Who is involved with the demo? How is money budgeted? What is the decision process, and what is the procurement process? If you are reacting to every customer demand and request without knowing the steps you need to win the business, you are functioning on hope. Understand all the steps necessary to close business up front. Once you know all the steps, you can keep yourself and your customer on track to close the order. Always be aware of the next step. Trusted salespeople can move deals along. The customer will have fluctuating concerns throughout the buying cycle. While you must align with these concerns, you must also continue to bring to the forefront why they are working on this process. They have an issue; you are just trying to help them solve it. If you keep the customer focused on the pain, the time-sensitive, compelling event will move the process along.

Controlling this process can demonstrate more business trust than any other portion of the sale. First, understand every step. Then, take ownership of the customer's problem. Show dedication to getting that problem solved. This involves holding the customer accountable for their portion of getting the deal done. Move your customer along; always keep them going to the next steps you define together. As you learn more about your customer's decision process over time, you can take complete control of this process. A trusted advisor can sometimes know the customer's process better than the customer. At this point, not only is trust strong, but the customer begins to rely on the salesperson to help him get things done.

Now that I have addressed the most important aspects of managing an opportunity, it's time to discuss how to track and report on them.

Forecasting

Accurate forecasting should be a simple process. I also believe any administrative work a salesperson has to accomplish should also be a tool in helping them close business. All too often, forecasting becomes a chore that has to be done, and since it's a chore, minimal effort is put forth. Therefore, the forecast is inaccurate. If you can use forecasting as a tool to drive business, you'll try harder, and more accurate forecasting will be the result.

This discussion is meant to be a guideline for creating a forecasting system. Some companies have three levels of commitment, and some have four. I am using the more simple three levels.

- Pipeline—Something held in forecast as a placeholder.

- Upside—There is a clear path to closed business, but not all the elements of the sales equation are satisfied.

- Commit—Each element of the sales equation is satisfied. A purchase order is imminent.

The age-old challenge is how to create accurate forecasts. It's as simple as asking four questions of your existing customers, and five questions of new customers.

If the answers to all four or five questions are yes, then the opportunity is a commit. If there are three or four yeses, then it's an upside. Anything less makes it a pipeline opportunity. It's the sales equation!

The first four questions are opportunity based:

- Does the compelling event land inside your forecast window?

- Do you have a yes from power?

- Does the customer see value? Or, is there an ROI showing value?

- Does the decision and purchase process put you inside the forecast window?

For new customers, there is one additional question.

- Have you made a conscious effort to address each of the trust elements? You can't determine whether the customer trusts you, you can only know what actions you have taken.

The good news is you should be working only on deals that you have a great chance to close. You should be in upside with any deal that enters into the evaluation stage, because you can have most of these elements checked off.

- Is there a compelling event? If not, why are you and the customer wasting time?

- Do you understand the decision and purchase processes before evaluation?

- Does the customer see value? He should. The evaluation stage is about demonstrating that you can deliver the value you promised.

- Can you get a yes from power? This is really the only item left for a commitment.

- Lastly, you should have developed a certain level of trust before you enter into opportunity discussions.

I like this method because it helps you close the deal. It tells you and management exactly what needs to be done to close the deal. If the answer is no to any of the questions above, you need to get a yes. So, a no helps you define what is the next step in the sales effort. If there is no compelling event, can you create one? If you don't understand the decision process, or it's beyond the forecast window, can you change it?

The missing element from most forecasting methods is time. Each of these questions needs to be posed against a timeframe. You might have everything in place, but the decision process puts the deal into the next quarter. Well, that's a "no" for that question in this quarter, but a "yes" in the next. Is there a chance that the decision process can be accelerated into this quarter? If yes, keep it upside, if no, it becomes a commit for the following quarter. This method allows you to be more accurate beyond your immediate month or quarter.

Lastly, do not inflate forecasts! Work on improving your odds of winning. Do not waste time managing deals that you have very little chance of closing.

Summary

Know the sales equation. It is the map you need to control the sales cycle. It is the tool you need to forecast accurately. When dealing with new customers, ensure you are inspecting for trust on each deal. Even though there are many sales processes out there, my suggestion is that you add the element of trust to it. If you do not have a process in place, you can download a simple sales process worksheet from my website at www.huntingwithtrust.com.

You learned about managing opportunities in ideal situations in this chapter. In the next chapter, you learn how to determine if you are winning or losing, and use strategies to turn a losing situation around.

Are You Winning or Losing?

Avoid Becoming Column Fodder

I think self-awareness is probably the most important thing towards being a champion.

—Billie Jean King

When you gain access to customers, you are focused on qualifying them, but your overall goal is to find opportunity.

It is crucial that you view opportunities with new customers with extra skepticism. I discussed the idea of "column fodder" in Chapter 2. As you consider these opportunities, you need to determine what category you are in. Knowing how the customer views you within the sales cycle will help you determine how to engage with the customer about a particular opportunity.

When to Engage—or Not Engage—the Customer

Customers put vendors in one of four categories: the preferred vendor (Vendor A), the vendor they can live with (Vendor B), and vendors they use (Vendors C or D; also called column fodder) to get better terms or pricing from the preferred vendors. Which category are you in?

The difference between Vendors C and D is that Vendor C understands he is in a weak position and can change his strategy. Vendor D remains confident that he has a chance of winning, but nothing is further from the truth. Traditionally you have only a few data points to determine which vendor you are. With your new focus on relationship and trust, you will have better data, which will give you more confidence in positioning and negotiating (see Figure 20-1).

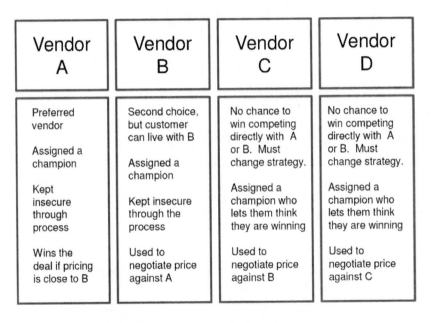

Vendor A	Vendor B	Vendor C	Vendor D
Preferred vendor Assigned a champion Kept insecure through process Wins the deal if pricing is close to B	Second choice, but customer can live with B Assigned a champion Kept insecure through the process Used to negotiate price against A	No chance to win competing directly with A or B. Must change strategy. Assigned a champion who lets them think they are winning Used to negotiate price against B	No chance to win competing directly with A or B. Must change strategy. Assigned a champion who lets them think they are winning Used to negotiate price against C

Figure 20-1. Vendor categories and positions with the customer

The most common method way to determine which vendor you are is to analyze the criteria the customer is using to make a purchase decision. Did your company set the criteria or are you reacting to it?

Criteria is based on the pain(s) the customer is trying resolve. The three levels of pain are latent pain, admitted pain, and actively seeking a specific solution. Latent pain occurs when the customer is not aware of the issue(s) they are facing or they feel there is not a reasonable solution to the problem. Vendor A helps the customer identify and better define the problem(s).

Vendor A also shows the customer options for solving this issue. The customer calls Vendor A first after a trigger event.

Admitted pain is when the customer has identified a need or a problem, and has reached out to a vendor to help solve the problem. This is Vendor B or C.

The final level of pain is when the customers are actively looking to source a solution. They know exactly what they want. This can be indicated by the customers sending out a request for proposal (RFP) or asking for a quote. The temptation in this scenario is for the seller to be excited. Vendor D might think, "Yes, the customer needs something," or "short sales cycle," or "easy business." This is the worst position to be in, Vendor D, because it is nothing more than false hope.

The vendor ratings, the pain, and the trust levels are dependent characteristics. Remember the buyer's strategy. The customer needs Vendors C and D for pricing comparison against Vendors B and A. Who are they going to use in this manner—the vendors that have established trust or have taken an interest in establishing a relationship, or the vendors they don't know very well? When you are asked to quote and have little to no history with the customer, most likely you are Vendor C or D.

Which Vendor Are You?

Determining which vendor you are takes some art and some gut instinct. With the trust meter, you now have other data points to help you (Figure 20-2). The amount of time you've spent with a customer is always an indication, but now you must ask yourself whether that time was spent building business value or buying lunch. Be honest when assessing where you are on the trust meter; have you actively addressed each element of trust?

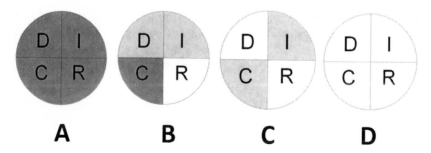

Figure 20-2. Assumed trust levels of the vendors

A strong indicator that you are Vendor A is that you are the incumbent. You helped the customer develop their pain. The solution to be evaluated is based on criteria that you developed jointly with the customer. Even then, you need to think through your trust meter. After your last deal/project, did you come back after the sale and measure results? Were the results as expected? Or, was the last time you saw the customer when you took your last order? How strong of an incumbent are you?

Vendor A

If you are Vendor A, the customer might say, "We had a vendor in here the other day, and they say there is a new solution for X. Do you know anything about this new technology? We are having some issues here." So, an incumbent may never get blind-sided by a request for a quote. But if you are an incumbent and the customer asks you to quote something very specific and you did not help define the solution, you need to quickly understand the changing competitive environment. The customer is working with another vendor.

Take a moment to think about how this might have impacted your trust meter. It goes back to, "Why did you not tell us about this solution?" Your intent, capability, and dedication are in question. Did this new vendor just lessen your dedication or capability, or lower your intent level?

Vendor B

A strong indicator that you are Vendor B is when you have spent time showing the customer value. You may have done some business with the customer in another area. You helped define the solution with the customer. Yes, you can help define the solution and not be Vendor A. If there is a strong incumbent, you may only get a starting position of Vendor B even when you provide real value. Remember, as Vendor B, you do have a chance to win the bid if you show a unique offering, or if Vendor A slips. There are many examples of a new vendor coming into a customer and helping the customer identify a need, or position a new solution. Then the customer just takes the idea to their other business partner, Vendor A, and asks if they can provide the same solution.

Lastly, have you built trust? Vendor B's trust meter shows that you still have some work to do. Have you used the strategies in this book to build trust?

Vendors C and D

A strong indication that you are Vendor C or D is that you are presented with opportunities but you have no special relationship with this customer. They call for a quote, or they send an RFP. On your first call or two, the customer says,

"Yes, we are looking for a solution to solve X." This is the worst position to be in. You pretty much have no chance to win, but the deal feels so tangible that most salespeople do not have the discipline to walk away. The questions you need to ask yourself include, "Do we have enough trust to compete? Are we established enough with this customer for them to trust us with this business?" The greater the opportunity, the more you need to ask if you have earned this chance. Are you trying to build trust with this first opportunity?

If you have been asked to respond to an RFP, and had no input as to its contents, you are most likely Vendor C or D. There are instances when answering an RFP might make sense. If the customer is bound to use the lowest bidder, you have a chance. Government and educational accounts typically require three bidders, and they have to go with the lowest bid. However, they usually have a preferred vendor, and sometimes will share another's lower pricing with their preferred vendor in the hopes that they can match it.

If you are Vendor C or D, don't despair. You know exactly what you must do: build trust. This book provides a roadmap for doing just that.

What If You Are in the Wrong Column?

You won't likely be the preferred vendor very often during the first year in a new territory. The goal of this section is to think through a strategy for every situation. You analyze the customer for long-term potential, level of trust you've built, and effort (time) required by the customer decision process. The matrix (Figure 20-3) serves as a guide to help you get on track when you find yourself in the wrong column.

Customer Quality	Trust Built	Effort	Strategy/Points to Consider
High	High	High	Try to win.
High	High	Low	Try to win.
High	Low	High	Try to say that you want to do business with this customer, but you don't know enough about them to provide a proper solution this early.
High	Low	Low	If the customer is requesting a proposal, and it will help them with their job, work the deal, or bid. In this case your intent is to help them, but your chances of winning are slim.
Low	High	High	Maybe, but need to ask why you spent time to build trust with a low-qualified customer to begin with.
Low	High	Low	Work the deal. However, you need to ask yourself why you have spent time building trust with a lower-qualified customer.
Low	Low	High	No bid. Your time is best spent with another customer.
Low	Low	Low	Maybe, if you have large competitive advantage. This might be the one area to consider lower pricing as a strategy.

Figure 20-3. Decision matrix to determine level of effort needed for sales cycle

Higher-Qualified Customers

Since this assumes an earlier engagement with the customer, the scenarios you need to consider more closely are when you have low trust. When you have low trust, a highly qualified customer, and need to expend a lot of effort to win a deal, the last thing you want to do is get completely out of alignment with a customer. Your chance of winning is low, but your chance of damaging trust beyond repair can be high in this situation. You have qualified this customer as having great long-term potential; don't risk damaging the relationship. Your best strategy may be to try to back out of this opportunity. This doesn't mean you don't want to do business with this customer; it means you don't think this particular opportunity is right. You can say something like, "We are early in our relationship, and it is hard to start such an important project without first understanding your business and project in much more detail. While I want to build a long-term relationship with you, starting with the opportunity might not be in your best interest. You do not know our capabilities, and we just do not know your business well enough to make proper recommendations."

Your trust quotient will greatly increase. Your intent is to help the customer. They might this and say, "Great, let's work on the next one together." They might say, "Okay, let's get more detailed with our requirements." Or, you might have a customer who says, "If you want to do business with us, you will provide a quote." If this is their response, you may have just qualified this customer as someone you do not want a relationship with. This is the type of customer who likes to make vendors jump through hoops. Time wasters! They have also just solidified you as Vendor C or D. If they rank strong on your customer target list, you might just have to quote something, but have proper expectations. Do not damage trust with a low-ball quote.

Low-ball quotes show desperation. They show that you do not value your products or services. If you happen to win on price, you will be able to compete only on price going forward. It takes discipline to walk away from a deal, or to quote straight up when you are not in a position to win. But for the long-term relationship, it is the best avenue.

The next situation is a highly qualified customer, low trust, and low effort on the deal. Effort is low, because you know you don't really have the trust built to make the sale. If the intent is to help the customer with their decision process, work the deal. Again, set realistic expectations—you are helping the customer and don't have much of a chance to win the bid. Do not try to win on price in this situation. Your goal is a long-term relationship; do not start it off by diminishing your value.

Lower-Qualified Customers

Next is the lower-qualified customer, low trust, and high effort to win a deal. Walk away; this is a waste of time.

What if you have a lower-qualified customer, low trust, and low effort situation? Work the deal if you feel you have a large competitive advantage that benefits the customer. This is the one situation where leading with price may be acceptable. You don't care as much about the long-term relationship, winning on price does not take much effort, and you are not worried about damaging trust. This situation becomes more about the opportunity versus the customer relationship.

Example

A large company, Acme Outdoors, invites three vendors to develop and present solutions to solve an issue. Each vendor partners with one of their resellers to develop solutions to present to the customer. Vendor 1, being smart, partners with an incumbent reseller, Reseller A. Based on technical capabilities and the Reseller A relationship, the customer chooses Vendor 1. However, the customer is required by its purchasing department to get three quotes. So, the customer asks the chosen vendor to provide names of two more resellers to get quotes from. The customer then reaches out to the two resellers, one who is known to the customer but very new (called Reseller B).

Acme Outdoors shares the requirements of the project with each reseller, and each is told to use products from Vendor 1. Reseller B reaches out to the vendor, who confirms they are already working with the incumbent reseller. Reseller B, realizing they are in a weak position, goes back to the customer to try to change the requirements of the project. (I will discuss this strategy later in the chapter.) The customer is firm about the requirements. At this point, Reseller B tries to back out of the deal politely. They state that they want to business with the customer, but the timing of the deal is not great. The customer comes clean and says, "We are required by purchasing to provide three quotes. Would you mind helping with that?"

Reseller B replies to the customer, "We don't mind helping, but we don't want to have to develop a new solution. Can you provide us the list of what you need quoted?" The customer agrees. Reseller B cannot change the requirements, and cannot win on price since Reseller A is getting registered pricing with Vendor 1. So, they spend one morning quoting a solution to help the customer.

Reseller C is also new to the customer, and does not realize that they are Reseller C. They only see an opportunity. Reseller C spends the next two weeks on whiteboards, designing a new solution for the customer. They present to the customer, who is half listening in the meeting, because they know they are going with Reseller A. Reseller C thinks they have a superior solution; they were able to tweak the design to save the customer some money. They also quote the customer with an extremely low profit margin. Line item for line item, Reseller C's option is still more expensive than Reseller A's, but less expensive than Reseller B's. Feeling that they provided a better solution, Reseller C forecasts the deal as probable. Two weeks go by, and the deal is awarded to Reseller A. At this point, the customer informs all parties. They tell Resellers B and C they lost on price. Reseller C tries to lower the price again, and tries to go above the contact's head.

Although the obvious winner is the incumbent, who came in a strong second? Definitely Reseller B. They played it smart:

- They are new to this customer. They realize they have not earned enough trust to compete.

- They are competing with an incumbent who provided the original design. They recognize they are column fodder.

- They tried to change the rules, but were unsuccessful.

- They see weeks of effort with very little chance to win.

- They choose not to waste their time or the customer's. Instead, they submit a courtesy quote that costs them a few hours' time.

Reseller B came out way ahead:

- They did not waste weeks.

- They did not inflate forecasts.

- They got the customer to be up front with their intentions, and gave the customer what they asked for. The customer only wanted a bid to please purchasing. This may come back to their credit later; give to get.

- They did not present themselves as the low-cost provider.

- The Reseller B sales rep was able to spend those four weeks looking for new opportunities, rather than working that bad deal.

- Reseller B eventually wins the trust of the customer, and ends up winning a new deal a month later in a different division.

Reseller C, on the other hand:

- Wasted weeks of time.

- Did desperate things to try to win the deal, and in the end hurt their trust with the customer, and their partner vendor.

- Lost any chance to do business with the customer going forward.

Change the Rules

I will talk about working opportunities in the next section, but the strategy is pretty much the same if you decide to work an opportunity when you are not the preferred vendor. In order to increase your chances of winning, you need to redefine the criteria of the deal. I have talked about aligning with the customer, but this is the one time you need to get the customer to align with you. When you are Vendor C or D, you engage the customer pretty close to when they are going to purchase. You need to get them from that point (Point A on Figure 20-4) back to needs analysis (Point B). The only chance of winning is by changing the focus of the decision, and redefining the needs in your favor.

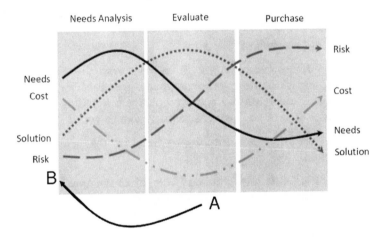

Figure 20-4. Moving a customer to the beginning of the buyer cycle

This is defined in sales as *changing the rules*.

Viewed through the lens of the traditional sales process, if you have each element in the following list in your favor, you can win the deal:

- Budget
- Pain
- Compelling event
- Decision process
- Access to power

Remember the sales formula, though. You need to take trust into account—and it counts more than any of the other elements:

$$CE \times V \times P \times DP \times (D+I+C+R)^2 = Sale$$

In order to win deals when you are not Vendor A, you must change the elements of this equation. The compelling event is fixed. Budget can be slightly flexible if your solution offers a much better value. The decision process can be changed by going above the level of the current decision-maker. This is a risky maneuver. If you have a solid relationship with someone higher in the organization, you should have been used that relationship before the company chose a preferred vendor. You risk alienating future decision makers with this approach.

Changing the rules also means that you find another pain or problem to solve. You can expand the deal to include pains you know Vendor A cannot solve. You must have some trust with the customer for them to allow you to bring the sales cycle back to the qualify or needs analysis stages. If they do allow this, it means you have a good chance to win.

Be creative in changing the deal. The real reason you are Vendor B, C, or D is that you have a lower level of trust. It's not necessarily about price or product features. Do not compete head-to-head on price or features. You will lose.

If you are not allowed to change the rules, you should not waste your time. Always remember—if this is a high-value customer, do not hurt your chances for future business.

Change Your Trust Levels

I mentioned, prior to change the rules, that one way to increase trust is to actually walk away. This might be the best strategy for developing a long-term relationship with the customer. What if you are in a situation where you must work the deal? Maybe they buy your type of solution once every four years, and you can't wait four years for another chance. You are new to the customer, and you know you have bad timing. You do not have nearly enough trust built to win against an incumbent.

You must show proper intent, capability, dedication, and results, and do so quickly. There are two ways to accomplish this. The first it way is to partner for trust. This was discussed in the Chapter 5, Trust. You can find a partner in the account that is an incumbent and has developed trust with the customer. The second way to elevate trust is to help the customer from day one. Implement your solution at no cost, no risk, and no time commitment.

One of the ways to determine if you are the chosen vendor is to determine whether the customer has "skin in the game" with you. With this method you know you are not Vendor A, so in this situation all the skin is yours. It goes beyond a proof of concept. It is about letting the customer experience what they are going to buy first. If it works, they pay for it.

Building trust quickly is not easy, but it can be done through partnering or providing the customer with working products at no cost. This is the redefined sales cycle all over again.

Figure 20-5 shows how this method changes the sales cycle.

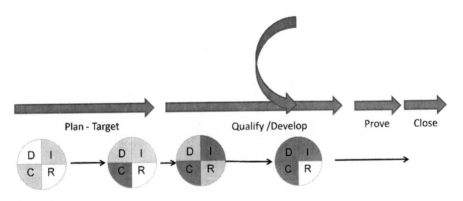

Figure 20-5. Build trust before an opportunity

Let's look at the trust elements:

- *Intent* – You give the customer a solution that shows your intent is to help. You show the customer that you are willing to go "all in" with them.

- *Capability* – You demonstrate that you are confident in your ability to deliver what you are selling in a specific time frame.

- *Dedication* – You are dedicated to customer success. You are dedicated to your company. This is not giving the customer the solution; it is allowing them to test drive with the intent to buy.

- *Results* – No results, no deal. You prove results before they purchase.

This is a last-ditch effort, but it can work effectively. You have to be sure you have the resources to deliver, and you have to be sure the deal has enough profit to cover the extended terms. This method has to be discussed closely with management, as it introduces revenue recognition issues that have to be carefully weighed.

Summary

This chapter is about using your time wisely once you have gained access to a customer. The first thing you must remember is that the first opportunity you find should not determine the long-term relationship you have with the customers. The first opportunity might be the opportunity trap I have discussed so frequently. Answer this question honestly, "Am I in a position to win this deal; have I earned their trust yet?" Use the chart that defines customer quality, effort to work the opportunity, and perceived trust levels you have built to guide you. Build trust before you try to compete. The first opportunity does not define your long-term relationship, but it can destroy your chances of establishing any trust.

In the last chapter, you learn how to build a 30-60-90-day plan for you and management to achieve rapid success.

Wrapping Up
Hunt with Trust, Hunt with Purpose

While skills can take years to master, strategy can be learned in the morning and executed in the afternoon.

—Dave Monty

I started with the term *hunter.* Yes, you are hunting new logos and new customers. I hope I debunked the ego-dominated myth of a hunter and helped you understand that in order to bring down new game, it is more about your ability to understand the land than it is about your skill in aiming a rifle. Selling is a patient game. It requires that you trust the method and focus on the customer. This patient approach actually gives you a much more powerful position with the customer. It allows for an atmosphere of trust to develop, and with trust comes power.

I start with a second look at two examples from earlier in the book that used many of these strategies. This is a great place to wrap up the book and show you the way to a win. Then I summarize most of the material in a 30-60-90-day plan. This chapter discusses the salesperson's plan as well as the role that management and marketing must take in assisting the salesperson.

Insurance Company Example

A large manufacturer was trying to win some business at a large insurance company. The manufacturer already did a lot of business with this company, but could not break into an important division. The manufacturer was assigning their fourth sales rep, in as many years, to this account. The new sales rep understood the customer enough to bargain with his own company to give him two years to win this business. This may sound like a lot, but let's review the situation again.

- The equipment they were selling was upgraded every four years, and the customer just purchased new equipment two years ago.

- They replace each sales rep as they start to make some headway.

- The customer is sick of revolving salespeople.

- The insurance company moves at its own slow pace. They have an "if it's not broke, don't fix it" mentality.

This is a difficult challenge for the salesperson. He has a reluctant customer and aggressive sales management. He needs a plan.

- Learn as much as he can about any issue the customer is experiencing.

- Find a way to build some trust. Trust has been burnt many times over by previous sales efforts.

- Find a niche play.

Without getting technical, the salesperson learns about a situation in which the customer wants to build a new IT environment to handle the testing of some applications. This environment is pathetically small compared to the full production environment the manufacturer has been trying to win. However, the salesperson understands that their products have some features that are perfect for this project. His competitor cannot provide this advantage. The customer is reluctant because eventually the applications will have to be placed into production using the incumbent's gear. Even though the new equipment from the manufacturer is better, and perfect for this environment, the customer is leaning toward the incumbent. They know how to use the technology and think they can live with the drawbacks.

The salesperson knows this is his way to get his foot in the door. So, he arranges with the customer to have his company install the equipment, manage the environment, and train the customer engineers over the course of six months. The customer will not be billed for anything during those six months. If they decide to keep the equipment, they will be billed only for the equipment, not any of the services.

I understand that not all companies are in a position or willing to implement up front. Maybe in this case a simple proof of concept would have worked. However, due to the nature of the past relationships, the manufacturer agreed to this aggressive "try and buy."

This giveaway works. The salesperson gets the new technology into the customer's office, and they are able to demonstrate results with the basic and advanced features. The proof of concept ends just as the sales cycle for the larger production equipment refresh starts. The salesperson has shown intent by helping the customer. He has shown better capability with features, shown dedication by absorbing the risk in the project, and most importantly, produced results. He is now in a position to compete for the production equipment. Nine months from starting with the customer, not two years, he wins his first order for their production equipment. By picking a niche product and being willing to give some to get much more in return, the salesperson was able to secure this business.

My Loss Example

In the Chapter 5, "Trust," I talk about a large data storage deal that I lost to the incumbent because I had not established trust. Typically, as a vendor, after losing a deal, I would move on to the next customer. The business I was in was highly transactional. As stated earlier, I led with the product or solution before I established trust. However, throughout the sales process, my relationship did strengthen. I did not want all my work to go to waste. This had been a long battle with the incumbent. When the customer told me that I had lost the business, I knew that I had *lost*. It was not an angle to get better pricing. The tone of his voice was somber, so I knew a last-ditch effort would be fruitless. At this point, many salespeople, including management, would start throwing grenades; lower the price, offer better incentives, or bash the competition. When the customer called me, I was caught off guard. I basically was short with the customer, "Sorry it worked out this way; good luck with the project." I felt like I should have said more.

In the meantime, I told my manager what happened. At first, he wanted to get aggressive, but I explained the entire situation. To his credit, he allowed me to take the approach I was suggesting. The customer met the ideal profile of our company. I could also tell there was a personality fit. That afternoon I called the customer back.

"I just wanted to say I enjoyed working with your team. I hope this is a start of a business relationship, not the end."

The customer was cautious; he was not sure where this was going, "Well, Dave we enjoyed working with you, but…"

I cut him off, "I am not trying to win this bid. I respect the decision you made. And I understand why you made your decision. All I wanted to say is that we stand by our technology, and if you happen to have an issue with the equipment you are about to purchase, we will step in and help in any way possible. I promise no 'I told you so's.' "

He was appreciative. Over the next six months, I kept in touch with the him, updating him about new technologies, and staying close to his issues. While staying close, I learned of a larger deal for my type of technology in a different department. I was in a position of strength. My competitor was still having deployment issues. My primary contact in the account introduced me to the other department like so, "This is Dave. He has worked with us over the last six months and he understands our business. For your project, I feel his technology would be a perfect fit. We even did extensive testing on the performance issues." We had instant trust with this internal referral.

Meanwhile, the other incumbent was so busy trying to get something they sold working, which they knew would not work, they never had a chance to compete for this new business. It was the shortest sales cycle in my career; we went into the division, listened to their business and technical needs, and configured a proper solution. Within a few weeks, we took an order three times the size of the deal I had lost.

After a smooth installation with this new department, we established even more trust by producing results. My original customer at the account came back to us and said, "The incumbent technology is just not giving us the performance we need and it's impacting our production. Can you help?"

If I had lost sight of the fact that this could be a great customer, I would have moved on after losing the original opportunity, and I would never have had a chance to win these deals. I analyzed the account for future potential, and did not let the loss discourage me from maintaining the strong relationships I was forming. While my competitor was busy losing trust, I was busy building it.

When your competition is focused on opportunities, and in some cases losing credibility to win opportunities, you concentrate on building relationships and trust. Sales will come.

Where to Start: A 30-60-90-Day Plan

You can, of course, implement any of the topics discussed in this book individually. However, your company, its management, and the marketing department play a role in accelerating individual success in the first year. The 30-60-90-day plan recaps and organizes the major topics of this book, as well as assigns responsibility of each task to the proper person.

Pre-Day Zero

New reps must have the tools for success on day one. Ideally, management must give the sales rep the following:

- *An ideal customer profile.* This is the list of traits that the rep can use to rank prospects and qualify customers. What is the ideal revenue target? What are the ideal titles the salesperson must gain access to? The list can be endless.

- *Elevator hook.* Reduce the company presentation down to the elevator hook. Remember that it's in the form of a question. "Do you know how hard it is to ...?" You goal is to prompt a "yes" from the customer. Help identify the common pains that customers deal with. The pains need to be defined at the buyer's level, or to the job-specific needs of the customer.

- *Find a niche.* Have an idea where the salesperson should spend their training time. Ideally you want a new person to lead with a new concept, niche product, or service. Do not automatically train on the best product. Help them select something with a unique value or benefit. Focus training and marketing efforts in this area. This will give the salesperson focus in training, messaging, and measuring results. It will result in a more realistic pipeline, and it will help the salesperson avoid opportunity traps. The training should be at the story level—how does the service help the customer? What pains does it solve; what questions can the salesperson ask; what story can the salesperson tell to differentiate herself in the market?

You can also take steps before stepping foot in the door, day one. Specifically, clean up your online presence. Google yourself. Clean up your Facebook account. Have your LinkedIn profile ready for customers to view. Again, your LinkedIn profile should not be a resume, but should instead contain information about how you can help your customers. List the pains you can help solve for potential customers.

Days 0–30

Train. Learn the elevator hooks, and learn the products or services you sell. If management has identified a niche offering, concentrate your training there. When learning about the product, do not focus on the features and benefits, or on the speeds and feeds. Learn the technical or business problems you solve; learn the business advantages you bring. Learn the questions you need to ask the customer. If you have a good story of how all this works, use that story. Or develop your own story. Customers will remember if you allowed them to talk, and whether you had a conversation, and they will remember a cohesive story.

Gather customer data. You should be presented with an ideal customer profile by management. If not, ask them to help develop one. You can use the generic attributes used in developing the examples in this book, but it is best to create your own. Using data from the company, trade publications, information from partners, your own territory knowledge, and purchased customer lists, start to populate your ranking worksheet. Use your ranking worksheet to focus your prospecting efforts.

Partners (other salespeople in the supply chain). Meet with your partners. When you meet with partners for the first time, you are there to learn what you can about the territory. Focus on populating your ranking worksheet. Remember, once you are engaged with customers, they may help you fill in gaps on your trust meter. For example, if you are a manufacturer, a VAR (value-added reseller) might have an established relationship. Management should be able to help facilitate meetings with partners.

Internal resources. You are building a team around you. Meet the technical staff, the customer service people, and the order entry people. Meet the people you will work with on a daily basis, and the people that might interface with your customers. Learn what makes their jobs easier so they can support you better. This team helps you build the trust element of capability.

Marketing. Learn how marketing helps you with lead generation or with penetrating accounts. Does marketing have an internal team that helps generate appointments? Do they have messaging or promotions that will help you with your own prospecting efforts? Share some of the cold-calling ideas from this book with marketing. Do they have events that you can use to help drive attendance?

Start your prospecting efforts. With your ranked prospect list, now identify at least four people in each account you can target. Use the prospecting methods in this book to secure first appointments.

Days 30–60

Continue the efforts from days 0–30. Prospecting never stops. Keep track of the methods you have tried. What is working and what isn't? Remember to play the new sales numbers game; increase your odds at every step of the process.

Online. Start becoming more active with the online forums in your industry. Start sharing ideas in forums that customers often visit.

First sales calls. Follow the sales skills guidance in this book. You should spend as much time qualifying the customer as you do looking for and qualifying an opportunity.

Ranking worksheet. Use this as a guide for questions to ask your customers. You are looking for qualified customers. If you have a proper ideal customer profile, the qualifying questions should match the data you need to maintain your ranking worksheet. Your prospecting list should slowly migrate to a qualified customer list. The more qualified customers you have, the fewer prospecting efforts are required.

Opportunity inspection. This is a joint effort with management and the salesperson. For the manager, not all inspection is equal. The level of inspection is determined by the level of relationship the company has with the customer. With a new salesperson, most of their customers will be new to them and/or the company. The first level of inspection is to the customer profile, or ranking worksheet. Is your salesperson spending time with the right customers? When inspecting where the salesperson is spending time, you need to understand if the customer is qualified against the ideal customer profile. This is a discussion that you should have with the salesperson in order to justify time spent. You are not necessarily inspecting for opportunity yet.

The next level of inspection is business trust. Inspect and strategize tangible actions that are directed at developing intent, capability, dedication, and results in the customer's eyes. When inspecting deals with new customers, you have to focus not only on opportunity qualifications but on developing relationship and trust.

The last level of inspection is the opportunity. With all the best intentions, the shareholders need guidance about revenue projects, so the CEO turns to the VP of sales and asks for a number. The best way to understand the number is to drill down to the biggest deals affecting the quarter. The VP of sales holds his forecast call, and conducts an inspection of the regional managers by opportunity. With the best CRM and forecasting tools and metrics in place to help regional managers accurately forecast, they go to their sales people and "inspect" the business. A lot of responsibility falls on the shoulders of the regional manager to interpret the dialogue each salesperson has during a deal. Accurate management and reporting become subjective.

So how should the sales manager assess an opportunity? Forget the background story to determine the forecast category. Here is what you need to win a deal. Hold your team to knowing these elements of the deal.

- Compelling event
- Budget
- Yes from someone with buying authority

- Purchase process determined

- Especially for new customers—*trust*

If one of these is missing, don't commit to the deal. If two are missing, it is at maximum a potential upside for that inspection period. If inspection covers these basics, the forecast accuracy of the deals increases. The benefit of an approach like this is that you can determine if the salesperson is having the right conversations with the customers. Also, you can help the salesperson strategize about how to move the sales cycle to the next level by addressing the elements that are not in place. This style of inspection will start to drive some basic sales behavior.

Last Example: Tom "Two"

As stated earlier, while conducting research for this book, I was a regional manager with an IT reseller. Here is an example of putting the tactics to work with a salesperson who was going down the wrong path and chasing opportunities. One of the salespeople I inherited from the previous manager was almost a carbon copy of "Tom," discussed in Chapter 2. So I will call him Tom 2. Tom 2 was a 20-year veteran of sales, but his behavior was almost exactly like Tom. He was new to his territory, he was hard working, he knew the company, the products, and had a very large pipeline. Unfortunately, he was also closing very little business and deals were continually slipping. He had been in the territory for about three quarters and his results were less than desirable. Looking at Tom 2's experience, and knowing his qualities, this was kind of shocking.

During our first business review together, about two weeks after I took over as manager, we ended the session by reviewing his pipeline. He provided commentary about each deal. I stopped him. I suggested we do three things. First analyze each deal relative to the five questions—do they have a compelling event, do they have budget, does he have access to power (dealing with a decision maker), does he understand each step needed to close the deal, and finally, has he addressed the four elements of trust?

This is a new concept to Tom 2, so I review with him the actions that can show intent, dedication, capability, and results. After the review, we realized that he probably had only five or six deals out of the 40 on his forecast that seem to have a realistic chance to close.

Then we quickly picked five traits that we would put into an ideal customer profile. We went back down the list analyzing the customers he had visited and determined how they stacked up against those traits. Also, I asked Tom 2 to identify when he had a personal relationship or when he felt he "clicked" with the customer. We determined that there were probably another 15 customers who deserved more time and attention. With those accounts, we developed a strategy to show intent, capability, dependability, and results.

Lastly, we reviewed our product line and picked a niche technology with which we could focus his efforts with these new customers. The results were great. Within the first quarter, he closed four of six deals. With the focus customers, he was able to drive another six opportunities that we determined would have a great chance to close. So, we saw immediate results. Within two quarters, he was on pace to make quota.

With most systems or sales processes, inspection is opportunity focused; this may be adequate with existing customers, when you are the incumbent. But, *one size does not fit all.* When you're inspecting deals with new customers, you need to go deeper than inspecting just the opportunity. Inspection needs to go to the level of trust in the relationship.

It is easy to understand the elements you need for an order. What elements do you need for a successful business relationship? Is your new salesperson executing the right strategy? What questions can you ask to ensure they are executing the proper strategy?

Here are the qualities and activities of successful business relationships that you can inspect:

1. The salesperson has multiple engagement points with the customer:

   a. Number of different people

   b. Number of different departments

2. The salesperson has high-level relationships, like titles to like titles

3. The salesperson has multiple discussion points

4. The salesperson is seen as a business partner, not a vendor

5. The salesperson logs face time

6. The salesperson understands their business

7. The salesperson's personality matches the customer's

8. The salesperson has been able to demonstrate intent, capability, dedication, and results

If you inspect to these elements, you are asking the salesperson to understand the customer business, push for multiple contact points, discuss many projects, discuss business issues and not just products, and spend time with the right customers. You are asking them to *qualify* the customer. Not only can you use these metrics as a way to understand if the salesperson is performing, but you can use these metrics to determine if a customer is worth spending time with. Through inspection, you are forcing them to think about how they are advancing their trust in the account.

By not immediately pushing for opportunities, and instead spending the time to get to know the customer, you actually help the salesperson establish the trust they need to engage in real opportunities.

It is up to the sales manager to set the culture of customer-centric selling versus opportunity-based selling. New salespeople will take your lead. To use the hunting analogy, you must first put them in fertile hunting grounds, during hunting season, and equip them with the right weapons.

Days 60–90

Time management. After you hit day 60, disciplining your time is of the utmost importance. At this point, most salespeople start to migrate all their time to working opportunities. During your first year, you must always have a balanced approach with your time. Allocate your time for working opportunities, prospecting, and most importantly building trust with qualified customers.

Build trust with qualified customers. Keep abreast of new industry ideas, and share these with customers, whether they are URLs or whitepapers. Call your customers to discuss, and then follow up with emails. Work with marketing to develop lunch and learns.

Broaden the number of contacts. Do not become myopic with customers. With qualified customers, start meeting more people within the organization.

Close business. This will happen quite naturally if you build trust.

10 RULES FOR DEVELOPING A TERRITORY

1. Understand your territory and what your ideal customer should look like, both from a business and personal sense.

2. Work the strategies mentioned in this book to gain entry to the customer.

   - Online presence

   - Marketing

   - Cold calling

   - Referrals

   - Partners

3. Once you're in the door, listen and ask questions. Learn about your customer, and remember your number one job is to establish trust.

4. Beware of hunting out of season. Be extra diligent about opportunities you run across very early in the relationship. Understand that you could be column fodder.

5. Continually offer value to your customer and don't just ask for business. Give to receive.

6. Position a niche product or service. Find something new your customer is not currently buying or using. Understand your deals might be small to begin with.

7. Forecast accurately' do not inflate forecasts for any reason. This will just waste everyone's time and give you a false sense of security.

8. Have fun. I see this on every sales managers presentation; it almost sounds cliché. But why is this important? Your customers sense if you are struggling, or if you are desperate for a sale. If you are desperate, they will feel the pressure and instantly your intent is in question.

9. Remember the elements of trust: intent, capability, dedication, and results. Continually ask yourself how you can advance each in every aspect of the sales process.

10. This is your career. Treat it like a career, not a job. Even though it sometimes takes years to master, keep learning about sales and keep sharpening your sales skills.

I hope you see that my intention was to help you, not to sell you something. I hope you see my capabilities and dedication to the sales process. Lastly, I hope you produce the results you desire.

Resources

I have found the following books extremely helpful in my sales career; I believe you will too.

Bettger, Frank. *How I Raised Myself from Failure to Success in Selling.* New York, NY: Fireside, 1947.

Bosworth, Michael T. *Solution Selling: Creating Buyers in Difficult Selling Markets.* New York, NY: McGraw-Hill, 1995.

Brodie, Richard. *Virus of the Mind.* Carlsbad, California: Hay House Publishing, 1996.

Carnegie, Dale. *How to Win Friends and Influence People.* New York, NY: Pocket Books, a division of Simon and Schuster, 1936.

Cialdini, Robert B., Ph.D. *Influence: The Psychology of Persuasion.* New York, NY: Collins Business, HarperCollins Publishers, 1984.

Covey, Stephen M. R. *The Speed of Trust.* New York, NY: Free Press, 2006.

Dixon, Matthew and Adamson, Brent. *The Challenger Sale.* New York, NY: Penguin Group, 2011.

Dyer, Wayne W., Dr. *Excuses Begone!* Carlsbad, California: Hay House Publishing, 2009.

Eades, Keith M. *The New Solution Selling.* New York, NY: McGraw-Hill, 2004.

Elias, Craig and Shanto, Tibor. *Shift: Turn Prospects Into Customers.* Bloomington, IN: iUniverse, 2010.

Holland, John R., and Tim Young, *Rethinking the Sales Cycle.* New York, NY: McGraw Hill, 2010.

Lipton, Bruce, Ph.D. *The Biology of Belief.* Carlsbad, California: Hay House Publishing, 2005.

Moore, Geoffrey A. *Crossing the Chasm.* New York, NY: Harper Business, 1998.

Sittig-Rolf, Andrea. *The Seven Keys to Effective Business-to-Business Appointment Setting.* New York, NY: Thomson/Aspatore, 2006.

Index

Get the eBook for only $10!

Now you can take the weightless companion with you anywhere, anytime. Your purchase of this book entitles you to 3 electronic versions for only $10.

This Apress title will prove so indispensible that you'll want to carry it with you everywhere, which is why we are offering the eBook in 3 formats for only $10 if you have already purchased the print book.

Convenient and fully searchable, the PDF version enables you to easily find and copy code—or perform examples by quickly toggling between instructions and applications. The MOBI format is ideal for your Kindle, while the ePUB can be utilized on a variety of mobile devices.

Go to www.apress.com/promo/tendollars to purchase your companion eBook.

Other Apress Business Titles You Will Find Useful

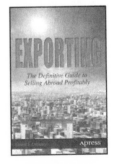